Microsoft

Step by Step

Microsoft®
Excel
Version 2002 Microsoft® Office XP Application

Curtis Frye

PUBLISHED BY
Microsoft Press
A Division of Microsoft Corporation
One Microsoft Way
Redmond, Washington 98052-6399

Library of Congress Cataloging-in-Publication Data
Frye, Curtis, 1968-
        Microsoft Excel Version 2002 Step by Step / Curtis Frye.
            p. cm.
        Includes index.
        ISBN 0-7356-1296-X
        1. Microsoft Excel for Windows.   2. Business--Computer programs.   3. Electronic
        spreadsheets.   I. Title.

    HF5548.4M523 F79 2001
    005.369--dc21   2001030646

Printed and bound in the United States of America.

7 8 9   QWT   6 5 4 3

Distributed in Canada by H.B. Fenn and Company Ltd.

A CIP catalogue record for this book is available from the British Library.

Microsoft Press books are available through booksellers and distributors worldwide. For further information about international editions, contact your local Microsoft Corporation office or contact Microsoft
Press International directly at fax (425) 936-7329. Visit our Web site at mspress.microsoft.com. Send
comments to *mspinput@microsoft.com*.

Acquisitions Editor: Kong Cheung
Project Editor: Jenny Moss Benson
Technical Editor: Marc Young
Manuscript Editor: Shawn Peck
Principal Compositor: Paula Gorelick

Body Part No. X08-06202

Contents

1 Getting to Know Excel   1

2 Setting Up a Workbook   22

3 Performing Calculations on Data   34

4 Changing Document Appearance   48

Contents

10 Creating Charts 148

11 Printing 168

12 Automating Repetitive Tasks with Macros 186

13 Working with Other Microsoft Office Programs 204

14 Working with Database Data 218

What's New in Microsoft Excel 2002

You'll notice some changes as soon as you start Microsoft Excel 2002. The toolbars and menu bar have a new look, and there's a new task pane on the right side of your screen. But the features that are new or greatly improved in this version of Excel go beyond just changes in appearance. Some changes won't be apparent to you until you start using the program.

To help you quickly identify features that are new or greatly enhanced with this version, this book uses the icon in the margin whenever new features are discussed or shown. If you want to learn about only the new features of the program, you can skim through the book, completing only those topics that show this icon.

The following table lists the new features that you might be interested in, as well as the chapters in which those features are discussed.

To learn how to	Using this new feature	See
Get help from the main Excel window	Ask A Question Box	Chapter 1, page 3
Perform common tasks with a single click	Task Pane	Chapter 1, page 3
Set the properties of pasted data	Paste Options	Chapter 1, page 6
Set the properties of AutoFill and FillSeries data	Auto Fill Options	Chapter 1, page 11
Locate data with a specific format	Find Format	Chapter 1, page 16
Set the properties of inserted columns, rows, or cells	Insert Options	Chapter 2, page 25
Get information about an error	Error Options	Chapter 3, page 45
Draw borders with new tools	Borders	Chapter 4, page 51
Add a graphic to a header or footer	Header Graphic	Chapter 4, page 65
Create PivotTables with an easier-to-use dialog box	PivotTables	Chapter 9, page 130
Link to data in a PivotTable	Link to PivotTable Cell	Chapter 9, page 138
Hide errors in a printed worksheet	Suppress Errors	Chapter 11, page 173
Avoid printing blank pages at the end of a workbook	Intelliprint	Chapter 11, page 178

(continued)

To learn how to	Using this new feature	See
Update Web files whenever the source workbook is saved	AutoRepublish	Chapter 15, page 235
Create a Web query	Copy Paste Web Query	Chpater 15, page 241
Link cell data to related data on the Web	Smart Tags	Chapter 15, page 243
Work with structured (XML) data	XML	Chapter 15, page 245

For more information about the Excel product, see *http://www.microsoft.com/office/xp.*

Getting Help

Every effort has been made to ensure the accuracy of this book and the contents of its CD-ROM. If you do run into problems, please contact the appropriate source for help and assistance.

Getting Help with This Book and Its CD-ROM

If your question or issue concerns the content of this book or its companion CD-ROM, please first search the online Microsoft Knowledge Base, which provides support information for known errors in or corrections to this book, at the following Web site:

http://mspress.microsoft.com/support/search.htm

If you do not find your answer at the online Knowledge Base, send your comments or questions to Microsoft Press Technical Support at:

mspinput@microsoft.com

Getting Help with Microsoft Excel 2002

If your question is about a Microsoft software product, including Excel, and not about the content of this Microsoft Press book, please search the Microsoft Knowledge Base at:

http://support.microsoft.com/directory

In the United States, Microsoft software product support issues not covered by the Microsoft Knowledge Base are addressed by Microsoft Product Support Services. The Microsoft software support options available from Microsoft Product Support Services are listed at:

http://support.microsoft.com/directory

Outside the United States, for support information specific to your location, please refer to the Worldwide Support menu on the Microsoft Product Support Services Web site for the site specific to your country:

http://support.microsoft.com/directory

Using the Book's CD-ROM

The CD-ROM inside the back cover of this book contains all the practice files you'll use as you work through the exercises in the book. By using practice files, you won't waste time creating samples and typing spreadsheet data—instead, you can jump right in and concentrate on learning how to use Microsoft Excel 2002.

Important

This book does not contain the Excel 2002 software. You should purchase and install that program before using this book.

System Requirements

To use this book, you will need:

- **Computer/Processor**

   Computer with a Pentium 133-megahertz (MHz) or higher processor

- **Memory**

   RAM requirements depend on the operating system used.

   - **Microsoft Windows 98, or Windows 98 Second Edition**

      24 MB of RAM plus an additional 8 MB of RAM for each Microsoft Office program (such as Microsoft Word) running simultaneously

   - **Microsoft Windows Me, or Microsoft Windows NT**

      32 MB of RAM plus an additional 8 MB of RAM for each Office program (such as Microsoft Word) running simultaneously

   - **Windows 2000 Professional**

      64 MB of RAM plus an additional 8 MB of RAM for each Office program (such as Microsoft Word) running simultaneously

- **Hard Disk**

   Hard disk space requirements will vary depending on configuration; custom installation choices may require more or less hard disk space.

   - 245 MB of available hard disk space with 115 MB on the hard disk where the operating system is installed. (Users without Windows 2000, Windows Me, or Office 2000 Service Release 1 [SR-1] require an extra 50 MB of hard disk space for System Files Update.)

   - An additional 3 MB of hard disk space is required for installing the practice files.

■ **Operating System**

Windows 98, Windows 98 Second Edition, Windows Millennium Edition (Windows Me), Windows NT 4 with Service Pack 6 (SP6) or later, or Windows 2000 or later. (On systems running Windows NT 4 with SP6, the version of Microsoft Internet Explorer must be upgraded to at least version 4.01 with SP1.)

■ **Drive**

CD-ROM drive

■ **Display**

Super VGA (800 × 600) or higher-resolution monitor with 256 colors

■ **Peripherals**

Microsoft Mouse, Microsoft IntelliMouse, or compatible pointing device

■ **Applications**

Excel 2002, Microsoft Access 2002, and Microsoft PowerPoint 2002

Installing the Practice Files

You need to install the practice files on your hard disk before you use them in the chapters' exercises. Follow these steps to prepare the CD's files for your use:

1 Insert the CD-ROM into the CD-ROM drive of your computer.

A menu screen appears.

Important

If the menu screen does not appear, start Windows Explorer. In the left pane, locate the icon for your CD-ROM and click the icon. In the right pane, double-click the file StartCD.

2 Click **Install Practice Files**.

3 Click **OK** in the initial message box.

4 If you want to install the practice files to a location other than the default folder (C:\SBS\Excel), click the **Change Folder** button, select the new drive and path, and then click **OK**.

5 Click the **Continue** button to install the selected practice files.

6 After the practice files have been installed, click **OK**.

Within the installation folder are subfolders for each chapter in the book.

7 Remove the CD-ROM from the CD-ROM drive, and return it to the envelope at the back of the book.

Using the Practice Files

Each chapter's introduction lists the files that are needed for that chapter and explains any file preparation that you need to take care of before you start working through the chapter.

Each topic in the chapter explains how and when to use any practice files. The file or files that you'll need are indicated in the margin at the beginning of the procedure above the CD icon, as shown here:

GoalSeek

The following table lists each chapter's practice files.

Chapter	Folder	Files
1	GettingToKnowXL	FileOpen, ZeroIn, DataEntry, and Replace
2	SettingUpWorkbook	Easier, DataRead, and AddPicture
3	PerformingCalculations	NameRange, Formula, and FindErrors
4	ChangingDocAppearance	Formats, CreateNew, EasyRead, Conditional, Follow, and Margins
5	UsingFilters	Filter, Calculations, and Validate
6	MultipleSources	TemplateStart, January, February, March, Linking, 2001Q1, Consolidate, TotalByHour2001, Y2001Q1, and Y2001ByMonth
7	ReorderingAndSummarizing	Sorting and Levels
8	AnalyzingAlternativeDataSets	Defining, Multiple, and GoalSeek
9	PivotTable	CreatePivot, EditPivot, Export, and External
10	Charts	CreateChart, Customize, TrendLine, and Dynamic
11	Printing	Printing, Part, and PrintChart
12	Macros	View, Record, Toolbar, Menu, and RunOnOpen
13	OtherPrograms	Include, YearEndSummary, Worksheet, SalesByCategory, Hyperlink, ProductList, PasteChart, and ChartTarget

(continued)

Chapter	Folder	Files
14	Database	Lookup, Query, and Products
15	Web	Saving, Publish, Pivot, WebData, Smart, Structured, and PivotXML
16	Collaborating	Sharing, Comments, Tracking, MergeTarget, Owner, Buyer, and Protection

Uninstalling the Practice Files

After you finish working through this book, you should uninstall the practice files to free up hard disk space.

1 On the Windows taskbar, click the **Start** button, point to **Settings**, and then click **Control Panel**.

2 Double-click the **Add/Remove Programs** icon.

3 Click **Microsoft Excel 2002 SBS Files**, and click **Add/Remove**. (If you're using Windows 2000 Professional, click the **Remove** or **Change/Remove** button.)

4 Click **Yes** when the confirmation dialog box appears.

Important

If you need additional help installing or uninstalling the practice files, please see the section "Getting Help" earlier in this book. Microsoft's product support does not provide support for this book or its CD-ROM.

Conventions and Features

You can save time when you use this book by understanding how the Step by Step series shows special instructions, keys to press, buttons to click, and so on.

Convention	Meaning
1 **2**	Numbered steps guide you through hands-on exercises in each topic.
●	A round bullet indicates an exercise that has only one step.
(CD icon)	This icon at the beginning of a chapter lists the files that the lesson will use and explains any file preparation that needs to take place before starting the lesson.
FileName (CD icon)	Practice files that you'll need to use in a topic's procedure are shown above the CD icon.
Ex2002-3-5 (MICROSOFT OFFICE SPECIALIST icon) Approved Courseware	This icon indicates a section that covers a Microsoft Office Specialist (MOS) exam objective. The numbers above the icon refer to the specific MOS objective.
new for **Office**XP	This icon indicates a new or greatly improved feature in this version of Microsoft Excel.
Tip	This section provides a helpful hint or shortcut that makes working through a task easier.
Important	This section points out information that you need to know to complete the procedure.
Troubleshooting	This section shows you how to fix a common problem.
Save (Save button icon)	When a button is referenced in a topic, a picture of the button appears in the margin area with a label.

(continued)

Convention	Meaning
`Alt`+`Tab`	A plus sign (+) between two key names means that you must press those keys at the same time. For example, "Press `Alt`+`Tab`" means that you hold down the `Alt` key while you press `Tab`.
Boldface type	Program features that you click or press are shown in black boldface type.
Blue boldface type	Terms that are explained in the glossary at the end of the book are shown in blue boldface type within the chapter.
Red boldface type	Text that you are supposed to type appears in red boldface type in the procedures.

MOS Objectives

Each Microsoft Office Specialist (MOS) certification level has a set of objectives, which are organized into broader skill sets. To prepare for the MOS certification exam, you should confirm that you can meet its respective objectives.

This book will prepare you fully for the MOS exam at either the core or the expert level because it addresses all the objectives for both exams. Throughout this book, content that pertains to a MOS objective is identified with the following MOS logo and objective number in the margin:

Ex2002-3-2

Approved Courseware

Core MOS Objectives

Objective	Skill	Page
Ex2002-1	**Working with Cells and Cell Data**	
Ex2002-1-1	Insert, delete, and move cells	24
Ex2002-1-2	Enter and edit cell data, including text, numbers, and formulas	16, 245
Ex2002-1-3	Check spelling	16
Ex2002-1-4	Find and replace cell data and formats	16
Ex2002-1-5	Work with a subset of data by filtering lists	74
Ex2002-2	**Managing Workbooks**	
Ex2002-2-1	Manage workbook files and folders	234
Ex2002-2-2	Create workbooks using templates	87
Ex2002-2-3	Save workbooks using different names and file formats	4
Ex2002-3	**Formatting and Printing Worksheets**	
Ex2002-3-1	Apply and modify cell formats	50
Ex2002-3-2	Modify row and column settings	24, 25, 29
Ex2002-3-3	Modify row and column formats	24, 29

(continued)

Objective	Skill	Page
Ex2002-3-4	Apply styles	53
Ex2002-3-5	Use automated tools to format worksheets	132
Ex2002-3-6	Modify Page Setup options for worksheets	64, 68, 170, 178
Ex2002-3-7	Preview and print worksheets and workbooks	173, 177
Ex2002-4	**Modifying Workbooks**	
Ex2002-4-1	Insert and delete worksheets	86
Ex2002-4-2	Modify worksheet names and positions	23, 90
Ex2002-4-3	Use 3-D references	93
Ex2002-5	**Creating and Revising Formulas**	
Ex2002-5-1	Create and revise formulas	38, 40, 42
Ex2002-5-2	Use statistical, date and time, financial, and logical functions in formulas	39
Ex2002-6	**Creating and Modifying Graphics**	
Ex2002-6-1	Create, modify, position, and print charts	150, 156, 181
Ex2002-6-2	Create, modify, and position graphics	31
Ex2002-7	**Workgroup Collaboration**	
Ex2002-7-1	Convert worksheets to Web pages	232
Ex2002-7-2	Create hyperlinks	211
Ex2002-7-3	View and edit comments	253

Expert MOS Objectives

Objective	Skill	Page
Ex2002e-1	**Importing and Exporting Data**	
Ex2002e-1-1	Import data into Excel	223
Ex2002e-1-2	Export data from Excel	232
Ex2002e-1-3	Publish worksheets and workbooks on the Web	234
Ex2002e-2	**Managing Workbooks**	
Ex2002e-2-1	Create, edit, and apply templates	86
Ex2002e-2-2	Create workspaces	100
Ex2002e-2-3	Use data consolidation	97

Taking a MOS Exam

As desktop computing technology advances, more employers rely on the objectivity and consistency of technology certification when screening, hiring, and training employees to ensure the competence of these professionals. As an employee, you can use technology certification to prove that you meet the standards set by your current or potential employer. The Microsoft Office Specialist (MOS) program is the only Microsoft-approved certification program designed to assist employees in validating their competence using Microsoft Office applications.

About the MOS Program

A Microsoft Office Specialist is an individual who has certified his or her skills in one or more of the Microsoft Office desktop applications of Microsoft Word, Microsoft Excel, Microsoft PowerPoint, Microsoft Outlook, Microsoft Access, Microsoft FrontPage, or Microsoft Project. The Microsoft Office Specialist Program typically offers certification exams at the "core" and "expert" skill levels. (The availability of Microsoft Office Specialist certification exams varies by application, application version, and language. Visit *http://www.microsoft.com/officespecialist* for exam availability.) The Microsoft Office Specialist Program is the only Microsoft-approved program in the world for certifying proficiency in Microsoft Office desktop applications and Microsoft Project. This certification can be a valuable asset in any job search or career advancement.

What Does This Logo Mean?

Approved Courseware

This MOS logo means this courseware has been approved by the Microsoft Office Specialist Program to be among the finest available for learning Excel 2002. It also means that upon completion of this courseware, you may be prepared to become a Microsoft Office Specialist.

Selecting a MOS Certification Level

In selecting the MOS certification(s) level that you would like to pursue, you should assess the following:

- The Office application and version(s) of the application with which you are familiar
- The length of time you have used the application
- Whether you have had formal or informal training

Candidates for the core-level MOS certification exams are expected to successfully complete a wide range of standard business tasks, such as formatting a document. Successful candidates generally have six or more months of experience with the application, including either formal instructor-led training with a MOS Authorized Instructor or self-study using MOS-approved books, guides, or interactive computer-based materials.

Candidates for expert-level certification, by comparison, are expected to complete more complex business-oriented assignments utilizing the application's advanced functionality, such as importing data and recording macros. Successful candidates generally have two or more years of experience with the application, again including formal instructor-led training with a MOS Authorized Instructor or self-study using MOS-approved materials.

MOS Exam Objectives

Every MOS certification exam is developed from a list of exam objectives, which are derived from studies of how the Office application is actually used in the workplace. Because these objectives dictate the scope of each exam, they provide you with critical information on how to prepare for MOS certification.

Tip

See the previous section, "MOS Objectives," for a complete list of objectives for Excel.

MOS Approved Courseware, including the Microsoft Press Step by Step series, is reviewed and approved on the basis of its coverage of the MOS exam objectives.

The Exam Experience

The MOS certification exams are unique in that they are performance-based examinations that allow you to interact with a "live" version of the Office application as you complete a series of assigned tasks. All the standard menus, toolbars, and keyboard shortcuts are available—even the Help menu. MOS exams for Office XP applications consist of 25 to 35 questions, each of which requires you to complete one or more tasks using the Office application for which you are seeking certification. For example:

Prepare the document for publication as a Web page by completing the following three tasks:

1   Convert the memo to a Web page.
2   Title the page **Revised Company Policy**.
3   Name the memo **Policy Memo.htm**.

The duration of MOS exams ranges from 45 to 60 minutes, depending on the application. Passing percentages range from 70 to 80 percent correct.

The Exam Interface and Controls

After you fill out a series of information screens, the testing software starts the exam and the respective Office application. You will see the exam interface and controls, including the test question, in the dialog box in the lower right corner of the screen.

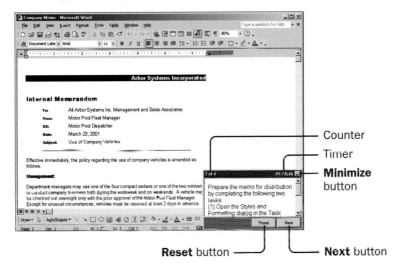

- If the exam dialog box gets in the way of your work, you can hide it by clicking the **Minimize** button in the upper right corner, or you can drag it to another position on the screen.

- The timer starts when the first question appears on your screen and displays the remaining exam time. If the timer and the counter are distracting, click the timer to remove the display.

Important

The timer will not count the time required for the exam to be loaded between questions. It keeps track of only the time you spend answering questions.

- The counter tracks how many questions you have completed and how many remain.

- The **Reset** button allows you to restart work on a question if you think you have made an error. The **Reset** button will *not* restart the entire exam or extend the exam time limit.

- When you complete a question, click the **Next** button to move to the next question.

Important

It is not possible to move back to a previous question on the exam.

Test-Taking Tips

- Follow all instructions provided in each question completely and accurately.

- Enter requested information as it appears in the instructions but without duplicating the formatting. For example, all text and values that you will be asked to enter will appear in the instructions as **bold** and **underlined**; however, you should enter the information without applying this formatting unless you are specifically instructed to do otherwise.

- Close all dialog boxes before proceeding to the next exam question unless you are specifically instructed otherwise.

- There is no need to save your work before moving on to the next question unless you are specifically instructed otherwise.

- Do not cut and paste information from the exam interface into the application.

- For questions that ask you to print a document, spreadsheet, chart, report, slide, and so forth, nothing will actually be printed.

- Responses are scored based on the result of your work, not the method you use to achieve that result (unless a specific method is explicitly required), and not the time you take to complete the question. Extra keystrokes or mouse clicks do not count against your score.

- If your computer becomes unstable during the exam (for example, if the application's toolbars or the mouse no longer functions) or if a power outage occurs, contact a testing center administrator immediately. The administrator will then restart the computer, and the exam will return to the point before the interruption occurred.

Certification

At the conclusion of the exam, you will receive a score report, which you can print with the assistance of the testing center administrator. If your score meets or exceeds the minimum required score, you will also be mailed a printed certificate within approximately 14 days.

For More Information

To learn more about becoming a Microsoft Office Specialist, visit *www.Microsoft.com/ officespecialist*.

To purchase a Microsoft Office Specialist certification exam, visit *http://www.microsoft.com/traincert/mcp/officespecialist/officespecialist_locator.asp*.

To learn about other Microsoft Office Specialist–approved courseware from Microsoft Press, visit *http://www.microsoft.com/mspress/certification/officespecialist*.

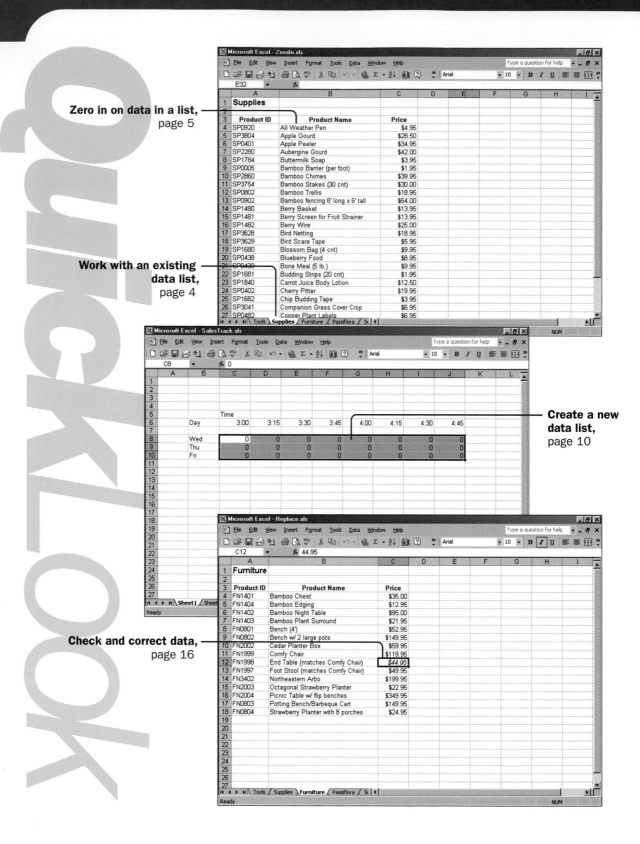

Zero in on data in a list, page 5

Work with an existing data list, page 4

Create a new data list, page 10

Check and correct data, page 16

Chapter 1
Getting to Know Excel

After completing this chapter, you will be able to:

✔ **Work with an existing data list.**

✔ **Zero in on data in a list.**

✔ **Create a data list.**

✔ **Check and correct data.**

One thing all businesses have in common is the need to keep accurate records. As the range of products, services, and customers expands, businesses require a computer-based system to keep up with an avalanche of financial and other data.

Microsoft Excel is a spreadsheet program that lets you organize your data into lists and then summarize, compare, and present your data graphically. For example, you can have Excel find the sum, average, or maximum value for sales on a given day; create a graph showing what percentage of sales were in a particular range; and show how the total sales compared with the total sales of other days in the same week. In short, Excel saves you from having to create these summaries by hand.

The exercises in this book are based on data for The Garden Company, the fictional business used in the *Step by Step* series. In addition to taking care of the plants and gardening supplies offered by the company, the owner, Catherine Turner, and her employees need to maintain the data lists that let Catherine and The Garden Company's head buyer make informed decisions about the products the company carries.

In this chapter, you'll learn how to work with an existing data list and specific data within a data list, create a data list, and check and correct data.

 This chapter uses the practice files FileOpen, ZeroIn, DataEntry, and Replace that you installed from this book's CD-ROM. For details about installing the practice files, see "Using the Book's CD-ROM" at the beginning of this book.

Important

Depending on the screen resolution you have set on your computer and which toolbar buttons you use most often, it's possible that not every button on every toolbar will appear on your Excel toolbars. If a button mentioned in this book doesn't appear on a toolbar, click the **Toolbar Options** down arrow on that toolbar to display the rest of the buttons available on that toolbar.

Introducing Excel

When you start Excel, a blank document appears. From this point, you can add data, change how the data looks, have Excel summarize data, or find information in Excel's help files. The following graphic points out the most important parts of Excel, the last two of which are new in Excel 2002: the workbook window, the main menu bar, the formula bar, the Standard and Formatting toolbars, the status bar, and (new in this version) the Ask A Question box and the task pane.

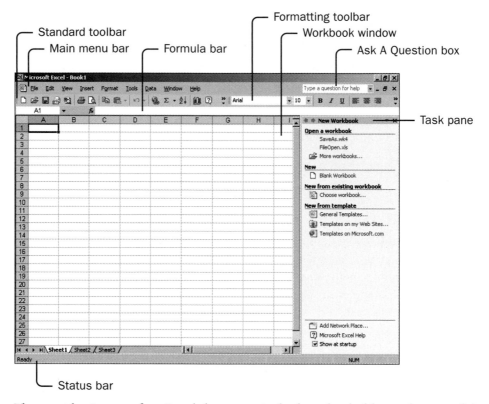

The most basic part of an Excel document is the box that holds an element of data—in Excel, that box is called a **cell**. Each cell is at the intersection of a **row** (a sequence of cells along a horizontal line) and a **column** (a sequence of cells along a vertical line); rows are identified by a number and columns by a letter. The row number and column letter that designate a specific cell are called a **cell reference**. For example, the cell in the upper left corner of the workbook window has the cell reference A1. A single set of columns and rows makes up a **worksheet**, which appears as a page in an Excel document. A **workbook**, in turn, is a collection of one or more worksheets.

Tip

When you create an Excel document, you create a workbook with three worksheets.

The workbook that owner Catherine Turner has developed for The Garden Company has three worksheets, with each worksheet holding data about products available at the company's retail location. She has named the workbook *Products*, and she records data about furniture items on one worksheet, gardening supplies on another worksheet, and tools on a third worksheet. On each worksheet, she uses three columns to record each product's identification code, description, and price. This collection of related information is called a data list.

You can include more than three categories in a workbook for a given subject by simply creating additional worksheets; if you want to store data about an entirely different subject, however, you must create a new workbook. For example, if Catherine wanted to record more data about different categories of products sold by The Garden Company, such as varieties of plants, she could create a new worksheet in the *Products* workbook and add the data to the worksheet. However, if she wanted to store data on a different subject, perhaps her customers and their contact information, she would need to create a new workbook.

Tip

Each workbook should contain information about a unique subject, such as Products, Customers, or Sales, while each worksheet should hold information about a subset of items in that category, meaning different types of products, preferred customers vs. non-preferred customers, or sales information for a given month.

Ask A Question
new for
OfficeXP

The Ask A Question box is new in this version of Excel. Rather than get help through the **Help** menu, you can now type a question in the Ask A Question box and have Excel display the help topics that match your request. The benefit of placing the Ask A Question box in the main Excel window is that you can quickly and easily get help while your question is fresh in your mind, without adding any steps that might distract you from your question.

Task pane
new for
OfficeXP

The task pane, also new in this version of Excel, lets you open files, paste data from the Clipboard, create blank workbooks, and create Excel workbooks based on existing files. A great advantage of the task pane is that it groups many common actions, such as opening or creating new files, in one place and lets you perform them with a single mouse click. The only drawback of the task pane is that it takes up valuable screen space. Fortunately, you can show or hide the task pane easily. On the **View** menu, click **Task Pane**; Excel hides the task pane if it is currently displayed or shows it if it is currently hidden.

Important

If you haven't done so yet, you should install this book's practice files so you can work through the exercises in this chapter. You can find instructions for installing the practice files in the "Using the Book's CD-ROM" section at the front of this book.

Working with an Existing Data List

When you start Excel, the program displays a blank worksheet and has the task pane open on the right side of the screen. You can begin to enter data in the worksheet's cells or open an existing workbook. In the exercises that follow, you'll be working with some of the workbooks that have already been created for The Garden Company. After you've made any desired changes to a workbook, you should save the workbook.

When you save a file, you overwrite the previous copy of the file. If you have made changes that you want to save but you want to keep a copy of the file as it was previously, you can use the **Save As** command to specify a name for the new file.

Tip

Readers frequently ask, "How often should I save my files?" It's good practice to save your changes every half hour, or even every five minutes, but the best time to save a file is whenever you have made a change you would hate to have to make again.

Ex2002-2-3

Approved Courseware

You can also use the controls in the **Save As** dialog box to specify a different format for the new file. For example, Catherine Turner, the owner of The Garden Company, might want to save an Excel file in a different format if she needs to share the file with the company's accountant, who happens to use another spreadsheet program.

FileOpen

In this exercise, you start Excel from the **Start** menu and then use the **Open** dialog box to open an existing workbook. Once you have opened the workbook, you update the price of an item and save the workbook twice: once as an Excel workbook and again as a Lotus file.

1 On the taskbar, click the **Start** button, point to **Programs**, and then click **Microsoft Excel**.

The main Excel program window appears.

Open

2 On the Standard toolbar, click the **Open** button.

The **Open** dialog box appears.

Tip

When the task pane is displayed, you can also open a file by looking under the **Open a Workbook** heading and either clicking the name of the workbook you want to open or clicking **More Workbooks** to display the **Open** dialog box.

3 Click the **Look In** down arrow, and select the hard disk where you installed the Step by Step practice files.

The files and folders on your hard disk appear.

4 Locate the SBS folder, and then double-click the **Excel** folder.

The files and folders in the Excel folder appear.

5 Double-click the **GettingToKnowXL** folder.

The files and folders in the GettingToKnowXL folder appear.

6 Double-click the **FileOpen.xls** file.

The FileOpen.xls file opens.

7 Click cell C16, and type **15.95**.

The data in cell C16 changes to $15.95.

Save

8 On the Standard toolbar, click the **Save** button.

Excel saves your changes.

9 On the **File** menu, click **Save As**.

The **Save As** dialog box appears.

10 Click in the **File name** box, delete the existing file name, and type **SaveAs**.

11 Click the **Save as type** down arrow to expand the list, and click **WK4 (1-2-3) (*.wk4)**.

12 Click the **Save** button.

A dialog box appears, indicating that some features might be lost. Click **Yes** to have Excel save a new copy of your data in a Lotus file named SaveAs.wk4.

Zeroing In on Data in a List

Once you have opened a workbook, you can examine and modify its contents. To change specific data, such as the price of a pair of shears, you can move to that cell directly and then make your changes. Once in that cell, you can move to another cell in the same worksheet or move to another worksheet in the workbook. Moving to another worksheet is accomplished by clicking its **sheet tab**, located at the lower left edge of the workbook window.

You can move to a specific cell in lots of ways, but the most direct method is to click the cell to which you want to move. The cell you click will be outlined in black, and its contents, if any, will appear in the formula bar. When a cell is outlined, it is the **active cell**, meaning that you can modify its contents. You use a similar method to select multiple cells (referred to as a **cell range**)—just click the first cell in the range, and drag the mouse pointer over the remaining cells you want to select. Once you have selected the cell or cells you want to work with, you can cut, copy, delete, or change the format of the contents of the cell or cells. For instance, Catherine Turner, the owner of The Garden Company, might want to copy the prices of her five most popular garden furniture pieces to a new page that summarizes the best-selling items in each product category that the company offers.

Important

If you select a group of cells, the first cell you click is designated the active cell.

You're not limited to selecting cells individually or as part of a range. For example, you might need to move a column of price data one column to the right to make room for a column of headings that indicate to which product category (Furniture, Tools, Supplies, and so forth) items belong. To move an entire column (or entire columns) of data at a time, you click the column's header, located at the top of the worksheet. Clicking a column header highlights every cell in that column and lets you copy or cut the column and paste it elsewhere in the workbook.

Paste Options
new for
OfficeXP

A new feature in this version of Excel is the **Paste Options** button that appears next to data you copy from a cell and paste into another cell.

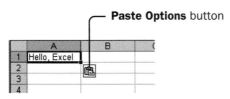

— **Paste Options** button

Clicking the **Paste Options** button displays a list of actions Excel can take regarding the pasted cells. The options in the list are summarized in the following table.

Option	Action
Keep Source Formatting	Paste the contents of the Clipboard (which holds the last information selected via Cut or Copy) into the target cells, and format the data as it was formatted in the original cells.
Match Destination Formatting	Paste the contents of the Clipboard into the target cells, and format the data using the existing format in the target cells.

Option	Action
Values and Number Formatting	Paste the contents of the Clipboard into the target cells, keeping any numeric formats.
Keep Source Column Widths	Paste the contents of the Clipboard into the target cells, and resize the columns of the target cells to match the widths of the columns of the source cells.
Formatting Only	Apply the format of the source cells to the target cells, but do not copy the contents of the source cells.
Link Cells	Display the contents of the source cells in the target cells, updating the target cells whenever the content of the source cells changes.
Values Only	Paste the values from a column into the target column; use the existing format of the target column.
Values and Source Formatting	Paste a column of cells into the target column; apply the format of the copied column to the new column.

Troubleshooting

If the **Paste Options** button doesn't appear, you can turn the feature on by clicking **Options** on the **Tools** menu. In the dialog box that appears, click the **Edit** tab and then select the **Show Paste Options buttons** check box.

Zeroln

In this exercise, you move from one worksheet to another to examine data about products The Garden Company sells and then select a range of cells whose contents you want to copy to the Summary sheet in your workbook. After you have copied and pasted that information, you select the first three columns of your Summary worksheet, copy them to the Clipboard, and move the columns (and their contents) over one column to make the first column available for text indicating which worksheet-specific sets of data came from.

1 Navigate to the GettingToKnowXL practice folder, and double-click the **Zeroln xls** file.

2 In the lower left corner of the Excel window, click the **Furniture** sheet tab.

The Furniture worksheet appears.

3 On the tab bar, right-click the arrow buttons and then, from the shortcut menu that appears, click **Passiflora**.

The Passiflora worksheet appears.

4 Click the **Tools** sheet tab to make the Tools worksheet the active worksheet in the workbook.

5 Click cell A3.

Cell A3 becomes the active cell in the worksheet. The value in cell A3, *Product ID*, appears in the formula bar, and the cell identifier appears in the Name box.

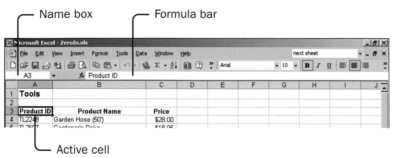

6 Drag from cell A3 to cell C6.

The selected cells are highlighted.

Copy

7 On the Standard toolbar, click the **Copy** button.

The contents of the selected cells are copied to the Clipboard. The selected cells retain their contents and are surrounded by a marquee outline (an outline that seems to move around the edge of the cells).

8 Click the **Summary** sheet tab.

Paste

9 The Summary sheet appears. Click cell A3, and then, on the Standard toolbar, click the **Paste** button.

The values in the cells you copied appear in cells A3 to C6 of the Summary worksheet.

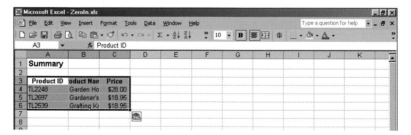

Tip

In previous versions of Excel, you had to select the cells that were the destination for the values you copied. If the destination area wasn't the same size as the copied area, Excel wouldn't let the paste proceed. In this version of Excel, all you need to do is click the cell in the upper left corner of the group of cells that you want to hold the data and then paste the data into the sheet. The exception, which you will encounter later in this chapter, occurs when you cut and paste entire columns or rows.

10 Click the **Tools** sheet tab.

The Tools worksheet appears.

11 Click the Name box.

The value in the Name box is highlighted.

12 In the Name box, type **B9** and press [Enter].

Cell B9 is highlighted with the value *Long-handled Loppers*.

13 Click the Name box, type **B14**, and press [Enter].

Cell B14 is highlighted with the value *Pruning Saw*.

14 Click the **Summary** sheet tab.

The Summary worksheet appears.

15 Click the column heading for column A.

Every cell in column A, including the column heading, is highlighted.

16 Drag to the column heading for column C.

Every cell in columns A through C, including the column headings, is highlighted.

Cut

17 On the Standard toolbar, click the **Cut** button.

18 Click the column heading for column B, and drag to the column heading for column D.

Every cell in columns B through D, including the column headings, is highlighted.

19 On the **Edit** menu, click **Paste**.

The contents of the Clipboard appear in columns B through D.

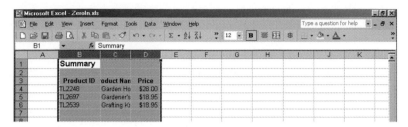

20 On the Standard toolbar, click the **Save** button to save your changes.

Close

21 Click the **Close** button to close ZeroIn.xls.

Tip

To select cell A1 in the active worksheet (that is, to return to the top of a worksheet immediately), press Ctrl + Home.

Creating a Workbook

Every time you want to gather and store data that isn't closely related to any of your existing data, you should create a new workbook. The default new workbook in the current version of Excel has three worksheets, although you can add more worksheets or delete existing worksheets if you want. Creating a new workbook is a straightforward process—you just click the appropriate button on the toolbar.

Once you have created a workbook, you can begin entering data. The simplest way to enter data is to click a cell and type a value, a method that works very well when you're entering a few pieces of data but that is less than ideal when you're entering long sequences or series of values. For example, Catherine Turner, the owner of The Garden Company, might want to create a worksheet listing hourly sales figures for the company from 1:00 p.m. to 7:00 p.m. for weekdays. To record those numbers, she would need to create a worksheet with the following layout.

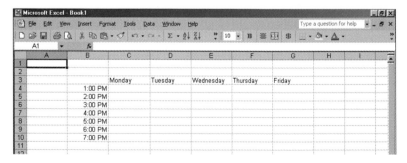

Typing the sequence *Monday, Tuesday, Wednesday, Thursday, Friday* repeatedly can be handled by copying and pasting the first occurrence of the sequence, but there's an easier way to do it using **AutoFill**. With AutoFill, you enter the first element in a recognized series, grab the **fill handle** at the lower right corner of the cell, and drag the fill handle until the series extends far enough to accommodate your data. A similar tool, **FillSeries**, lets you enter two values in a series and use the fill handle to extend the series in your worksheet. For example, if you want to create a series starting at 2 and increasing by two, you would put *2* in the first cell and *4* in the second cell, select both cells, and then use the fill handle to extend the series to your desired end value.

Other data entry techniques you'll use in this section are **AutoComplete**, which detects when a value you're entering is similar to previously entered values; **Pick from List**, which lets you choose a value from existing values in a column; and Ctrl+Enter, which lets you enter a value in multiple cells simultaneously.

The following table summarizes these data entry techniques.

Method	Action
AutoFill	Enter the first value in a recognized series, and use the fill handle to extend the series.
FillSeries	Enter the first two values in a series, and use the fill handle to extend the series.
AutoComplete	Type the first few letters in a cell, and if a similar value exists in the same column, Excel will suggest the existing value.
Pick from List	Right-click a cell, and from the shortcut menu that appears, choose **Pick from List**. A list of existing values in the cell's column will appear.
Ctrl + Enter	Select a range of cells to contain the same data, type the data in the active cell, and press Ctrl + Enter.

Auto Fill
Options
now for
OfficeXP

A new feature in the current version of Excel is the **Auto Fill Options** button that appears next to data you add to a worksheet using either AutoFill or FillSeries.

Clicking the **Auto Fill Options** button displays a list of actions Excel can take regarding the cells affected by your Fill operation. The options in the list are summarized in the following table.

Option	Action
Copy Cells	Copy the contents of the selected cells to the cells indicated by the Fill operation.
Fill Series	Fill the cells indicated by the Fill operation with the next items in the series.
Fill Formatting Only	Copy the format of the selected cell to the cells indicated by the Fill operation, but do not place any values in the target cells.
Fill Without Formatting	Fill the cells indicated by the Fill operation with the next items in the series, but ignore any formatting applied to the source cells.
Fill \<sequence\>	This option changes according to the series Excel detects and seems to have the same effect as the Fill Series option. If you do not use a recognized sequence, the option does not appear.

Troubleshooting

If the **Auto Fill Options** button doesn't appear, you can turn the feature on by clicking **Options** on the **Tools** menu. In the dialog box that appears, click the **Edit** tab and then select the **Show Paste Options buttons** check box.

DataEntry

In this exercise, you create a workbook to track the number of customers of The Garden Company making purchases during a two-hour period for three days. The workbook will eventually have sheets recording the total number of customers making purchases (by quarter hour), items sold, and number of items in a given transaction. You use the data entry methods described earlier in this section, such as AutoFill, FillSeries, and [Ctrl]+[Enter], to fill in the worksheets.

New

1 On the Standard toolbar, click the **New** button.

A blank workbook appears.

Save

2 On the Standard toolbar, click the **Save** button.

The **Save** dialog box appears.

3 If necessary, navigate to the SBS\Excel\GettingToKnowXL folder on your hard disk.

4 In the **File name** box, type **SalesTrack**.

Excel adds the .xls extension to your file.

5 Click **Save**.

Excel saves your file as SalesTrack.xls.

6 Click cell B6, and type **Day**.

7 Click cell C5, and type **Time**.

8 Click cell B8, and type **Wed**.

A black box appears around cell B8.

9 Move the mouse pointer over the lower right corner of cell B8.

The mouse pointer changes to a black plus sign.

10 Click the black plus sign at the lower right corner of cell B8, and drag it to cell B10.

Excel fills cell B9 with the value *Thu* and cell B10 with *Fri*. As you drag over cells B9 and B10, Excel displays a ScreenTip indicating which value will appear in each cell.

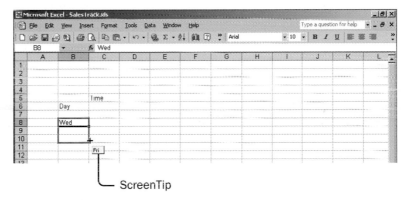

ScreenTip

11 Click cell C6, and type **3:00**; then click cell D6, and type **3:15**.

Tip

You give Excel two values when you use FillSeries: the first value sets the starting point for the series, and the second sets the increment. In this example, 3:15 is 15 minutes greater than the starting value of 3:00, so Excel adds 15 minutes to the current cell to generate the value for the next cell in the series.

12 Click cell C6, and drag to cell D6.

A black box appears around cells C6 and D6.

13 Move the mouse pointer over the lower right corner of cell D6.

When the mouse pointer is over the lower right corner of the cell, it changes to a black plus sign.

14 Click the black plus sign at the lower right corner of cell D6, and drag it to cell J6.

Excel fills the six cells from E6 through J6 with the next values in the series, namely 3:30 to 4:45, in 15-minute increments.

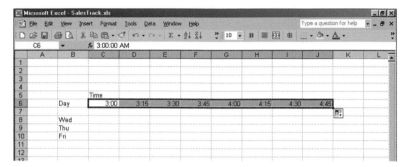

15 On the Standard toolbar, click the **Save** button to save your changes.

16 Click the **Close** button to close SalesTrack.xls.

Open

17 On the Standard toolbar, click the **Open** button.

The **Open** dialog box appears.

18 Click **DataEntry**, and then click **Open**.

DataEntry.xls appears.

19 Click the **Sheet2** sheet tab.

Sheet2 appears.

20 Click cell C8 and type **Bamboo S**, but do not press Enter.

Just after you type the S, Excel searches the existing items in the column and, finding a match, adds the highlighted text *takes (30 cnt)* to the contents of the cell.

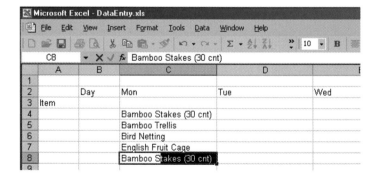

21 To accept the suggested value, *Bamboo Stakes (30 cnt)*, for the cell, press the ⌈Enter⌋ key.

Excel completes the cell entry.

Important

Pressing ⌈Del⌋ before pressing ⌈Enter⌋ (or ⌈Tab⌋) will delete the highlighted text and keep *Bamboo S* as the value of the cell you were editing.

22 Click cell C9 and type **Bamboo T**, but do not press ⌈Enter⌋.

Just after you type the *T*, Excel adds the highlighted text *rellis*.

23 Press ⌈Tab⌋ to accept the suggested value, *Bamboo Trellis*.

Bamboo Trellis appears in cell C9.

24 Right-click cell C10, and on the shortcut menu that appears, click **Pick from List**.

A list of existing values in the column appears.

25 Click **Bird Netting**.

Bird Netting appears in cell C10.

26 Click the **Sheet1** sheet tab.

Sheet1 appears.

27 Drag from cell C8 to cell J10.

Excel highlights the cells in the rectangle defined at the upper left by cell C8 and at the lower right by cell J10. Note that cell C8 is still the active cell.

28 Type **0**, and press ⌈Ctrl⌋+⌈Enter⌋.

The value *0* appears in every selected cell.

29 On the Standard toolbar, click the **Save** button to save your changes.

Close

30 Click the **Close** button.

DataEntry.xls closes.

Checking and Correcting Data

Ex2002-1-2
Ex2002-1-3
Ex2002-1-4

Approved Courseware

Once you've entered your data, you should take the time to check and correct it. You do need to verify visually that each piece of numeric data is correct, but you can make sure that the text is spelled correctly by using Excel's spelling checker. When the spelling checker encounters a word it doesn't recognize, it will highlight the word and offer suggestions representing its best guess as to the correct word. You can then edit the word directly, pick the proper word from the list of suggestions, or have the spelling checker ignore the misspelling. You can also use the spelling checker to add any words that aren't in the standard dictionary so that Excel will recognize them later, saving you time by not requiring you to identify the words as correct every time they occur in your worksheets. Once you've made a change, you can remove the change as long as you haven't closed the workbook where you made the change. To undo a change, you click the appropriate toolbar button or open the **Edit** menu and choose the **Undo** command. If you decide you want to keep a change, you can use the **Redo** command to restore it.

Find Format

new for
OfficeXP

You can use a distinct text format to identify data you may need to change later. As an example, a sales representative for one of The Garden Company's suppliers might give The Garden Company's owner, Catherine Turner, a list of prices for upcoming products, with a note that those prices could change at any time. Catherine could format the changeable prices differently from the rest of the prices in the worksheet and call the representative to update her worksheet just before the products became available. After she got the new prices, she could use **Find Format** in the **Find and Replace** dialog box to locate the old prices and then change them by hand.

Replace

In this exercise, you have just found out that the manufacturer of the *Comfy Chair* has changed the name of the product to the *Cushy Chair*. You use **Find** to determine whether there are any occurrences of the word *Comfy*, and if there are, you use **Replace** to change them to *Cushy*. After you have made that change, you use **Find Format** to locate specially formatted data and change it. Finally you use the spelling checker to ensure that your text data has been entered correctly.

Open

1 On the Standard toolbar, click the **Open** button.

The **Open** dialog box appears.

2 Click **Replace.xls**, and then click **Open**.

Replace.xls appears.

3   If necessary, click the **Furniture** sheet tab to display the Furniture worksheet.

4   On the **Edit** menu, click **Find**.

The **Find and Replace** dialog box appears and opens to the **Find** tab.

Tip

You can also open the **Find and Replace** dialog box by pressing [Ctrl]+[F].

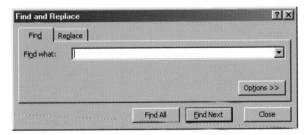

5   In the **Find what** box, type **Comfy** and then click **Find Next**.

The first cell containing *Comfy* is highlighted.

6   In the **Find and Replace** dialog box, click **Find Next** again.

The second cell containing *Comfy* is highlighted.

Tip

Clicking **Find All** would generate a list of matching cells and their contents below the dialog box. Clicking one of the matches moves you to that instance of the matching word or phrase.

7   Click the **Replace** tab.

The **Find what** box still shows the word *Comfy*.

8   In the **Replace with** box, type **Cushy**.

9   Click **Replace All**.

A dialog box appears, indicating that Excel has completed the operation and that three replacements were made.

10   Click **OK**.

The three occurrences of the word *Comfy* have been switched to *Cushy*.

Important

You can change the occurrences of the word *Comfy* one at a time by clicking the **Replace** button instead of the **Replace All** button. You might do so to ensure that there are no instances in which you don't want to replace the original word.

11 In the **Find and Replace** dialog box, click the **Find** tab.

The **Find** tab page appears.

12 Clear the **Find what** box.

13 Click the **Options** button to expand the options on the **Find** tab page.

The **Find** tab page options appear.

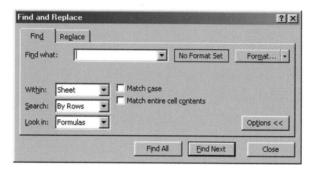

14 Click the **Format** button.

The **Find Format** dialog box appears.

15 If necessary, click the **Font** tab.

The **Font** tab page appears.

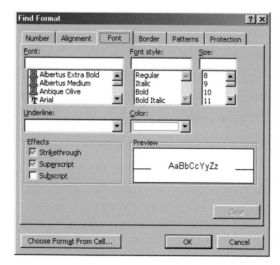

16 In the **Font style** list, click **Italic**, and then click **OK**.

The **Find Format** dialog box disappears.

17 In the **Find and Replace** dialog box, click **Find Next**.

Excel highlights the first cell containing italicized text.

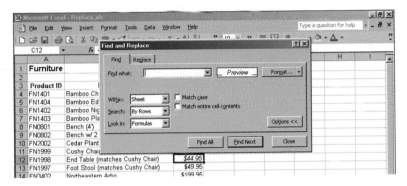

18 Click cell C12.

Italic

I

19 On the Formatting toolbar, click the **Italic** button.

Excel removes italics from the text in the selected cell.

20 Type **47.95**.

Excel replaces the previous value in the cell with the value you just entered. You will now undo the change you just made.

Undo

21 On the Standard toolbar, click the **Undo** button.

The contents of cell C12 revert to 44.95.

22 Click the **Undo** button.

The contents of cell C12 are once again italicized.

Redo

23 Click the **Redo** button.

The contents of cell C12 are no longer italicized.

24 On the **Tools** menu, click **Spelling**.

The **Spelling** dialog box appears. The first misspelled word Excel detects appears in the **Not in Dictionary** box, while the list of suggested replacements appears in the **Suggestions** list.

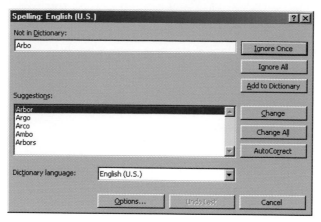

25 If necessary, in the **Suggestions** list, click **Arbor** and then click **Change**.

Excel changes *Arbo* to *Arbor* and displays a dialog box indicating that it found no more misspellings.

26 Click **OK**.

The dialog box disappears.

Tip

If you click **Change**, Excel inserts the suggested word. If you wanted Excel to ignore this occurrence of *Arbo*, you could have clicked **Ignore Once**; clicking **Ignore All** would cause Excel to skip over any occurrence of *Arbo* in the worksheet. Clicking **Add to Dictionary** means Excel would forever recognize *Arbo* as a word that did not need to be corrected.

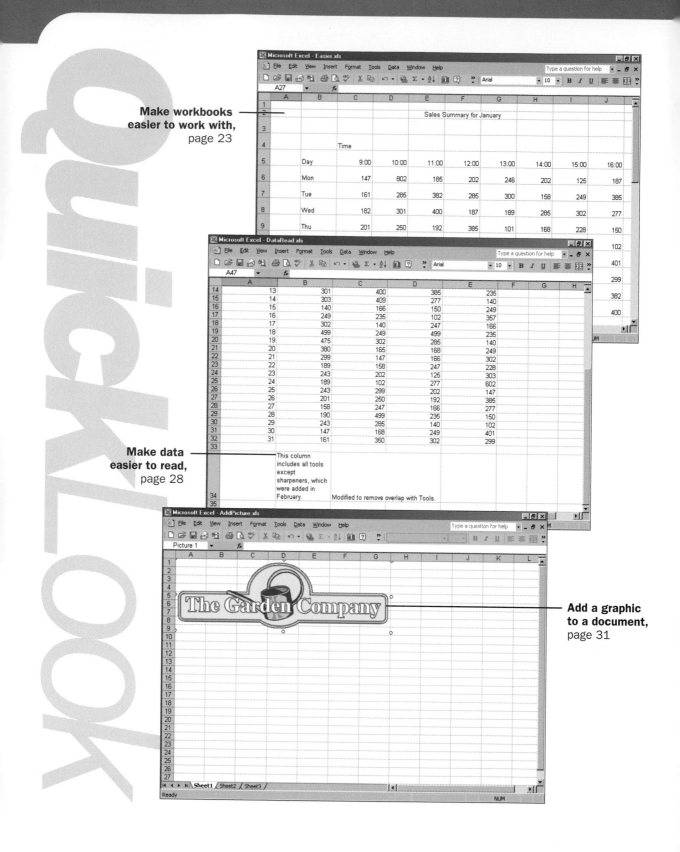

Make workbooks
easier to work with,
page 23

Make data
easier to read,
page 28

Add a graphic
to a document,
page 31

Chapter 2
Setting Up a Workbook

After completing this chapter, you will be able to:

✔ **Make workbooks easier to work with.**

✔ **Make data easier to read.**

✔ **Add a graphic to a document.**

One of the real strengths of Microsoft Excel is that the program helps you manage large quantities of data with ease. Part of the reason managing large data collections is so easy with Excel is that you can change how Excel displays your data within a worksheet. If you want more space between the rows or columns of a worksheet, want to temporarily limit which data is shown on the screen, or even just want to add descriptions that make it easier for you and your colleagues to understand the data that's stored on a worksheet, you can do so quickly. You can also change how those descriptions appear in a cell, setting them apart from the data in the worksheet.

Another way you can customize your worksheets is to add graphics, such as your company's logo or the image of a product, to a worksheet. Adding graphics to worksheets promotes awareness of your company, identifies the data as belonging to your company, and, in the case of a product image, gives viewers valuable information they need to make a purchase decision.

In this chapter, you'll learn how to make workbooks easier to work with, make data easier to read, and add a graphic to a document.

This chapter uses the practice files Easier, DataRead, and AddPicture that you installed from this book's CD-ROM. For details about installing the practice files, see "Using the Book's CD-ROM" at the beginning of this book.

Making Workbooks Easier to Work With

Ex2002-4-2

Approved Courseware

An important component of making workbooks easy to work with is to give users an idea where to find the data they're looking for. Excel gives you several ways to set up signposts directing users toward the data they want. The first method, discussed in Chapter 1, "Getting to Know Excel," is to give each workbook a descriptive name. Once users have opened the proper workbook, you can guide them to a specific worksheet by giving each worksheet a name; the names are displayed on the sheet tabs in the lower left corner of the workbook window. To change a worksheet's name, you right-click the sheet tab of the worksheet you want and, from the shortcut menu that appears, choose **Rename**. Choosing **Rename** opens the worksheet name for editing. You can also change the order of worksheets in a workbook by dragging the sheet tab of a worksheet to the desired position on the navigation bar, bringing the most popular worksheets to the front of the list.

Ex2002-3-3

Approved Courseware

After you have put up the signposts that make your data easy to find, you can take other steps to make the data in your workbooks easier to work with. For instance, you can change the width of a column or the height of a row in a worksheet by dragging the column or row's border to the desired position. Increasing a column's width or a row's height increases the space between cell contents, making it easier to select a cell's data without inadvertently selecting data from other cells as well.

Tip

You can apply the same change to more than one row or column by selecting the rows or columns you want to change and then dragging the border of one of the selected rows or columns to the desired location. When you release the mouse button, all of the selected rows or columns will change to the new height or width.

Ex2002-3-2
Ex2002-3-3

Approved Courseware

Changing column width and row height can make a workbook's contents easier to work with, but you can also insert a row or column between the edge of a worksheet and the cells containing the data. Adding space between the edge of a worksheet and cells, or perhaps between a label and the data to which it refers, makes the workbook's contents less crowded and easier to work with. You insert rows by clicking a cell and then, on the **Insert** menu, clicking **Rows**. Excel inserts a row above the active cell. You insert a column in much the same way, but you click **Columns** on the **Insert** menu. When you do, Excel inserts a column to the left of the active cell.

Ex2002-1-1

Approved Courseware

Likewise, you can insert individual cells into a worksheet. To insert a cell, click the cell currently in the position where you want the new cell to appear, and on the **Insert** menu, click **Cells** to display the **Insert** dialog box. In the **Insert** dialog box you can choose whether to shift the cells surrounding the inserted cell down (if your data is arranged as a column) or to the right (if your data is arranged as a row). When you click **OK**, the new cell appears and the contents of affected cells shift down or to the right, as appropriate.

Tip

The **Insert** dialog box also includes option buttons you can select to insert a new row or column.

Merge and Center

Sometimes changing a row's height or a column's width isn't the best way to improve your workbook's usability. For instance, even though a worksheet's label might not fit within a single cell, increasing that cell's width (or every cell's width) might throw off the worksheet's design. While you can type individual words in cells so that the label fits in the worksheet, another alternative is to merge two or more cells. Merging cells tells Excel to treat a group of cells as a single cell as far as content and formatting go. To merge cells into a single cell, you click the **Merge and Center** toolbar button. As the name of the button implies, Excel centers the contents of the merged cell.

Tip

Clicking a merged cell and then clicking the **Merge and Center** toolbar button removes the merge.

Ex2002-3-2

Approved Courseware

If you want to delete a row or column, you right-click the row or column head and then, from the shortcut menu that appears, click **Delete**. You can temporarily hide a number of rows or columns by selecting those rows or columns and then, on the **Format** menu, pointing to **Row** or **Column** and then clicking **Hide**. The rows or columns you selected disappear, but they aren't gone for good, as they would be if you'd used **Delete**. Instead, they have just been removed from the display until you call them back; to return the hidden rows to the display, on the **Format** menu, point to **Row** or **Column** and then click **Unhide**.

Insert Options
new for
OfficeXP

When you insert a row, column, or cell in a worksheet with existing formatting, the **Insert Options** button appears. As with the **Paste Options** button and the **Auto Fill Options** button, clicking the **Insert Options** button displays a list of choices you can make about how the inserted row or column should be formatted. The options are summarized in the following table.

Option	Action
Format Same as Above	Apply the format of the row above the inserted row to the new row.
Format Same as Below	Apply the format of the row below the inserted row to the new row.
Format Same as Left	Apply the format of the column to the left of the inserted column to the new column.
Format Same as Right	Apply the format of the column to the right of the inserted column to the new column.
Clear Formatting	Apply the default format to the new row or column.

Easier

In this exercise, you make the worksheet containing last January's sales data easier to read. First you name the worksheet and bring it to the front of the list of worksheets in its workbook. Next you increase the column width and row height of the cells holding the sales data. In addition, you merge and center the worksheet's title and then add a row between the title and the row that holds the times for which The Garden Company recorded sales. Finally you add a column to the left of the first column of data and then hide rows containing data for all but the first week of the month.

Open

1 On the Standard toolbar, click the **Open** button.

The **Open** dialog box appears.

2 If necessary, navigate to the SBS folder, and then double-click the **Excel** folder to display its contents.

The files and folders in the Excel folder appear.

3 Double-click the **SettingUpWorkbook** folder.

The files in the SettingUpWorkbook folder appear.

4 Double-click the **Easier.xls** file.

The Easier.xls file opens.

5 In the lower left corner of the workbook window, right-click the **Sheet2** sheet tab.

6 From the shortcut menu that appears, click **Rename**.

Sheet2 is highlighted.

7 Type **January**, and press [Enter].

The name of the worksheet changes from *Sheet2* to *January*.

22	Thu	189	299	102	283	277
23	Fri	101	166	401	166	201
24	Sat	135	235	299	202	125
25	Sun	206	140	382	243	444
26	Mon	189	249	400	147	1028
27	Tue	161	302	357	158	247

⏮ ◀ ▶ ⏭ \ Sheet1 \ **January** / Sheet3 /

Ready

8 Click the **January** sheet tab, and drag it to the left of the **Sheet1** sheet tab.

The **January** sheet tab moves to the left of the **Sheet1** sheet tab. As the sheet tab moves, an inverted black triangle marks the sheet's location in the workbook.

9 Click the column head for column A, and drag to column M.

Columns A through M are highlighted.

10 Position the mouse pointer over the right edge of column A, and drag the edge to the right until the ScreenTip says *Width: 10.00 (75 pixels)*.

The width of the selected columns changes.

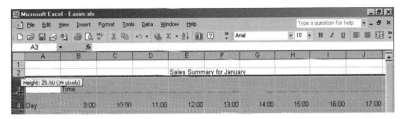

11 Select rows 3 through 35.

Rows 3 through 35 are highlighted.

12 Position the mouse pointer over the bottom edge of row 3, and drag the edge down until the ScreenTip says *Height: 25.50 (34 pixels)*.

The height of the selected rows changes.

13 Click cell E2, and drag to cell G2.

14 On the Formatting toolbar, click the **Merge and Center** toolbar button.

Cells E2, F2, and G2 are merged into a single cell, and the new cell's contents are centered.

Important

Depending on the screen resolution you have set on your computer and which toolbar buttons you use most often, It's possible that not every button on every toolbar will appear on your Excel toolbars. If a button mentioned in this book doesn't appear on a toolbar, click the **Toolbar Options** down arrow on that toolbar to display the rest of the buttons available on that toolbar.

15 Click cell A3.

16 On the **Insert** menu, click **Rows**.

A new row, labeled row 3, appears above the row previously labeled row 3.

17 On the **Insert** menu, click **Columns**.

A new column, labeled column A, appears to the left of the column previously labeled column A.

18 Select rows 13 through 36.

Rows 13 through 36 are highlighted.

19 On the **Format** menu, point to **Row**, and then click **Hide**.

Rows 13 through 36 disappear from the worksheet.

	A	B	C	D	E	F	G	H	I	J
1										
2							Sales Summary for January			
3										
4			Time							
5		Day	9:00	10:00	11:00	12:00	13:00	14:00	15:00	16:00
6		Mon	147	802	185	202	246	202	125	187
7		Tue	161	285	382	285	300	158	249	385
8		Wed	182	301	400	187	189	285	302	277
9		Thu	201	250	192	385	101	168	228	150
10		Fri	158	247	166	277	135	350	412	102
11		Sat	190	499	235	150	206	189	602	401
12		Sun	243	285	140	102	189	85	147	299

20 On the **Format** menu, point to **Row**, and then click **Unhide**.

The hidden rows reappear in the worksheet.

Save

21 On the Standard toolbar, click the **Save** button.

Excel saves the document.

Close

22 Click the **Close** button.

The file Easier.xls closes.

Making Data Easier to Read

After you have modified your worksheet so it is easier to work with, you can make the data easier to read by modifying how data is presented within the worksheet's cells. One case in which you might want to change how data is presented occurs if the data doesn't fit in a cell's boundaries and you don't want to merge the cells the data overlaps with. For instance, you could choose not to merge the cells because you might want to add data or comments to the neighboring cells later.

The following graphic shows what happens if there is a spillover in two adjacent cells.

161	350	302
This column include	Modified to remove overlap with Tools.	

If the right-hand cell were empty, the text in the left-hand cell would simply spill over into the right-hand cell. When there is data in the right-hand cell, however, Excel brings it to the front, hiding any data that spills over from the adjoining cell. To avoid hiding the text in the first cell behind the text in the second cell, you can have the text wrap within the first cell, as seen in the following graphic.

	This column includes all tools except sharpeners, which were added in February.	
34		Modified to remove overlap with Tools.

Tip

It may be tempting to just change a column's width to accommodate your data, but remember that widening a single column will make that column stand out in the worksheet, possibly making data in other columns harder to read.

Ex2002-3-3
Approved Courseware

Another way you can make your data easier to read is to distinguish any data labels by changing how the data appears in a cell. One way to separate data labels from the data that follows them is to change the **alignment** of the labels in their cells. For example, you can center the data labels in their cells, setting the labels apart from the right aligned data farther down in the column.

Ex2002-3-2
Approved Courseware

You can also make your worksheet data easier to read by ensuring that the data labels at the top of a column **freeze**, or remain on the screen regardless of how far down in the document you scroll. For instance, Catherine Turner, the owner of The Garden Company, might not remember which data is kept in which column on a worksheet. Freezing the data labels at the top of the column would let her scroll to the last row of the worksheet and still have the labels available as a reference. Excel marks the division between frozen and unfrozen cells with a **split bar**.

Split bar

	A	B	C	D	E	F
1		Tools	Supplies	Furniture	Passiflora	
13	12	285	382	208	166	
14	13	301	400	385	235	
15	14	303	409	277	140	
16	15	140	166	150	249	
17	16	249	235	102	357	
18	17	302	140	247	166	

Troubleshooting

When you tell Excel to freeze rows in your worksheet, Excel freezes the rows above the active cell. So if you want to freeze the top three rows of your worksheet, click a cell in the fourth row and then turn on the freeze.

DataRead

In this exercise, you prevent the text in a cell from spilling over into adjoining cells, allowing you to enter comments in those adjoining cells without obscuring the contents of the first cell. You then change the alignment of the cells containing the data labels for the columns in your worksheet and then freeze those data labels so that they remain at the top of the page as you scroll down through the worksheet.

Open

1 On the Standard toolbar, click the **Open** button.

The **Open** dialog box appears.

2 Double-click the **DataRead.xls** file.

DataRead.xls opens.

3 If necessary, click the **SalesbyCategory** sheet tab.

4 Click cell B34.

5 On the **Format** menu, click **Cells**.

The **Format Cells** dialog box appears.

6 If necessary, click the **Alignment** tab.

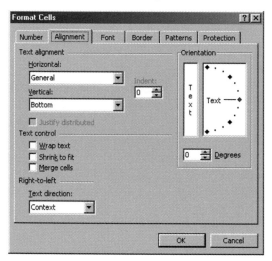

7 Select the **Wrap text** check box, and click **OK**.

The text in cell B34 wraps to fit within the original borders of the cell.

8 Click cell B1, and drag to cell E1.

Center

9 On the Formatting toolbar, click the **Center** button.

The contents of the selected cells are centered within those cells.

10 Click cell A2.

11 On the **Window** menu, click **Freeze Panes**.

A split bar appears between row 1 and row 2.

12 On the vertical scroll bar, click the down arrow.

Row 1 stays in place while the remaining rows scroll normally.

13 On the **Window** menu, click **Unfreeze Panes**.

The split bar disappears, and all rows scroll normally.

Save

14 On the Standard toolbar, click the **Save** button.

Excel saves your changes.

Close

15 Click the **Close** button.

The file DataRead.xls closes.

Adding a Graphic to a Document

Ex2002-6-2

Approved Courseware

An important part of establishing a strong business is creating a memorable corporate identity. Setting aside the obvious need for sound management, two important physical attributes of a strong retail business are a well-conceived shop space and an eye-catching, memorable logo. Once you or your graphic artist has created a logo, you should add the logo to all of your documents, especially any that might be seen by your customers. Not only does the logo mark the documents as coming from your company, it serves as an advertisement, encouraging anyone who sees your worksheets to call or visit your company.

One way to add a picture to a worksheet is to go through the **Insert** menu and click the **Picture** item. Clicking **Picture** shows a submenu that lists several sources from which you can choose which picture to add; in this case, you can click the **From File** item to open a dialog box that lets you locate the picture you want to add from your hard disk.

Once you've added the picture to your worksheet, you can change the picture's location on the worksheet by dragging it to the desired spot, or you can change the picture's size by right-clicking the picture and choosing **Format Picture** from the shortcut menu that appears.

Troubleshooting

You can also resize a picture by clicking the picture and then dragging one of the handles that appears on the graphic, but using the **Format Picture** dialog box helps ensure that the **aspect ratio**, or relationship between the picture's height and width, doesn't change. If you do accidentally resize a graphic by dragging a handle, just click the **Undo** button to remove your change.

AddPicture

In this exercise, you add the new logo for The Garden Company to an existing worksheet and then reduce the size of the graphic and move it to better fit on the worksheet.

Open

1 On the Standard toolbar, click the **Open** button.

The **Open** dialog box appears.

2 Double-click the **AddPicture.xls** file.

The AddPicture.xls file opens.

3 Click cell A1.

4 On the **Insert** menu, point to **Picture**, and then click **From File**.

The **Insert Picture** dialog box appears.

5 If necessary, navigate to the SettingUpWorkbook folder and then double-click **tgc_logo.gif**.

The chosen graphic appears in the AddPicture.xls file.

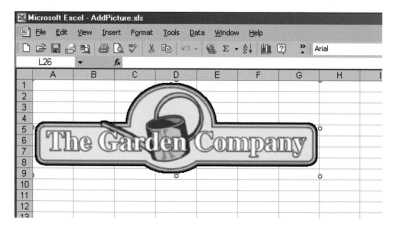

6 Right-click the graphic, and from the shortcut menu that appears, click **Format Picture**.

The **Format Picture** dialog box appears.

7 Click the **Size** tab.

The **Size** tab page appears. Notice that the **Lock aspect ratio** check box is selected.

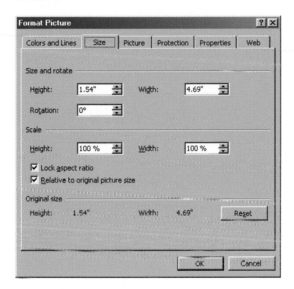

8 In the **Scale** section of the tab page, clear the contents of the **Height** box, type **50%**, and then click **OK**.

The picture is resized, maintaining the original aspect ratio.

9 Click the center of the graphic, and drag it so it is centered horizontally on the screen and the top of the graphic is just below row 1.

The graphic moves with your mouse pointer.

Troubleshooting

Remember that dragging one of the handles at the edge of the graphic will resize the graphic. To undo a change, click the **Undo** button.

Save

10 On the Standard toolbar, click the **Save** button.

Excel saves your changes.

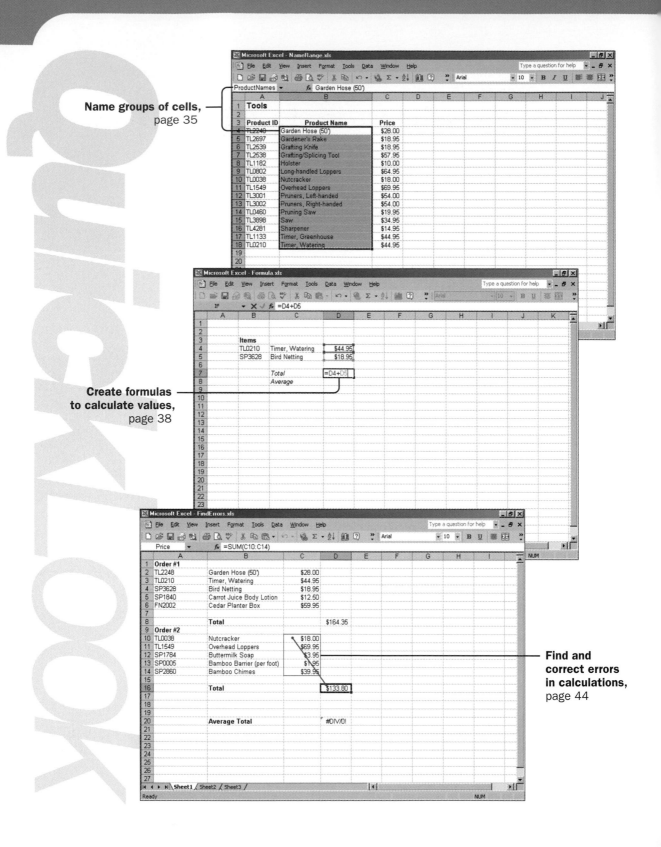

Name groups of cells,
page 35

Create formulas to calculate values,
page 38

Find and correct errors in calculations,
page 44

Chapter 3
Performing Calculations on Data

After completing this chapter, you will be able to:

✔ Name groups of cells.
✔ Create formulas to calculate values.
✔ Find and correct errors in calculations.

Microsoft Excel workbooks give you a handy place to store and organize your data, but you can do a lot more with your data in Excel. One important task you can perform in Excel is to calculate totals for the values in a series of related cells. You can also have Excel find out other things about the data you select, such as the maximum or minimum value in a group of cells. Finding the maximum or minimum value in a group can let you identify your best salesperson, product categories you might need to pay more attention to, or suppliers that consistently give you the best deal. Regardless of your bookkeeping needs, Excel gives you the ability to find the information you want. And if you should make an error, you can find the cause and correct it quickly.

Many times you can't access the information you want without referencing more than one cell, and it's also often true that you'll use the data in the same group of cells for more than one calculation. Excel makes it easy to reference a number of cells at once, letting you define your calculations quickly.

In this chapter, you'll learn how to streamline references to groups of data on your worksheets and how to create and correct formulas that summarize the sales and product data from The Garden Company.

This chapter uses the practice files NameRange, Formula, and FindErrors that you installed from this book's CD-ROM. For details about installing the practice files, see "Using the Book's CD-ROM" at the beginning of this book.

Naming Groups of Data

When you work with large amounts of data, it's easier to identify groups of cells that contain related data. In the following graphic, for example, cells C2 through C6 hold the prices of items from a customer's order.

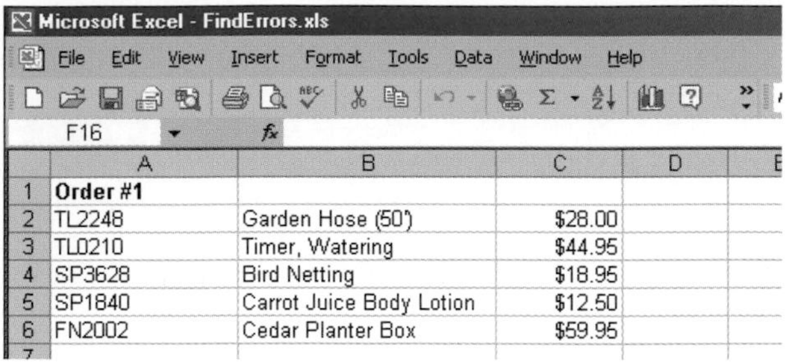

Rather than specify the cells individually every time you want to use the data they contain, you can define those cells as a **range** (also called a **named range**). For instance, you could group the items from the previous graphic into a range named *OrderItems1*. Whenever you wanted to use the contents of that range in a calculation, you could just use the name of the range instead of specifying each cell individually.

There are a number of ways to create a named range, two of which you can access through the **Insert** menu. The first method works well if you have a column of data with a label at the head of the column, as in the following graphic.

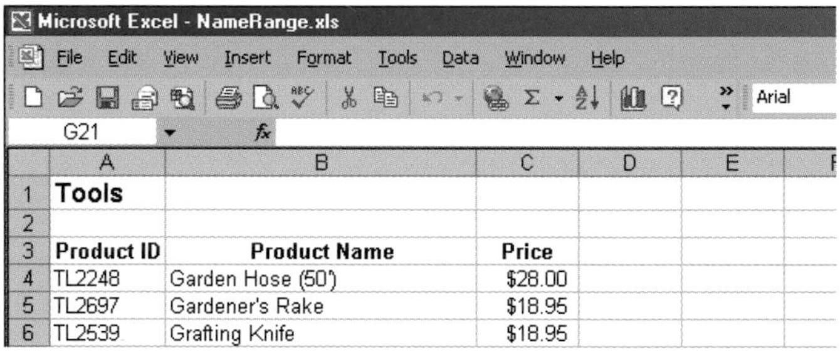

In this case, you access the **Create Name** dialog box by pointing to **Name** on the **Insert** menu and clicking **Create**. In the **Create Name** dialog box, you can define a named range by having Excel use the label in the top cell as the range's name. You can also create and delete named ranges through the **Define Name** dialog box, which you access by pointing to **Define** on the **Insert** menu and clicking **Name**.

A final way to create a named range is to select the cells you want in the range, click in the Name box next to the formula bar, and then type the name for the range. You can display the ranges available in a workbook by clicking the Name box's down arrow.

Important

Every range in a workbook must have a unique name. Assigning the name of an existing range to a new range removes the original reference, likely affecting how your worksheet behaves.

In this exercise, you will create named ranges to streamline references to groups of cells.

1   On the Standard toolbar, click the **Open** button.

The **Open** dialog box appears.

2   Navigate to the PerformingCalculations folder, and double-click the **NameRange.xls** file.

NameRange.xls opens.

3   If necessary, click the **Tools** sheet tab.

4   Click cell C3 and drag to cell C18.

The selected cells are highlighted.

5   On the **Insert** menu, point to **Name**, and then click **Create**.

The **Create Names** dialog box appears.

6   If necessary, select the **Top row** check box.

7   Click **OK**.

Excel assigns the name *Price* to the cell range.

8   In the lower left corner of the workbook window, click the **Supplies** sheet tab.

The Supplies worksheet appears.

9   Click cell C4 and drag to cell C29.

10   On the **Insert** menu, point to **Name**, and then click **Define**.

The **Define Name** dialog box appears.

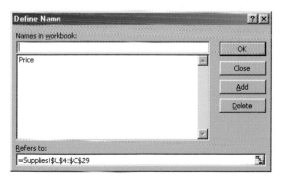

11   In the **Names in workbook** box, type **SuppliesPrice** and then click **OK**.

Excel assigns the name *SuppliesPrice* to the cell range, and the **Define Name** dialog box disappears.

12   In the lower left corner of the workbook window, click the **Furniture** sheet tab.

The Furniture worksheet appears.

13   Click cell C4 and drag to cell C18.

14   Click in the Name box.

The contents of the Name box are highlighted.

15   Type **FurniturePrice**, and press [Enter].

Excel assigns the name *FurniturePrice* to the cell range.

16   On the **Insert** menu, point to **Name**, and then click **Define**.

The **Define Name** dialog box appears.

17   In the lower pane of the **Define Name** dialog box, click **Price**.

Price appears in the **Names in workbook** box.

18   In the **Names in workbook** box, delete *Price*, type **ToolsPrice**, and then click **OK**.

The **Define Name** dialog box disappears.

Save

19   On the Standard toolbar, click the **Save** button.

Close

20   Click the **Close** button.

NameRange.xls closes.

Creating Formulas to Calculate Values

Ex2002-5-1

Approved Courseware

Once you've added your data to a worksheet and defined ranges to simplify data references, you can create a **formula**, or an expression that performs calculations on your data. For example, you can calculate the total cost of a customer's order, figure the average sales for all Wednesdays in the month of January, or find the highest and lowest daily sales for a week, month, or year.

To write an Excel formula, you begin the cell's contents with an equal sign—when Excel sees it, it knows that the expression following it should be interpreted as a calculation and not text. After the equal sign, you type the formula. For instance, you can find the sum of the numbers in cells C2 and C3 with the formula *=C2+C3*. After you have entered a formula into a cell, you can revise it by clicking the cell and then editing the formula on the formula bar. For example, you can change the preceding formula to *=C3-C2*, which calculates the difference of the contents of cells C2 and C3.

Troubleshooting

If Excel treats your formula as text, make sure you haven't accidentally put a space before the equal sign. Remember, the equal sign must be the first character!

Ex2002-5-2

Approved Courseware

Typing the cell references for 15 or 20 cells in a calculation would be tedious, but Excel makes it easy to handle complex calculations. To create a new calculation, you click **Function** on the **Insert** menu. The **Insert Function** dialog box appears, with a list of **functions**, or predefined formulas, from which you can choose.

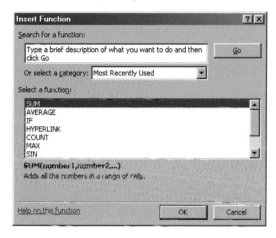

The most useful functions in the list are described in the following table.

Item	Description
SUM	Returns the sum of the numbers in the specified cells
AVERAGE	Finds the average of the numbers in the specified cells
COUNT	Finds the number of entries in the specified cells
MAX	Finds the largest value in the specified cells
MIN	Finds the smallest value in the specified cells

Two other functions you might use are the NOW() and PMT() functions. The NOW() function returns the time the workbook was last opened, so the value will change every time the workbook is opened. The proper form for this function is =NOW(); to update the value to the current date and time, just save your work, close the workbook, and then reopen it. The PMT() function is a bit more complex. It calculates payments due on a loan, assuming a constant interest rate and constant payments. To perform its calculations, the PMT() function requires an interest rate, the number of months of payments, and the starting balance. The elements to be entered into the function are called **arguments** and must be entered in a certain order. That order is written *PMT(rate, nper, pv, fv, type)*. The following table summarizes the arguments in the PMT() function.

Argument	Description
rate	The interest rate, to be divided by 12 for a loan with monthly payments
nper	The total number of payments for the loan
pv	The amount loaned (pv is short for present value, or principal)
fv	The amount to be left over at the end of the payment cycle (usually left blank, which indicates 0)
type	0 or 1, indicating whether payments are made at the beginning or at the end of the month (usually left blank, which indicates 0, or the end of the month)

If you wanted to borrow $20,000 at an 8 percent interest rate and pay the loan back over 24 months, you could use the PMT() function to figure out the monthly payments. In this case, the function would be written =PMT(8%/12, 24, 20000), which calculates a monthly payment of $904.55.

You can also add the names of any ranges you've defined to a formula. For example, if the named range *Order1* refers to cells C2 through C6, you can calculate the average of cells C2 through C6 with the formula =AVERAGE(Order1). If you want to include a series of contiguous cells in a formula but you haven't defined the cells as a named range, you can click the first cell in the range and drag to the last cell. If the cells aren't contiguous, hold down the Ctrl key and click the cells to be included. In both cases, when you release the mouse button, the references of the cells you selected appear in the formula.

Another use for formulas is to display messages when certain conditions are met. For instance, Catherine Turner, the owner of The Garden Company, might provide a free copy of a gardening magazine to customers making purchases worth more than $150. This kind of formula is called a **conditional formula** and uses the IF function. To create a conditional formula, you click the cell to hold the formula and open the **Insert Function** dialog box. From within the dialog box, you select IF from the list of available functions and then click **OK**. The **Function Arguments** dialog box appears.

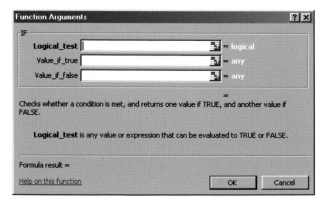

When you work with an IF function, the **Function Arguments** dialog box will have three boxes: **Logical_test**, **Value_if_true**, and **Value_if_false**. The **Logical_test** box holds the condition you want to check. To check whether the total for an order is greater than $150, the expression would be *SUM(Order1)>150*.

Now you need to have Excel display messages indicating whether the customer should receive a free magazine. To have Excel print a message from an IF function, you enclose the message in quotes in the **Value_if_true** or **Value_if_false** box. In this case, you would type *"Qualifies for a free magazine!"* in the **Value_if_true** box and *"Thanks for your order!"* in the **Value_if_false** box.

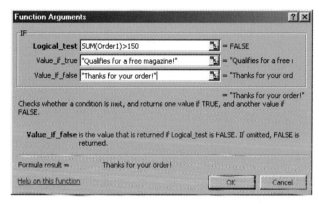

Once you've created a formula, you can copy it and paste it into another cell. When you do, Excel will try to change the formula so it works in the new cells. For instance, in the following graphic, cell D8 contains the formula *=SUM(C2:C6)*.

Clicking cell D8, copying the cell's contents, and then pasting the result into cell D16 writes *=SUM(C10:C14)* into cell D16. Excel has reinterpreted the formula so that it fits the surrounding cells! Excel knows it can reinterpret the cells used in the formula because the formula uses a relative reference, or a reference that can change if the formula is copied to another cell. Relative references are written with just the cell row and column (for example, *C14*). If you want a cell reference to remain constant when

Ex2002-5-1

Approved Courseware

the formula using it is copied to another cell, you can use an absolute reference. To write a cell reference as an absolute reference, you type *$* before the row name and the column number. If you wanted the formula in cell D16 to show the sum of values in cells C10 through C14 regardless of the cell into which it is pasted, you would write the formula as *=SUM($C$10:$C$14)*.

Tip

If you copy a formula from the formula bar, use absolute references, or use only named ranges in your formula, Excel won't change the cell references when you copy your formula to another cell.

Formula

In this exercise, you create a formula to find the total cost of an order, copy that formula to another cell, and then create a formula to find the average cost of items in the order. The cells with the cost of products in this order are stored in the named range *OrderItems*.

Open

1 On the Standard toolbar, click the **Open** button.

The **Open** dialog box appears.

2 Double-click **Formula.xls**.

Formula.xls opens.

3 Click cell D7.

D7 becomes the active cell.

4 On the formula bar, type **=D4+D5** and press [Enter].

The value *$63.90* appears in cell D7.

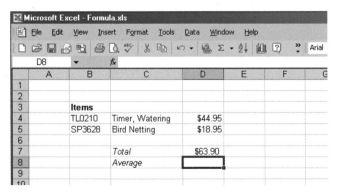

Copy

5 Click cell D7, and then, on the Standard toolbar, click the **Copy** button.

Excel copies the formula in cell D7 to the Clipboard.

Paste

6 Click cell D8, and then, on the Standard toolbar, click the **Paste** button.

The value *$18.95* appears in cell D8, and *=D5+D6* appears in the formula bar.

7 Press [Del].

The formula in cell D8 disappears.

8 On the **Insert** menu, click **Function**.

The **Insert Function** dialog box appears.

9 Click **AVERAGE**, and then click **OK**.

The **Function Arguments** dialog box appears, with the contents of the Number 1 box highlighted.

10 Type **OrderItems**, and then click **OK**.

The **Function Arguments** dialog box disappears, and *$31.95* appears in cell D8.

	A	B	C	D	E	F	G
				=AVERAGE(OrderItems)			
1							
2							
3		Items					
4		TL0210	Timer, Watering	$44.95			
5		SP3628	Bird Netting	$18.95			
6							
7			Total	$63.90			
8			Average	$31.95			
9							

11 Click cell C10.

12 On the **Insert** menu, click **Function**.

The **Insert Function** dialog box appears.

13 In the **Select a function** list, click **IF** and then click **OK**.

The **Function Arguments** dialog box appears.

14 In the **Logical_test** box, type **D7>50**.

15 In the **Value_if_true** box, type **"5% discount"**.

16 In the **Value_if_false** box, type **"No discount"** and then click **OK**.

The **Function Arguments** dialog box disappears, and *5% discount* appears in cell C10.

Microsoft Excel - Formula.xls

File Edit View Insert Format Tools Data Window Help

C10   fx =IF(D7>50,"5% discount","No discount")

	A	B	C	D	E	F	G
1							
2							
3		**Items**					
4		TL0210	Timer, Watering	$44.95			
5		SP3628	Bird Netting	$18.95			
6							
7			*Total*	$63.90			
8			*Average*	$31.95			
9							
10			5% discount				
11							
12							

Save

17 On the Standard toolbar, click the **Save** button.

Excel saves your changes.

Close

18 Click the **Close** button.

Formula.xls closes.

Finding and Correcting Errors in Calculations

Including calculations in a worksheet gives you valuable answers to questions about your data. As is always true, however, it is possible for errors to creep into your formulas. Excel makes it easy to find the source of errors in your formulas by identifying the cells used in a given calculation and describing any errors that have occurred. The process of examining a worksheet for errors in formulas is referred to as **auditing**.

Ex2002e-6-1

Approved Courseware

Excel identifies errors in several ways. The first way is to fill the cell holding the formula generating the error with an **error code**. In the following graphic, cell D8 has the error code *#NAME?*.

Microsoft Excel - FindErrors.xls

File Edit View Insert Format Tools Data Window Help   Arial

D11   fx

	A	B	C	D	E	F
1	**Order #1**					
2	TL2248	Garden Hose (50')	$28.00			
3	TL0210	Timer, Watering	$44.95			
4	SP3628	Bird Netting	$18.95			
5	SP1840	Carrot Juice Body Lotion	$12.50			
6	FN2002	Cedar Planter Box	$59.95			
7						
8		Total		#NAME?		
9	**Order #2**					
10	TL0038	Nutcracker	$18.00			

Error

When a cell with an erroneous formula is the active cell, an **Error** button appears next to it. You can click the button's down arrow to display a menu with options that provide information about the error and offer to help you fix it. The following table lists the most common error codes and what they mean.

Error button
new for
OfficeXP

Error Code	Description
#####	The column isn't wide enough to display the value.
#VALUE!	The formula has the wrong type of argument (such as text where a TRUE or FALSE value is required).
#NAME?	The formula contains text that Excel doesn't recognize (such as an unknown named range).
#REF!	The formula refers to a cell that doesn't exist (which can happen whenever cells are deleted).
#DIV/0!	The formula attempts to divide by zero.

Ex2002e-6-2

Approved Courseware

Another technique you can use to find the source of formula errors is to ensure that the appropriate cells are providing values for the formula. For example, you might want to calculate the total sales for a product category but accidentally create a formula referring to the products' names, not their prices. You can identify that kind of error by having Excel trace a cell's **precedents**, which are the cells with values used in the active cell's formula. Excel identifies a cell's precedents by drawing a blue tracer arrow from the precedent to the active cell.

Ex2002e-6-3

Approved Courseware

You can also audit your worksheet by identifying cells with formulas that use a value from a given cell. For example, you might have the total cost of a single order used in a formula that calculates the average cost of all orders placed on a given day. Cells that use another cell's value in their calculations are known as **dependents**, meaning that they depend on the value in the other cell to derive their own value. As with tracing precedents, you can point to **Formula Auditing** on the **Tools** menu, and click **Trace Dependents** to have Excel draw blue arrows from the active cell to those cells that have calculations based on that value.

If the cells identified by the tracer arrows aren't the correct cells, you can hide the arrows and correct the formula. To hide the tracer arrows on a worksheet, you point to **Formula Auditing** on the **Tools** menu and click **Remove All Arrows**.

FindErrors

In this exercise, you use the formula auditing capabilities in Excel to identify and correct errors in a formula.

Open

1 On the Standard toolbar, click the **Open** button.

The **Open** dialog box appears.

2 Double-click the **FindErrors.xls** file.

FindErrors.xls opens.

45

3 Click cell D8.

=SUM(C2:C6) appears in the formula bar.

4 On the **Tools** menu, point to **Formula Auditing**, and then click **Trace Precedents**.

A blue arrow appears between cell D8 and the group of cells from C2 to C6, indicating that cells in the C2:C6 range are precedents of the value in cell D8.

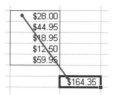

5 On the **Tools** menu, point to **Formula Auditing**, and then click **Remove All Arrows**.

The arrow disappears.

6 Click cell D20.

=AVERAGE(D7,D15) appears on the formula bar.

7 On the **Tools** menu, point to **Formula Auditing**, and then click **Trace Error**.

Blue arrows appear, pointing to cell D20 from cells D7 and D15. These arrows indicate that using the values (or lack of values, in this case) in the indicated cells is generating the error in cell D20.

	A	B	C	D
1	**Order #1**			
2	TL2248	Garden Hose (50')	$28.00	
3	TL0210	Timer, Watering	$44.95	
4	SP3628	Bird Netting	$18.95	
5	SP1840	Carrot Juice Body Lotion	$12.50	
6	FN2002	Cedar Planter Box	$59.95	
7				
8		**Total**		$164.35
9	**Order #2**			
10	TL0038	Nutcracker	$18.00	
11	TL1549	Overhead Loppers	$69.95	
12	SP1784	Buttermilk Soap	$3.95	
13	SP0005	Bamboo Barrier (per foot)	$1.95	
14	SP2860	Bamboo Chimes	$39.95	
15				
16		**Total**		$133.80
17				
18				
19				
20		**Average Total**	◇	#DIV/0!
21				
22				

Microsoft Excel - FindErrors.xls
File Edit View Insert Format Tools Data Window Help
D20   *fx* =AVERAGE(D7,D15)

8 On the **Tools** menu, point to **Formula Auditing**, and then click **Remove All Arrows**.

The arrows disappear.

9 In the formula bar, delete the existing formula, type **=AVERAGE(D8,D16)**, and press [Enter].

The value *$149.08* appears in cell D20.

Save

10 On the Standard toolbar, click the **Save** button.

Excel saves your changes.

Close

11 Click the **Close** button.

FindErrors.xls closes.

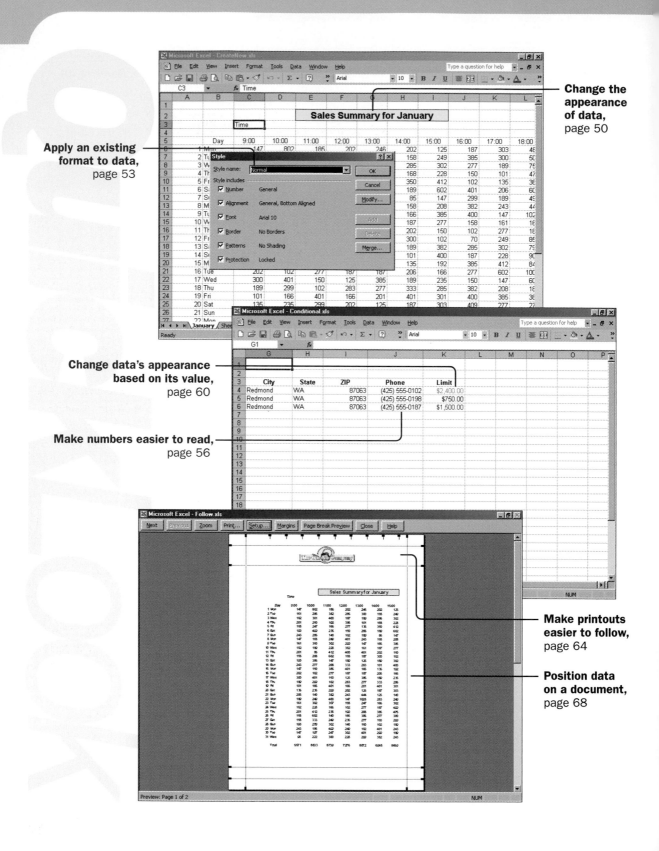

Change the appearance of data, page 50

Apply an existing format to data, page 53

Change data's appearance based on its value, page 60

Make numbers easier to read, page 56

Make printouts easier to follow, page 64

Position data on a document, page 68

Chapter 4
Changing Document Appearance

An important aspect of working with data entered into a workbook is ensuring that the data is easy to read. Microsoft Excel gives you a wide variety of ways to make your data easier to understand; for example, you can change the font, letter size, or color used to present a cell's contents. You can also change how your data appears on the printed page, such as by changing your printer's margins or adding information at the top or bottom of every page.

Changing how data appears on a worksheet helps set the contents of a cell apart from the contents of surrounding cells. The simplest example is that of a data label. If a column on your worksheet has a list of days, you can set a label—for example, *Day*—apart easily by presenting it in bold type that's noticeably larger than the type used to present the data to which it refers. To save time, you can define a number of custom formats and then apply them to the desired cells quickly.

You might also want to specially format a cell's contents to reflect the value in that cell. For instance, Catherine Turner, the owner of The Garden Company, might grant some of The Garden Company's better customers credit, use Excel to track each customer's purchases, and use that information to determine which customers are close to their credit limit. A quick way to distinguish when a customer is close to his or her credit limit is to change how their outstanding balance is presented in its cell. Catherine might, for example, change the color of the font from the standard black to blue when a customer is within 10 percent of his or her limit.

In addition to changing how data appears in your worksheets' cells, you can also use headers and footers to add page numbers, the current data, or graphics to the top and bottom of every printed page.

In this chapter, you'll learn how to change the appearance of data, apply existing formats to data, make numbers easier to read, change data's appearance based on its value, make printouts easier to follow, and position your data on the printed page.

 This chapter uses the practice files Formats, CreateNew, EasyRead, Conditional, Follow, and Margins that you installed from this book's CD-ROM. For details about installing the practice files, see "Using the Book's CD-ROM" at the beginning of this book.

Changing the Appearance of Data

Ex2002-3-1

Approved Courseware

Excel spreadsheets can hold and process lots of data, but when you manage numerous spreadsheets it can be hard to remember by a worksheet's title exactly what data is kept on that worksheet. Data labels give you and your colleagues information about data in a worksheet, but it's important to format the labels so they stand out visually. To make your data labels or any other data stand out, you can change the format of the cells in which the data is stored.

	Time			
Day		9:00 AM	10:00 AM	
1 Mon	$	147.00	$	802.00
2 Tue	$	161.00	$	285.00
3 Wed	$	182.00	$	301.00
4 Thu	$	201.00	$	250.00

Most of the tools you need to change a cell's format can be found on the Formatting toolbar.

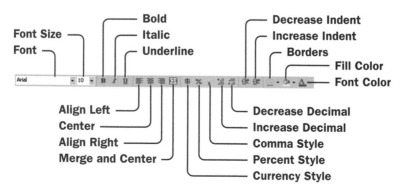

Important

Depending on the screen resolution you have set on your computer and which toolbar buttons you use most often, it's possible that not every button on every toolbar will appear on your Excel toolbars. If a button mentioned in this book doesn't appear on a toolbar, click the **Toolbar Options** down arrow on that toolbar to display the rest of its buttons.

Bold

You can apply the formatting represented by a toolbar button by selecting the cells to which you want to apply the style and then clicking the appropriate button. If you want to set your data labels apart by making them appear bold, click the **Bold** button. If you have already made a cell's contents bold, selecting the cell and clicking the **Bold** button will remove the formatting.

Tip

Deleting a cell's contents doesn't delete the cell's formatting. To delete a cell's formatting, select the cell and then, on the **Edit** menu, point to **Clear**, and click **Formats**.

Items on the Formatting toolbar that give you choices, such as the **Font Color** control, have a down arrow at the right edge of the control. Clicking the down arrow displays a list of options available for that control, such as the fonts available on your system or the colors you can assign to a cell.

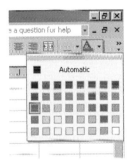

Borders

new for
OfficeXP

Another way you can make a cell stand apart from its neighbors is to add a border around the cell. In previous versions of Excel, you could select the cell or cells to which you wanted to add the border and use the options available under the Formatting toolbar's **Borders** button to assign a border to the cells. For example, you could select a group of cells and then choose the border type you wanted. That method of adding borders is still available in Excel, but it has some limitations. The most important limitation is that, while creating a simple border around a group of cells is easy, creating complex borders makes you select different groups of cells and apply different types of borders to them. The current version of Excel makes creating complex borders easy by letting you draw borders directly on the worksheet.

To use the new border-drawing capabilities, you display the Borders toolbar.

Erase Border ——————————┐   ┌—————— Line Style
Draw Border —————┐ | | ┌— Line Color

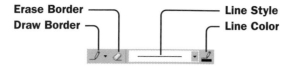

To draw a border around a group of cells, click the mouse pointer at one corner of the group and drag it to the diagonal corner. You will see your border expand as you move the mouse pointer. If you want to add a border in a vertical or horizontal line, drag the mouse pointer along the target grid line—Excel will add the line without expanding it to include the surrounding cells. You can also change the characteristics of the border you draw through the options on the Borders toolbar.

Another way you can make a group of cells stand apart from its neighbors is to change their shading, or the color that fills the cells. On a worksheet with monthly sales data for The Garden Company, for example, owner Catherine Turner could change the fill color of the cells holding her data labels to make the labels stand out even more than by changing the formatting of the text used to display the labels.

Formats

In this exercise, you emphasize a worksheet's title by changing the format of cell data, adding a border to a cell, and then changing a cell's fill color.

Open

1 On the Standard toolbar, click the **Open** button.

The **Open** dialog box appears.

2 Navigate to the ChangingDocAppearance folder, and double-click the **Formats.xls** file.

Formats.xls opens.

3 If necessary, click the **January** sheet tab.

4 Click cell G2.

Cell G2 is highlighted.

5 On the Formatting toolbar, click the **Font Size** down arrow and, from the list that appears, click **14**.

The text in cell G2 changes to 14-point type, and row 2 expands vertically to accommodate the text.

6 On the Formatting toolbar, click the **Bold** button.

The text in cell G2 appears bold.

7 Click the row head for row 5.

Row 5 is highlighted.

Center

8 On the Formatting toolbar, click the **Center** button.

The contents of the cells in row 5 are centered.

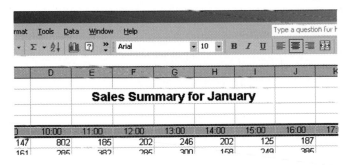

9   Click cell G2.

Cell G2 is highlighted.

Borders

10   On the Formatting toolbar, click the down arrow at the right of the **Borders** button and then, from the list that appears, click **Draw Borders**.

The Borders toolbar appears, and the mouse pointer changes to a pencil.

11   Click the left edge of cell G2 and drag to the right edge.

A border appears around cell G2.

Close

12   On the Borders toolbar, click the **Close** button.

The Borders toolbar disappears.

Fill Color

13   On the Formatting toolbar, click the **Fill Color** button.

The **Fill Color** color palette appears.

14   In the **Fill Color** color palette, click the yellow square.

Cell G2 fills with a yellow background.

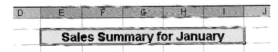

Save

15   On the Standard toolbar, click the **Save** button.

Excel saves your changes.

16   Click the **Close** button.

Formats.xls closes.

Applying an Existing Format to Data

Ex2002-3-4

Approved Courseware

As you work with Excel, you will probably develop preferred formats for data labels, titles, and other worksheet elements. Rather than add the format's characteristics one element at a time to the target cells, you can have Excel store the format and recall it as needed. You can find the predefined formats available to you in the **Style** dialog box.

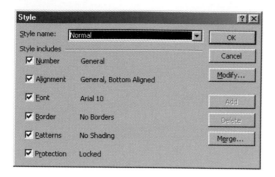

You can apply an existing style to a cell from within the **Style** dialog box. If none of the existing styles are what you want, you can create your own by typing the name of your new style in the **Style name** box and then clicking **Modify**. The **Format Cells** dialog box appears.

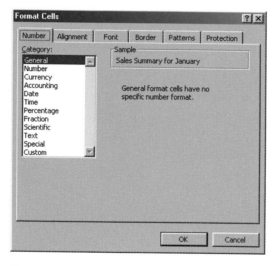

Once you've set the characteristics of your new style, you click **OK** to make your style available permanently.

Format Painter

The **Style** dialog box is quite versatile, but it's overkill if all you want to do is apply formatting changes you made to a cell to the contents of another cell. To do so, you can use the Standard toolbar's **Format Painter** button; just click the cell with the format you want to copy, click the **Format Painter** button, and select the target cells.

CreateNew

In this exercise, you create a style, apply the new style to a data label, and then use the Format Painter to apply the style to the contents of another cell.

Open

1   On the Standard toolbar, click the **Open** button.

The **Open** dialog box appears.

2   Double-click **CreateNew.xls**.

CreateNew.xls opens.

3   If necessary, click the **January** sheet tab.

4   Click cell C3.

5   On the **Format** menu, click **Style**.

The **Style** dialog box appears, with *Normal* in the **Style name** box.

6   In the **Style name** box, delete the existing value and then type **Emphasis**.

The **Add** button is activated.

7   Click **Modify**.

The **Format Cells** dialog box appears.

8   If necessary, click the **Font** tab.

The **Font** tab page appears.

9   In the **Font style** box, click **Bold Italic**.

The text in the Preview pane, in the lower right corner of the dialog box, changes to reflect your choice.

10   Click the **Alignment** tab.

The **Alignment** tab page appears.

11   In the **Horizontal** box, click the down arrow and, from the list that appears, click **Center**.

12   Click **OK**.

The **Format Cells** dialog box disappears.

13   Click **OK**.

The **Style** dialog box disappears, and the text in cell C3 takes on the chosen style.

14   On the Standard toolbar, click the **Format Painter** button.

The mouse pointer changes to a white cross with a paintbrush icon next to it.

15   Click cell B5.

Cell B5 takes on the format of cell C3.

Save

16 On the Standard toolbar, click the **Save** button.

Excel saves your changes.

Close

17 Click the **Close** button.

CreateNew.xls closes.

Making Numbers Easier to Read

Ex2002e-3-1

Approved Courseware

Changing the format of the cells in your worksheet can make your data much easier to read, both by setting data labels apart from the actual data and by adding borders to define the boundaries between labels and data even more clearly. Of course, using formatting options to change the font and appearance of a cell's contents doesn't help with idiosyncratic data types such as dates, phone numbers, or currency.

For example, consider U.S. phone numbers. These numbers are ten digits long and have a three-digit area code, a three-digit exchange, and a four-digit line number written in the form *(###) ###-####*. While it's certainly possible to type a phone number with the expected formatting in a cell, it's much simpler to type a sequence of ten digits and have Excel change the data's appearance.

You can tell Excel to expect a phone number in a cell by opening the **Format Cells** dialog box to the **Number** tab and displaying the formats available under the **Special** category.

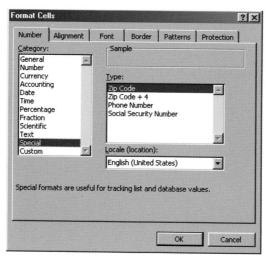

Clicking **Phone Number** from the **Type** list tells Excel to format ten-digit numbers in the standard phone number format. As you can see by comparing the contents of the active cell and the contents of the formula bar in the next graphic, the underlying data isn't changed, just its appearance in the cell.

B	C	D	E
	(425) 555-0122		

fx 4255550122

Troubleshooting

If you type a nine-digit number in a field that expects a phone number, you won't see an error message; instead, you'll see a two-digit area code. For example, the number 425555012 would be displayed as (42) 555-5012. Eleven-digit numbers are displayed with a four-digit area code.

Just as you can have Excel expect a phone number in a cell, you can also have it expect a date or a currency amount. You can make those changes from the **Format Cells** dialog box by choosing either the **Date** category or the **Currency** category. The **Date** category lets you pick the format for the date (and determine whether the date's appearance changes due to the **Locale** setting of the operating system on the computer viewing the workbook). In a similar vein, selecting the **Currency** category displays controls to set the number of places after the decimal point, the currency symbol to use, and the way in which Excel should display negative numbers.

Ex2002e 3-1

Approved Courseware

You can also create a custom numeric format to add a word or phrase to a number in a cell. For example, you can add the phrase *per month* to a cell with a formula that calculates average monthly sales for a year to ensure that you and your colleagues will recognize the figure as a monthly average. To create a custom number format, click **Cells** on the **Format** menu to open the **Format Cells** dialog box. Then, if necessary, click the **Number** tab to display the **Number** tab page.

In the **Category** list, click **Custom** to display the available custom number formats in the **Type** list. You can then click the base format you want and modify it in the **Type** box. For example, clicking the *0.00* format has Excel format any number in a cell as a number with two digits to the right of the decimal point.

Tip

The zeros in the format mean that that place in the format can accept any number as a valid value.

To customize the format, click in the **Type** box and add to the format any symbols or text you want. For example, typing a dollar sign to the left of the existing format and then typing *"per month"* to the right of the existing format causes the number 1500 to be displayed as *$1500.00 per month*.

Important

You need to enclose any text in quotes so that Excel recognizes the text as a string to be displayed in the cell.

EasyRead

In this exercise, you assign date, phone number, and currency formats to ranges of cells in your worksheet. After you assign the formats, you test them by entering customer data.

Open

1 On the Standard toolbar, click the **Open** button.

The **Open** dialog box appears.

2 Double-click the **EasyRead.xls** file.

EasyRead.xls opens.

3 Click cell B4.

4 On the **Format** menu, click **Cells**.

The **Format Cells** dialog box appears.

5 If necessary, click the **Number** tab.

6 In the **Category** list, click **Date**.

The **Type** list appears with a list of date formats.

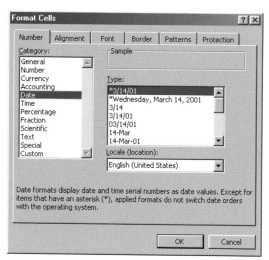

7 In the **Type** list, click ***3/14/01**.

8 Click **OK**.

Excel assigns the chosen format to the cell.

Format Painter

9 On the Standard toolbar, click the **Format Painter** button.

Cell B4 is highlighted with a marquee outline.

10 Click cell B5 and drag to cell B23.

Excel assigns the format from cell B4 to cells B5:B23.

11 Click cell J4.

12 On the **Format** menu, click **Cells**.

The **Format Cells** dialog box appears.

13 In the **Category** list, click **Special**.

The **Type** list appears with a list of Special formats.

14 In the **Type** list, click **Phone Number** and then click **OK**.

The **Format Cells** dialog box disappears.

15 On the Standard toolbar, click the **Format Painter** button.

Cell J4 is highlighted with a marquee outline.

16 Click cell J5 and drag to cell J23.

Excel assigns the format from cell J4 to cells J5:J23.

17 Click cell K4.

18 On the **Format** menu, click **Cells**.

The **Format Cells** dialog box appears.

19 In the **Category** list, click **Custom**.

The contents of the **Type** list are updated to reflect your choice.

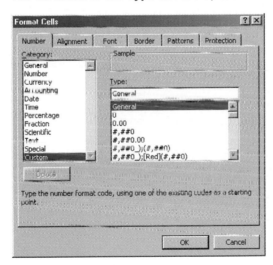

20 In the **Type** list, click the **#,##0.00** item.

#,##0.00 appears in the **Type** box.

21 In the **Type** box, click to the left of the existing format and type **$**, and then click to the right of the format and type **"total"**.

22 Click **OK**.

The **Format Cells** dialog box disappears.

23 On the Standard toolbar, click the **Format Painter** button.

Cell K4 is highlighted with a marquee outline.

24 Click cell K5 and drag to cell K23.

Excel assigns the format from cell K4 to cells K5:K23.

25 In cell B4, type **January 25, 2001**, and press ⎆Enter⎆.

The contents of cell B4 change to 1/25/01, matching the format you set earlier.

26 In cell C4, type **C100001**.

27 In cell D4, type **Steven**.

28 In cell E4, type **Levy**.

29 In cell F4, type **6789 Elm Street**.

30 In cell G4, type **Redmond**.

31 In cell H4, type **WA**.

32 In cell I4, type **87063**.

33 In cell J4, type **4255550102**.

The contents of the cell change to *(425) 555-0102*, matching the format you chose earlier.

34 In cell K4, type **2400**.

The contents of the cell change to *$2,400.00 total*, matching the format you created earlier.

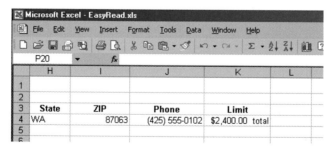

35 On the Standard toolbar, click **Save** to save your changes.

Close

36 Click the **Close** button to close EasyRead.xls.

Changing Data's Appearance Based on Its Value

Recording sales, credit limits, and other business data in a worksheet lets you make important decisions about your operations. And as you saw earlier in this chapter, you can change the appearance of data labels and the worksheet itself to make interpreting your data easier.

Ex2002e-3-2

Approved Courseware

Another way you can make your data easier to interpret is to have Excel change the appearance of your data based on its value. These formats are called **conditional formats** because the data must meet certain conditions to have a format applied to it. For instance, if owner Catherine Turner wanted to highlight any Saturdays on which daily sales at The Garden Company were over $4,000, she could define a conditional format that tests the value in the cell recording total sales and that will change the format of the cell's contents when the condition is met.

To create a conditional format, you click the cells to which you want to apply the format and open the **Conditional Formatting** dialog box. The default configuration of the **Conditional Formatting** dialog box appears in the following graphic.

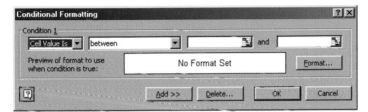

The first list box lets you choose whether you want the condition that follows to look at the cell's contents or the formula in the cell. In almost every circumstance, you will use the contents of the cell as the test value for the condition.

Tip

The only time you would want to set a formula as the basis for the condition would be to format a certain result, such as a grand total, the same way every time it appeared in a worksheet.

The second list box in the **Conditional Formatting** dialog box lets you select the comparison to be made. Depending on the comparison you choose, the dialog box will have either one or two boxes in which you enter values to be used in the comparison. The default comparison, *between*, requires two values, whereas comparisons such as *less than* require one.

After you have created a condition, you need to define the format to be applied to data that meets that condition. You do that in the **Format Cells** dialog box. From within this dialog box, you can set the characteristics of the text used to print the value in the cell. When you're done, a preview of the format you defined appears in the **Conditional Formatting** dialog box.

You're not limited to creating one condition per cell. If you like, you can create additional conditions by clicking the **Add** button in the **Conditional Formatting** dialog box. When you click the **Add** button, a second condition section appears.

Important

Excel doesn't check to make sure your conditions are logically consistent, so you need to be sure you enter your conditions correctly.

Excel evaluates the conditions in the order you entered them in the **Conditional Formatting** dialog box and, upon finding a condition the data meets, stops its comparisons. For example, suppose Catherine wanted to visually separate the credit limits of The Garden Company's customers into two different categories: those with limits under $1,500 and those with limits from $1,500 to $2,500. She could display her customers' credit limits with a conditional format using the conditions in the following graphic.

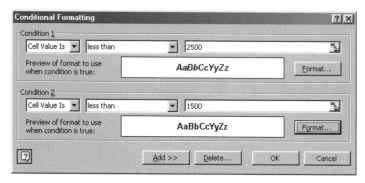

In this case, Excel would compare the value *1250* with the first condition, *<2500*, and assign that formatting to the cell containing the value. That the second condition, *<1500*, is "closer" is irrelevant—once Excel finds a condition the data meets, it stops comparing.

Tip

You should always enter the most restrictive condition first. In the preceding example, setting the first condition to *<1500* and the second to *<2500* would result in the proper format.

Conditional

In this exercise, you create a series of conditional formats to change the appearance of data in worksheet cells displaying the credit limit of The Garden Company's customers.

Open

1   On the Standard toolbar, click the **Open** button.

The **Open** dialog box appears.

2   Double-click the **Conditional.xls** file.

Conditional.xls opens.

3 If necessary, click cell K4.

4 On the **Format** menu, click **Conditional Formatting**.

The **Conditional Formatting** dialog box appears.

5 In the second list box, click the down arrow and then, from the list that appears, click **between**.

The word *between* appears in the second list box.

6 In the first argument box, type **1000**.

7 In the second argument box, type **2000**.

8 Click the **Format** button.

The **Format Cells** dialog box appears.

9 If necessary, click the **Font** tab.

The **Font** tab page appears.

10 In the **Color** box, click the down arrow and then, from the color palette that appears, click the blue square.

The color palette disappears, and the text in the Preview pane changes to blue.

11 Click **OK**.

The **Format Cells** dialog box disappears.

12 Click the **Add** button.

The **Condition 2** section of the dialog box appears.

13 In the second list box, click the down arrow and then, from the list that appears, click **between**.

The word *between* appears in the second list box.

14 In the first argument box, type **2000**.

15 In the second argument box, type **2500**.

16 Click the **Format** button.

The **Format Cells** dialog box appears.

17 In the **Color** box, click the down arrow and then, from the color palette that appears, click the green square.

The color palette disappears, and the text in the Preview pane changes to green.

18 Click **OK**.

The **Format Cells** dialog box disappears.

19 Click **OK**.

The **Conditional Formatting** dialog box disappears.

Auto Fill Options

20 In cell K4, click the fill handle, and drag it to cell K6.

The contents of cells K5 and K6 change to $2,400.00, and the **Auto Fill Options** button appears.

21 Click the **Auto Fill Options** button, and from the list that appears, click **Fill Formatting Only**.

The contents of cells K5 and K6 revert to their previous values, and Excel applies the conditional formats to the selected cells.

I	J	K	L	M
ZIP	Phone	Limit		
87063	(425) 555-0102	$2,400.00		
87063	(425) 555-0198	$750.00		
87063	(425) 555-0187	$1,500.00		

22 On the Standard toolbar, click the **Save** toolbar button to save your changes.

Close

23 Click the **Close** button to close Conditional.xls.

Making Printouts Easier to Follow

Changing how your data appears in the body of your worksheets can make your data much easier to understand, but it doesn't communicate when the worksheet was last opened or who it belongs to. You could always add that information to the top of every printed page, but you would need to change the current date every time you opened the document; and if you wanted the same information to appear at the top of every printed page, any changes to the body of your worksheets could mean you would need to edit your workbook so the information appeared in the proper place.

Ex2002-3-6

Approved Courseware

If you want to ensure that the same information appears at the top or bottom of every printed page, you can do so using headers or footers. A header is a section that appears at the top of every printed page, while a footer is a section that appears at the bottom of every printed page. To create a header or footer in Excel, you open the **Page Setup** dialog box to the **Header/Footer** tab.

Important

Everything you will learn about creating headers in this section applies to creating footers as well. Also, you can have both headers and footers in the same document.

The list boxes on the **Header/Footer** tab page will hold a number of standard headers and footers, such as page numbers by themselves or followed by the name of the workbook. You can create your own headers by opening the **Header** dialog box.

Header Graphic
new for
OfficeXP

In the **Header** dialog box, you can add your own text or use the box's buttons to change the appearance of the text in the header or to insert a date, time, or page number. Excel 2002 offers a new option when you create a header or footer: adding a graphic. Adding a graphic such as a company logo to a worksheet lets you identify the worksheet as referring to your company and helps reinforce your company's identity if you include the worksheet in a printed report distributed outside your company. After you insert a graphic into a header or footer, the **Format Picture** button will become available. Clicking that button will open a dialog box with tools to edit your graphic.

Follow

In this exercise, you create a custom header and a custom footer for a workbook. You add a graphic to the footer and then edit the graphic using the **Format Picture** dialog box.

Open

1 On the Standard toolbar, click the **Open** button.

The **Open** dialog box appears.

2 Double-click the **Follow.xls** file.

Follow.xls appears.

3 On the **View** menu, click **Header and Footer**.

The **Page Setup** dialog box appears, opened to the **Header/Footer** tab page.

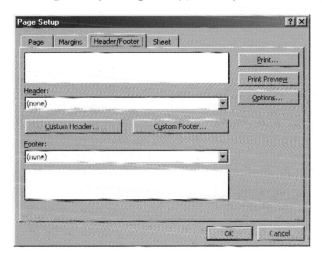

4 Click the **Custom Footer** button.

The **Footer** dialog box appears.

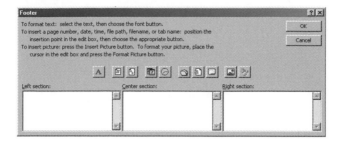

5 Click anywhere in the **Center section** box, and then click the **Insert Picture** button.

The **Insert Picture** dialog box appears.

6 Navigate to the ChangingDocAppearance folder, and then double-click the **tgc_logo.gif** file.

The **Insert Picture** dialog box disappears, and *&[Picture]* appears in the **Center section** box.

Format Picture

7 Click the **Format Picture** button.

The **Format Picture** dialog box appears.

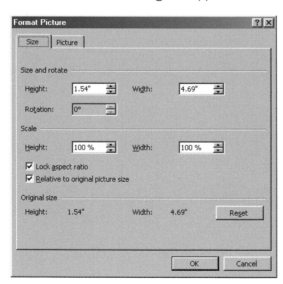

8 If necessary, select the **Lock aspect ratio** check box.

9 In the **Height** box, type **50%** and then click **OK**.

The **Format Picture** dialog box disappears.

10 In the **Footer** dialog box, click **OK**.

The **Footer** dialog box disappears, and part of the graphic you added appears in the footer section of the **Page Setup** dialog box.

11 Click the **Custom Header** button.

The **Header** dialog box appears.

Date

12 Click anywhere in the **Left section** box, and then click the **Date** button.

&[Date] appears in the **Left section** box.

Page Number

13 Click anywhere in the **Right section** box, and then click the **Page Number** button.

&[Page] appears in the **Right section** box.

14 Click **OK**.

The **Header** dialog box disappears.

15 Click the **Print Preview** button.

The Print Preview window appears.

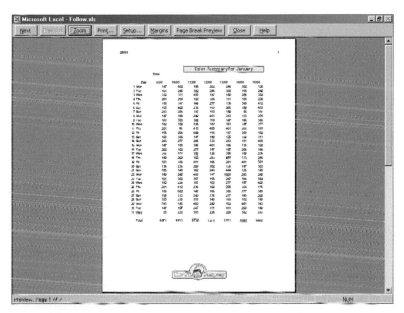

16 Click **Close**.

The Print Preview window and the **Page Setup** dialog box disappear.

17 Click cell G2.

18 On the **Edit** menu, point to **Clear**, and then click **All**.

The contents of the merged cell disappear, and the cells are unmerged.

Save

19 On the Standard toolbar, click the **Save** button to save your changes.

Close

20 Click the **Close** button to close Follow.xls.

Positioning Data on a Printout

Once you have your data and any headers or footers in your workbook, you can change your workbook's properties to ensure that your worksheets display all of your information and that the printing is centered on the page.

One of the workbook properties you can change is its margins, or the boundaries between different sections of the printed page. You can view a document's margins and where the contents of the header, footer, and body appear in relation to those margins in the Print Preview window.

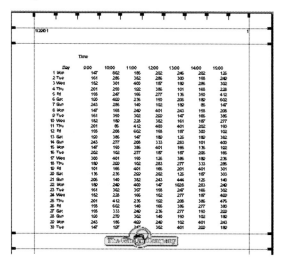

In the above graphic, the logo in the footer spills over the top margin of the footer and obscures some of the data in the worksheet. To remove the overlap, you can move the footer's top margin up, increasing the amount of space devoted to the footer. Increasing the size of the footer reduces the size of the worksheet body, meaning fewer rows can be printed on a page.

Another issue when printing worksheets is that the data in worksheets tends to be wider horizontally than a standard sheet of paper. For example, the data in the worksheet in the previous graphic is several columns wider than a standard piece of paper. You can use the controls in the **Page Setup** dialog box to change the alignment of the rows and columns on the page. When the columns follow the long edge of a piece of paper, the page is laid out in **portrait mode**; when the columns follow the short edge of a piece of paper, it is in **landscape mode**. The following graphic displays the contents of the previous worksheet laid out in landscape mode.

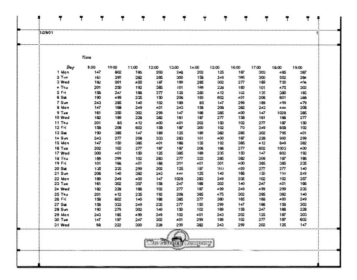

This is a better fit, but not all the data fits on the printed page. Once again, the **Page Setup** dialog box comes to the rescue. From within that dialog box, you can have Excel reduce the size of the worksheet's contents until the entire worksheet can be printed on a single page and also have Excel center the printed matter on the page so that there is an even margin around the printing.

Margins

In this exercise, you change the margins in a workbook to stop the graphic in the footer from overlapping with the data in the body of the worksheet. You then change the alignment of the workbook so that its contents are laid out in landscape mode and centered on the printed page.

1 On the Standard toolbar, click the **Open** button.

The **Open** dialog box appears.

2 Double-click the **Margins.xls** file.

Margins.xls opens.

Print Preview

3 On the Standard toolbar, click the **Print Preview** button.

The Print Preview window opens.

4 Click **Margins**.

Margin lines appear.

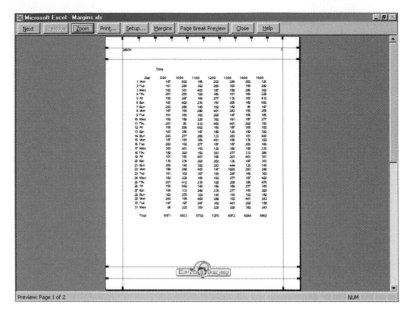

5 Drag the second margin line from the bottom of the page up until it clears the graphic.

The top edge of the footer moves above the graphic.

6 Click **Setup**.

The **Page Setup** dialog box appears.

7 If necessary, click the **Page** tab.

8 Select the **Landscape** option button.

9 Select the **Fit to** option button.

The default setting for the **Fit to** option is to fit the contents of a worksheet to one printed page.

10 Click the **Margins** tab.

The **Margins** tab page appears.

11 In the **Center on page** section of the tab page, select both the **Horizontally** check box and the **Vertically** check box.

12 Click **OK**.

The **Page Setup** dialog box disappears. The document view in the Print Preview window changes to reflect the new settings.

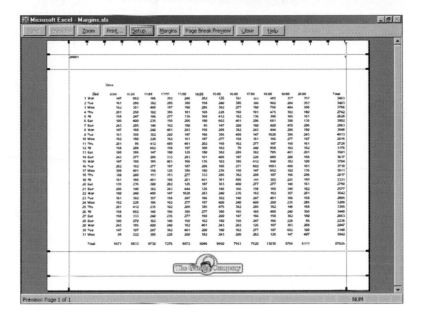

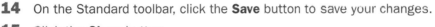

Save

Close

13 Click **Close**.

The Print Preview window disappears.

14 On the Standard toolbar, click the **Save** button to save your changes.

15 Click the **Close** button.

Margins.xls closes.

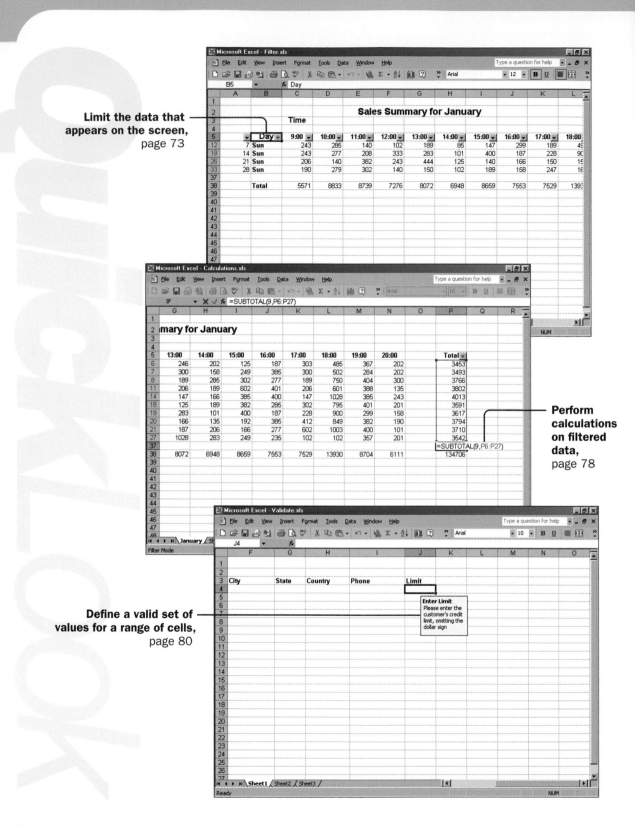

Limit the data that appears on the screen, page 73

Perform calculations on filtered data, page 78

Define a valid set of values for a range of cells, page 80

Chapter 5
Focusing on Specific Data Using Filters

After completing this chapter, you will be able to:

✔ Limit the data that appears on the screen.
✔ Perform calculations on filtered data.
✔ Define a valid set of values for a range of cells.

An important aspect of working with large amounts of data is the ability to zero in on the most important data in a worksheet, whether that data represents the best ten days of sales in a month or slow-selling product lines that you may need to reevaluate. In Microsoft Excel, you have a number of powerful, flexible tools with which you can limit the data displayed in your worksheet. Once your worksheet displays the subset of your data you need to make a decision, you can perform calculations on that data. You can discover what percentage of monthly sales were made up by the ten best days in the month, find your total sales for particular days of the week, or locate the slowest business day of the month.

Just as you can limit the data displayed by your worksheets, you can limit the data entered into them as well. Setting rules for data entered into cells lets you catch many of the most common data entry errors, such as entering values that are too small or too large, or attempting to enter a word in a cell that requires a number.

In this chapter, you'll learn how to limit the data that appears in your worksheets, perform calculations on the remaining data, and limit the data that can be entered into specific cells.

 This chapter uses the practice files Filter, Calculations, and Validate that you installed from this book's CD-ROM. For details about installing the practice files, see "Using the Book's CD-ROM" at the beginning of this book.

Limiting the Data That Appears on the Screen

Excel spreadsheets can hold as much data as you need them to, but you may not want to work with all of the data in a worksheet at the same time. For example, you might want to see the sales figures for your company during the first third, second third, and final third of a month. You can limit the data shown on a worksheet by creating a **filter**, which is a rule that selects rows to be shown in a worksheet.

Ex2002-1-5

Approved Courseware

To create a filter, you click the cell in the group you want to filter and use the **Data** menu to turn on **AutoFilter**. When you turn on AutoFilter, which is a built-in set of filtering capabilities, a down arrow button appears in the cell that Excel recognizes as the column's label.

Important

When you turn on filtering, Excel treats the cells in the active cell's column as a range. To ensure that the filtering works properly, you should always add a label to the column you want to filter.

Clicking the down arrow displays a list of values and options. The first few items in the list are filtering options, such as whether you want to display the top ten values in the column, create a custom filter, or display all values in the column (that is, remove the filter). The rest of the items on the list are the unique values in the column—clicking one of those values displays the row or rows containing that value.

Choosing the **Top 10** option from the list doesn't just limit the display to the top ten values. Instead, it opens the **Top 10 AutoFilter** dialog box. From within this dialog box, you can choose whether to show values from the top or bottom of the list, define the number of items you want to see, and choose whether the number in the middle box indicates the number of items or the percentage of items to be shown when the filter is applied. Using the **Top 10 AutoFilter** dialog box, you can find your top ten salespeople or identify the top five percent of your customers.

Ex2002e-7-2

Approved Courseware

When you choose **Custom** from the **AutoFilter** list, you can define a rule that Excel uses to decide which rows to show after the filter is applied. For instance, you can create a rule that only days with total sales of less than $2,500 should be shown in your worksheet. With those results in front of you, you might be able to determine whether the weather or another factor resulted in slower business on those days.

Two related things you can do in Excel are to choose rows at random from a list and to display the unique values in a column in the worksheet (not in the down arrow's list, which you can't normally work with). Generating a list of unique values in a column can give you important information, such as from which states you have customers or which categories of products sold in an hour.

Selecting rows randomly is useful for selecting customers to receive a special offer, deciding which days of the month to audit, or picking prize winners at an employee party. To choose rows, you can use the RAND function, which generates a random value and compares it with a test value included in the statement. A statement that returns a TRUE value 30 percent of the time would be *RAND()<=30%*; you could use this statement to select each row in a list with a probability of 30 percent.

Filter

In this exercise, you create a filter to show the top five sales days in January, show sales figures for Mondays during the same month, display the days with sales of at least $3,000, pick random days from the month to audit, and then generate a list of unique values in one of the worksheet's columns.

Open

1 On the Standard toolbar, click the **Open** button.

The **Open** dialog box appears.

2 Navigate to the UsingFilters folder, and double-click the **Filter.xls** file.

Filter.xls opens.

3 If necessary, click the **January** sheet tab.

4 Click cell P5.

5 On the **Data** menu, point to **Filter**, and then click **AutoFilter**.

A down arrow appears in cell P5.

6 In cell P5, click the down arrow and, from the list that appears, click **(Top 10...)**.

The **Top 10 AutoFilter** dialog box appears.

7 Click in the middle box, delete *10*, type **5**, and click **OK**.

Only the rows containing the five largest values in column P are shown.

8 On the **Data** menu, point to **Filter**, and then click **AutoFilter**.

The filtered rows reappear.

9 Click cell B5.

10 On the **Data** menu, point to **Filter**, and then click **AutoFilter**.

A down arrow appears in cell B5.

11 In cell B5, click the down arrow and, from the list of unique column values that appears, click **Mon**.

Only rows with *Mon* in column B are shown in the worksheet.

12 On the **Data** menu, point to **Filter**, and then click **AutoFilter**.

The filtered rows reappear.

13 Click cell P5, and then, on the **Data** menu, point to **Filter**, and then click **AutoFilter**.

A down arrow appears in cell P5.

14 In cell P5, click the down arrow and then, from the list that appears, click **(Custom...)**.

The **Custom AutoFilter** dialog box appears.

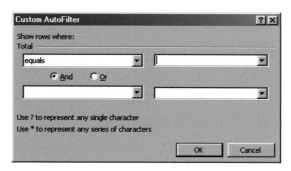

15 In the upper left box, click the down arrow and, from the list that appears, click **is greater than or equal to**.

16 In the upper right box, type **3000** and then click **OK**.

Only rows with totals of at least 3000 are shown in the worksheet.

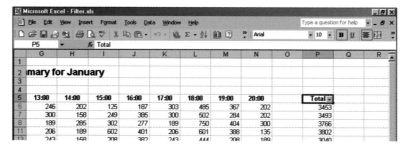

17 On the **Data** menu, point to **Filter**, and then click **AutoFilter**.

The filtered rows reappear.

18 On the **Data** menu, point to **Filter**, and then click **AutoFilter**.

A down arrow appears in cell P5.

19 In cell P5, click the down arrow and then, from the list of unique column values that appears, click **2236**.

All rows except the row containing 2236 in column P disappear.

20 On the **Data** menu, point to **Filter**, and then click **AutoFilter**.

The filtered rows reappear.

21 In cell Q5, type **Audit**.

22 In cell Q6, type **=RAND()<17%**.

If the result of the RAND function is less than *17%*, cell Q6 will display *TRUE*; otherwise, cell Q6 will display *FALSE*.

23 Drag the AutoFill handle from cell Q6 to cell Q36.

TRUE and *FALSE* values appear in the cells from Q6 to Q36 with a frequency of 16 percent and 84 percent, respectively.

24 Click cell B5 and drag to cell B36.

Cells B5 through B36 are highlighted.

25 On the **Data** menu, point to **Filter**, and then click **Advanced Filter**.

The **Advanced Filter** dialog box appears.

26 Select the **Unique records only** check box, and then click **OK**.

Rows with the first occurrence of a value are displayed in the worksheet.

27 On the **Data** menu, point to **Filter**, and then click **Show All**.

The filtered rows reappear.

Save

28 On the Standard toolbar, click the **Save** button.

Excel saves your changes.

Close

29 Click the **Close** button.

Filter.xls closes.

Performing Calculations on Filtered Data

When you filter your worksheet, you limit the data that appears. The ability to focus on the data that's most important to your current needs is important, but there are a few limitations. One limitation is that any formulas you have created don't change their calculations, even if some of the rows used in the formula are hidden by the filter.

There are two ways you can find the total of a group of filtered cells. The first method is to use AutoCalculate. To use AutoCalculate, you select the cells you want to find the total for. When you do, the total for the cells appears on the status bar, at the lower edge of the Excel window.

When you use AutoCalculate, you aren't limited to finding the sum of the selected cells. To display the other functions you can use, you right-click the AutoCalculate pane and select the function you want from the shortcut menu that appears.

AutoCalculate is great for finding a quick total or average for filtered cells, but it doesn't make the result available in the worksheet. To make the value available in your worksheet, you can create a SUBTOTAL function. As with AutoCalculate, you can choose the type of calculation the function performs.

Calculations

In this exercise, you use AutoCalculate to find the total of a group of cells in a filtered worksheet, create a SUBTOTAL function to make the same value available in the worksheet, and then edit the SUBTOTAL function so that it calculates an average instead of a sum.

Open

1 On the Standard toolbar, click the **Open** button.

The **Open** dialog box appears.

2 Double-click **Calculations.xls**.

Calculations.xls opens.

3 If necessary, click the **January** sheet tab.

4 Click cell P5.

5   On the **Data** menu, point to **Filter**, and then click **AutoFilter**.

A down arrow button appears in cell P5.

6   In cell P5, click the down arrow button and then, from the list that appears, click **(Top 10...)**.

The **Top 10 AutoFilter** dialog box appears.

7   Click **OK**.

Tip

Clicking **OK** here accepts the default setting of the **Top 10 AutoFilter** dialog box, which is to show the top ten values in the selected cells.

The **Top 10 AutoFilter** dialog box disappears, and the rows with the ten highest values in column P are displayed.

8   Click cell P6 and drag to cell P27.

The cells are selected, and on the status bar, in the lower right corner of the Excel window, *SUM=36781* appears in the AutoCalculate pane.

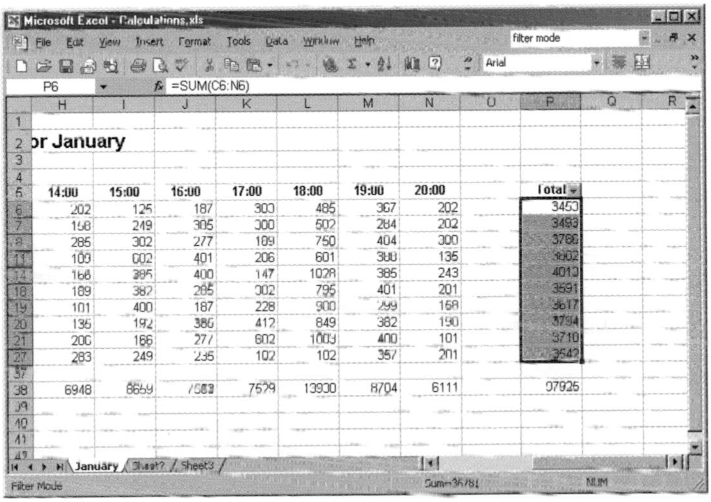

AutoSum

Σ

9   Click cell P37, and then, on the Standard toolbar, click the **AutoSum** button.

The formula *=SUBTOTAL(9,P6:P36)* appears on the formula bar.

10   Press [Enter].

The value *36781* appears in cell P37. The value in cell P38 also changes to *134706*, but that calculation includes the subtotal of the filtered cells in the column.

11   Click cell P37, and then, on the formula bar, edit the formula so that it reads *=SUBTOTAL(1,P6:P36)* and then press [Enter].

By changing the 9 to a 1 in the SUBTOTAL function, the function now calculates an average instead of a sum. The average of the top ten values in cells P6 through P36, *3678.1*, appears in cell P37. The value in cell P38 also changes to *101603.1*, but that calculation includes the average of the filtered cells in the column.

12   If necessary, click cell P37 and then press [Del].

Excel deletes the SUBTOTAL formula from cell P37, and the total in cell P38 changes to *97925*.

Save

13   On the Standard toolbar, click the **Save** button.

Excel saves your changes.

Close

14   Click the **Close** button.

Calculations.xls closes.

Defining a Valid Set of Values for a Range of Cells

Ex2002e-7-4

Approved Courseware

Part of creating efficient and easy-to-use worksheets is to do what you can to ensure that the data entered into your worksheets is as accurate as possible. While it isn't possible to catch every typographical or transcription error, you can set up a **validation rule** to make sure the data entered into a cell meets certain standards.

To create a validation rule, you open the **Data Validation** dialog box.

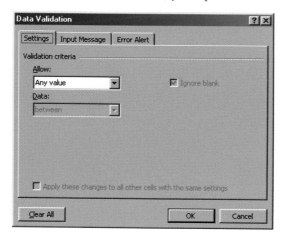

You can use the **Data Validation** dialog box to define the type of data that Excel should allow in the cell and then, depending on the data type you choose, to set the conditions data must meet to be accepted in the cell. In the following graphic, Excel knows to look for a whole number value between 1000 and 2000.

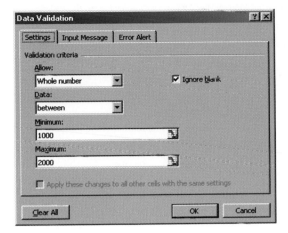

Setting accurate validation rules can help you and your colleagues avoid entering a customer's name in the cell designated to hold their phone number or setting a credit limit above a certain level. To require a user to enter a numeric value in a cell, display the **Settings** page of the **Data Validation** dialog box, click the **Allow** down arrow, and depending on your needs, choose either **Whole Number** or **Decimal** from the list that appears.

Of course, it's frustrating if you want to enter data into a cell and, when a message box appears, telling you the data you tried to enter isn't acceptable, you aren't given the rules you need to follow. Excel lets you create messages that tell the user what values are expected before the data is entered and then, if the conditions aren't met, reiterate the conditions in a custom error message.

You can turn off data validation in a cell by displaying the **Settings** page of the **Data Validation** dialog box and clicking the **Clear All** button in the lower left corner of the dialog box.

Validate

In this exercise, you create a data validation rule limiting the credit line of The Garden Company customers to $2,500, add an input message mentioning the limitation, and then create an error message should someone enter a value greater than $2,500. After you've created your rule and messages, you test them.

Open

1 On the Standard toolbar, click the **Open** button.

The **Open** dialog box appears.

2 Double-click the **Validate.xls** file.

Validate.xls opens.

3 Click cell J4.

4 On the **Data** menu, click **Validation**.

The **Data Validation** dialog box appears with the **Settings** tab page in front.

5 In the **Allow** box, click the down arrow and, from the list that appears, click **Decimal**.

Boxes labeled **Minimum** and **Maximum** appear below the **Data** box.

6 In the **Data** box, click the down arrow and, from the list that appears, click **less than or equal to**.

The **Minimum** box disappears.

7 In the **Maximum** box, type **2500**.

8 Clear the **Ignore blank** check box.

9 Click the **Input Message** tab.

The **Input Message** tab page appears.

10 In the **Title** box, type **Enter Limit**.

11 In the **Input Message** box, type **Please enter the customer's credit limit, omitting the dollar sign**.

12 Click the **Error Alert** tab page.

The **Error Alert** tab page appears.

13 In the **Style** box, click the down arrow and, from the list that appears, choose **Warning**.

The icon that will appear on your message box changes to the **Warning** icon.

14 In the **Title** box, type **Error**.

15 Click **OK**.

Tip

Leaving the **Error message** box blank causes Excel to use its default message: *The value you entered is not valid. A user has restricted values that can be entered into this cell.*

A ScreenTip with the title Enter Limit and the text *Please enter the customer's credit limit, omitting the dollar sign* appears near cell J4.

16 Type **2501**, and press `Enter`.

A warning box with the title **Error** and default text appears.

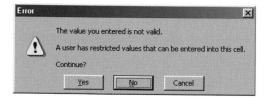

17   Click **Yes**.

The warning box disappears.

Important

Clicking **No** lets you edit the bad value, while clicking **Cancel** deletes the entry.

18   Click cell J4.

Cell J4 becomes the active cell, and the ScreenTip reappears.

19   Type **2500**, and press Enter.

Excel accepts your input.

20   Click cell J4.

21   On the **Data** menu, click **Validation**.

The **Data Validation** dialog box appears.

22   Click the **Settings** tab.

The **Settings** tab page appears.

23   In the **Allow** box, click the down arrow and, from the list that appears, click **Whole number**.

24   Click **OK**.

25   In cell J4, type **2499.95** and press Enter.

A warning box with the title **Error** and default text appears.

26   Click **No**.

The warning box disappears, cell J4 becomes the active cell, and the ScreenTip reappears.

27   Type **2500**, and press Enter.

Save

28   Excel accepts your input.

29   On the Standard toolbar, click the **Save** button.

Close

30   Click the **Close** button.

Validate.xls closes.

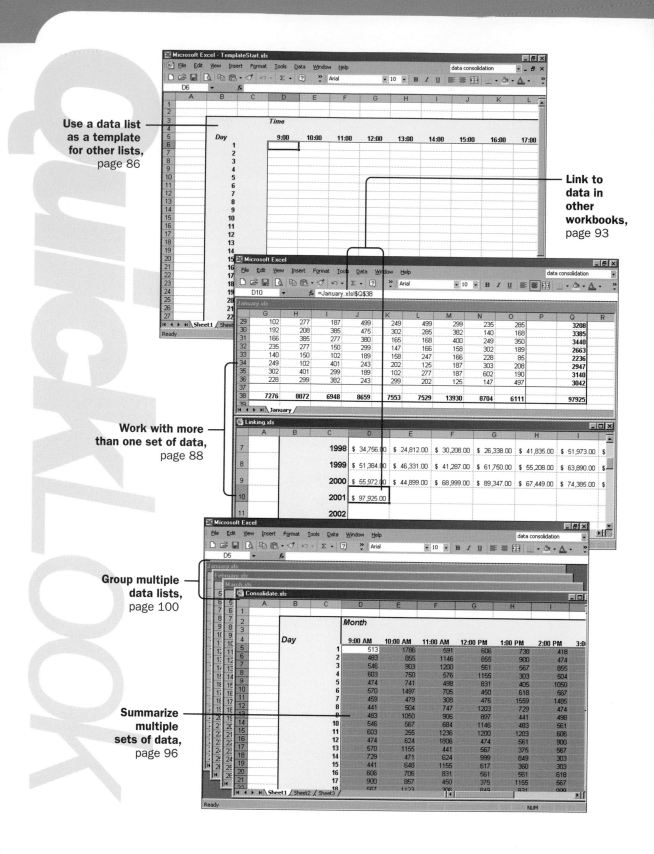

Use a data list as a template for other lists, page 86

Link to data in other workbooks, page 93

Work with more than one set of data, page 88

Group multiple data lists, page 100

Summarize multiple sets of data, page 96

Chapter 6
Combining Data from Multiple Sources

After completing this chapter, you will be able to:

✔ Use an existing data list as a template for other lists.

✔ Work with more than one set of data.

✔ Link to data in other workbooks.

✔ Summarize multiple sets of data.

✔ Group multiple data lists.

Microsoft Excel gives you a wide range of tools with which to format, summarize, and present your data. Once you have created a workbook to hold data about a particular subject, you can create as many worksheets as you need to make that data easier to find within the workbook. For instance, you can create a workbook to store sales data for a year, with each worksheet representing a month in that year. To ensure that the workbook for every year has a similar appearance, you can create a workbook with the desired characteristics (such as more than the standard number of worksheets, custom worksheet formatting, or a particular color for the workbook's sheet tabs) and save it as a pattern for similar workbooks you create in the future. The benefit of ensuring that all of your sales data worksheets have the same layout is that you and your colleagues will immediately know where to look for specific totals. Also, when you create a summary worksheet, you will know in advance which cells to include in your calculations.

If you work with the same workbooks repeatedly, you can group those workbooks in a special file, called a **workspace**. When you open the workspace, Excel knows to open the files you included in that workspace.

A consequence of organizing your data into different workbooks and worksheets is that you need ways to manage, combine, and summarize data from more than one Excel document. You can always copy data from one worksheet to another, but if the original value were to change, that change would not be reflected in the cell range to which you copied the data. Rather than remember which cells you need to update when a value changes, you can create a link to the original cell. That way, Excel will update the value for you whenever you open the workbook. If multiple worksheets hold similar values, you can use links to summarize those values in a single worksheet.

In this chapter, you'll learn how to use a data list as a template for other lists, work with more than one set of data, link to data in other workbooks, summarize multiple sets of data, and group multiple data lists.

This chapter uses the practice files TemplateStart, January, February, March, Linking, 2001Q1, Y2001Q1, Consolidate, TotalByHour2001, and Y2001ByMonth that you installed from this book's CD-ROM. For details about installing the practice files, see "Using the Book's CD-ROM" at the beginning of this book.

Using a Data List as a Template for Other Lists

Once you have decided on the type of data you want to store in a workbook and what that workbook should look like, you will probably want to be able to create similar workbooks without adding all the formatting and formulas again. For example, you might have settled on a design for your monthly sales tracking workbook.

Ex2002-4-1

Approved Courseware

When you have settled on a design for your workbooks, you can save one of the workbooks as a **template**, or pattern, for similar workbooks you create in the future. You should remove any existing data from a workbook you save as a template, both to avoid data entry errors and to remove any confusion as to whether the workbook is a template. You can also remove any worksheets you and your colleagues won't need by right-clicking the tab of an unneeded worksheet and, from the shortcut menu that appears, clicking **Delete**.

If you want your template workbook to have more than the standard number of worksheets (such as twelve worksheets to track sales for a year, by month), you can add worksheets by right-clicking any sheet tab, clicking **Insert** from the shortcut menu that appears, and then, on the **General** page of the **Insert** dialog box, double-clicking the **Worksheet** icon.

Ex2002e-2-1

Approved Courseware

To create a template from an existing workbook, you save the model workbook under the Template file type, which you can choose from the **Save as type** drop-down list in the **Save As** dialog box. If you ever want to change the template, you can open it like a standard workbook (that is, an Excel file with the .xls extension) and make your changes. When you have completed your work, resave the file normally—it will still be a template.

Important

When you change the file type to Template, Excel changes the active directory to the default Office XP templates directory. You need to save your template to this folder so that it will be available through the **Templates** dialog box.

Task pane new for **Office**XP

Once you have saved a workbook as a template, you can use it as a model for new workbooks. To create a workbook from a template in Excel, you open the task pane from the **View** menu.

Ex2002-2-2

Approved Courseware

The **New from template** section of the task pane has a list of any previously used templates as well as the **General Templates**, **Templates on my Web Sites**, and **Templates on Microsoft.com** options. Clicking either of the latter two items will take you to the Web and let you search for templates on the Internet or your company's intranet, or on Microsoft.com. Clicking **General Templates** lists the templates available on your computer.

From the **Templates** dialog box, you can double-click the template you want to use as the model for your workbook. Excel will create a new workbook with the template's formatting and contents in place.

Tip

The default file type for files created with a template is workbook (.xls), not template (.xlt).

TemplateStart

In this exercise, you create a template to track sales for a month at The Garden Company. You delete unneeded worksheets from the template, save the file with the Template file type, and then use your new template to create a workbook.

Open

1 On the Standard toolbar, click the **Open** button.

The **Open** dialog box appears.

2 Navigate to the MultipleSources folder, and double-click the **Template-Start.xls** file.

TemplateStart.xls opens.

3 On the tab bar, in the lower left corner of the workbook window, right-click the **Sheet2** tab and, from the shortcut menu that appears, click **Delete**.

The **Sheet2** worksheet disappears.

4 On the tab bar, in the lower left corner of the workbook window, right-click the **Sheet3** tab and, from the shortcut menu that appears, click **Delete**.

The **Sheet3** worksheet disappears.

5 On the **File** menu, click **Save As**.

The **Save As** dialog box appears.

6 Click the **Save as type** down arrow, and from the list that appears, click **Template (*.xlt)**.

The active directory changes to the default Microsoft Office XP templates directory.

7 In the **File name** box, delete the existing name and type **MonthlySales**.

8 Click **Save**.

The **Save As** dialog box disappears, and Excel saves your document as a template.

Close

9 Click the **Close** button.

MonthlySales.xlt closes.

10 On the **View** menu, click **Task Pane**.

The task pane appears.

11 In the **New from template** section of the task pane, click **General Templates**.

The **Templates** dialog box appears.

12 In the **Templates** dialog box, double-click **MonthlySales.xlt**.

A new workbook named MonthlySales1.xls appears.

Save

13 On the Standard toolbar, click the **Save** button.

The **Save As** dialog box appears, with the default Templates directory as the active directory.

14 Navigate to the MultipleSources exercise directory, and in the **File name** box, type **December**.

15 Click **Save**.

Excel saves your workbook, and the **Save As** dialog box disappears.

16 Click the **Close** button.

December.xls closes.

Working with More Than One Set of Data

An important part of managing your Excel data effectively is organizing it into workbooks by subject. For example, you can create a workbook to track sales for the new year or add a worksheet to a products workbook to maintain records of a new product category. When you store your data in more than one workbook, you need a way to work with multiple workbooks simultaneously. You can open more than one workbook at a time by accessing the **Open** dialog box multiple times, but you can also open more than one file from the **Open** dialog box at once.

In the **Open** dialog box, hold down the Ctrl key, click the files you want to open, and then click **Open**. For example, you might open the workbooks with the sales for the first three months in a year and compare the totals, both by day and by grand total.

Tip

The only limit to the number of Excel files you can have open at a time is the amount of memory in your computer. Of course, the practical limit for most tasks is much lower and probably doesn't exceed four or five open files.

When you open more than one Excel workbook, the active workbook often hides the inactive workbooks on the screen. You can use the buttons on the taskbar to move from file to file, but you can also arrange the workbooks within the Excel window. For example, you can split the screen horizontally and show one workbook in each portion of the window, as in the following graphic.

March.xls

Day		Time								
		9:00	10:00	11:00	12:00	13:00	14:00	15:00	16:00	17:00
1 Thu		183	492	203	202	246	108	97	84	18
2 Fri		161	285	382	285	300	158	249	385	300
3 Sat		182	301	400	187	189	285	302	277	10
4 Sun		201	250	192	385	101	168	228	150	10
5 Mon		158	247	166	277	135	350	412	102	13
6 Tue		190	499	235	150	206	189	602	401	20

January.xls

Day		Time								
		9:00 AM	10:00 AM	11:00 AM	12:00 PM	1:00 PM	2:00 PM	3:00 PM	4:00 PM	5:00
1 Mon		147	802	185	202	246	202	125	187	
2 Tue		161	285	382	285	300	158	249	385	
3 Wed		182	301	400	187	189	285	302	277	
4 Thu		201	250	192	385	101	108	228	150	
5 Fri		158	247	166	277	135	350	412	102	
6 Sat		190	499	235	150	206	189	602	401	

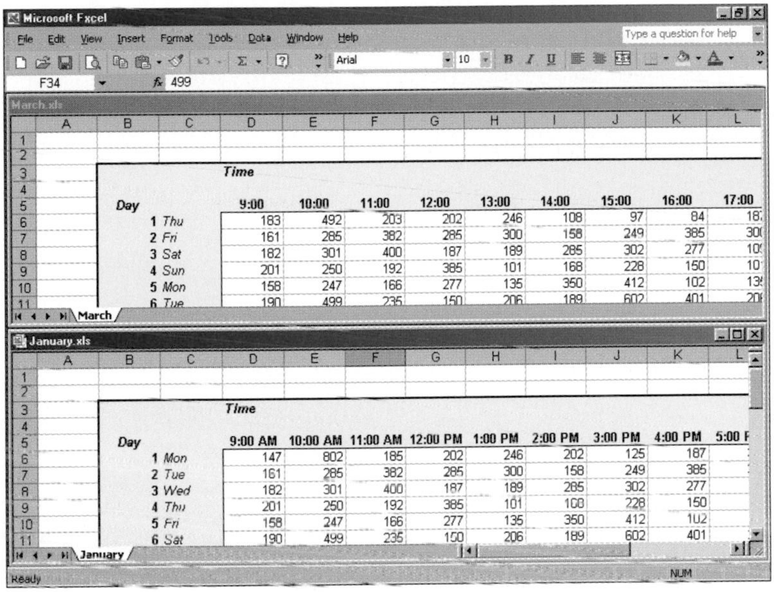

The problem with splitting the screen is that most of each workbook is hidden. You can arrange your workbooks within the Excel window so that most of the active workbook is shown but the others are easily accessible by clicking **Arrange** on the **Window** menu and, in the **Arrange Windows** dialog box, selecting the **Cascade** option. When you do, the windows will be arranged as in the following graphic.

January.xls

Day		Time								
		9:00 AM	10:00 AM	11:00 AM	12:00 PM	1:00 PM	2:00 PM	3:00 PM	4:00 PM	5:0
1 Mon		147	802	185	202	246	202	125	187	
2 Tue		161	285	382	285	300	158	249	385	
3 Wed		182	301	400	107	189	285	302	277	
4 Thu		201	250	192	385	101	168	228	150	
5 Fri		158	247	166	277	135	350	412	102	
6 Sat		190	499	235	150	206	109	602	401	
7 Sun		243	285	140	102	189	85	147	295	
8 Mon		147	168	249	401	243	158	208	382	
9 Tue		161	350	302	299	147	166	385	400	
10 Wed		182	189	228	382	161	187	277	158	
11 Thu		201	85	412	400	401	202	150	102	
12 Fri		158	208	602	150	187	300	102	70	
13 Sat		190	385	147	189	125	189	382	285	
14 Sun		243	277	208	333	283	101	400	187	
15 Mon		147	150	385	401	166	135	192	385	
16 Tue		202	102	277	187	187	206	166	277	
17 Wed		300	401	150	125	385	189	235	150	
18 Thu		189	299	102	283	277	333	285	382	
19 Fri		101	166	401	166	201	401	301	400	

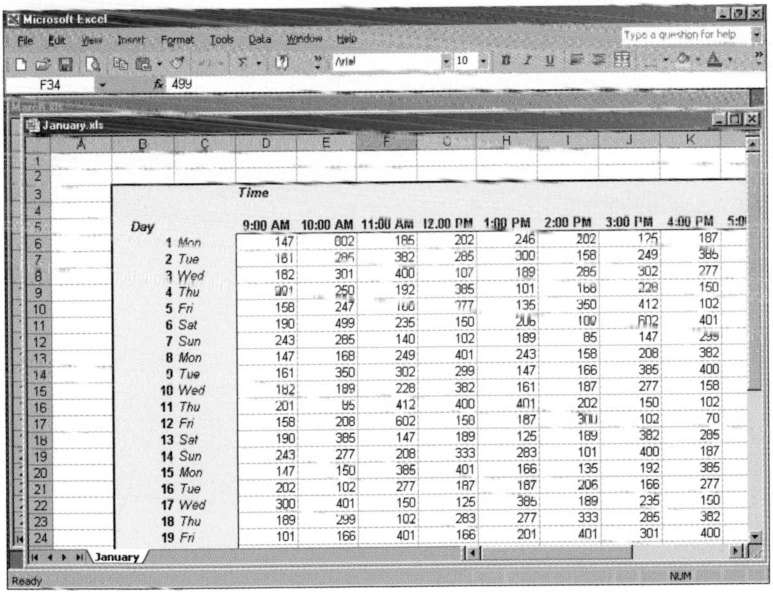

Ex2002-4-2

Approved Courseware

Another way you can work with more than one workbook is to copy a worksheet from another workbook to the current workbook. One circumstance in which you might consider copying worksheets to the current workbook would occur if you were to collect all monthly sales results for a year in one place. You can copy worksheets from another workbook by right-clicking the tab of the sheet you want to copy and, from the shortcut menu that appears, clicking **Move or Copy** to display the **Move or Copy** dialog box.

Tip

Selecting the **Create a copy** check box leaves the copied worksheet in its original workbook, while clearing the check box causes Excel to delete the worksheet from its original workbook.

Color-coded worksheet tabs
new for **Office**XP

Once the worksheets are in the target workbook, you can change their order to make the data easier to locate within the workbook. To change a worksheet's location in the workbook, you drag its sheet tab to the desired location on the tab bar. If you want a worksheet to stand out in a workbook, you can right-click its sheet tab and use the menu that appears to change the tab's color.

In this exercise, you open multiple workbooks, change how the workbooks are displayed, insert two worksheets into a workbook, reorder the worksheets, and then change the tab color of one of the worksheets.

January
February
March

Open

1 On the Standard toolbar, click the **Open** button.

The **Open** dialog box appears.

2 Hold down the Ctrl key while you click **January.xls**, **February.xls**, and **March.xls**, and then click **Open**.

January.xls, February.xls, and March.xls open.

3 Click the January.xls title bar.

January.xls becomes the active document.

4 On the **Window** menu, click **Arrange**.

The **Arrange Windows** dialog box appears.

5 Click the **Cascade** option button, and then click **OK**.

The windows of open Excel documents are cascaded within the Excel window.

6 Click the January.xls title bar.

7 On the **File** menu, click **Save As**.

The **Save As** dialog box appears.

8 In the **File name** box, type **FirstQuarter** and then click **Save**.

Excel saves the file under the name FirstQuarter.xls.

9 Click the February.xls title bar.

February.xls becomes the active document.

10 On the tab bar, right-click the **February** tab and then, from the shortcut menu that appears, click **Move or Copy**.

The **Move or Copy** dialog box appears.

11 Click the **To book** down arrow, and then, from the list that appears, click **FirstQuarter.xls**.

12 In the **Before sheet** list, click **(move to end)**.

13 At the bottom of the **Move or Copy** dialog box, select the **Create a copy** check box.

14 Click **OK**

The February worksheet appears in FirstQuarter.xls. Cells D38 through O38 contain an error marker in the upper left corner of each cell.

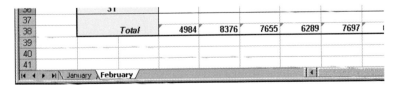

Error Options

15 Select cells D38 through O38.

An **Error Options** button appears.

Troubleshooting

The **Error Options** button appears because Excel asks whether the data in the cell above the top of the selected range should be included in the calculation. It's time data and shouldn't be included, so you can ignore the error message.

16 Click the **Error Options** button, and then, from the shortcut menu that appears, click **Ignore Error**.

The error markers disappear from the selected cells.

17 Click the March.xls title bar.

March.xls becomes the active document.

18 On the tab bar, right-click the **March** tab and then, from the shortcut menu that appears, click **Move or Copy**.

The **Move or Copy** dialog box appears.

19 Click the **To book** down arrow, and then, from the list that appears, click **FirstQuarter.xls**.

20 In the **Before sheet** list, click **February**.

21 At the bottom of the **Move or Copy** dialog box, select the **Create a copy** check box.

22 Click **OK**.

The March worksheet appears in FirstQuarter.xls, to the left of the February tab. Cells D38 through O38 contain an error marker in the upper left corner of each cell.

23 Select cells D38 through O38.

An **Error Options** button appears.

24 Click the **Error Options** button, and then, from the shortcut menu that appears, click **Ignore Error**.

The error markers disappear from the selected cells.

25 On the tab bar, drag the **February** tab to the left of the **March** tab. As you drag the **February** tab, a line will appear in the tab bar, marking the **February** tab's place.

The **February** tab moves to the left of the **March** tab.

26 On the tab bar, right-click the **March** tab, and then, from the shortcut menu that appears, click **Tab Color**.

The **Format Tab Color** dialog box appears.

27 Click the light orange square, and then click **OK**.

Excel assigns the light orange color to the **March** tab.

28 Click the **February** tab.

The February sheet is selected. Because the March sheet is in the background, the **March** tab turns light orange.

36	31					
37						
38	*Total*	4984	8376	7655	6289	7697
39						
40						
41						

|◄ ◄ ► ►|\ January \ **February** ⟨ March /

Save

29 On the Standard toolbar, click the **Save** button.

Excel saves your changes.

Close

30 Click the **Close** button.

FirstQuarter.xls closes, and March.xls becomes the active document.

31 Click the **Close** button.

March.xls closes, and February.xls becomes the active document.

32 Click the **Close** button.

February.xls closes.

Linking to Data in Other Workbooks

Cutting and pasting data from one workbook to another is a quick and easy way to gather related data in one place, but there is a substantial limitation: if the data from the original cell changes, the change is not reflected in the cell to which the data was copied. In other words, cutting and pasting a cell's contents doesn't create a relationship between the original cell and the target cell.

You can ensure that the data in the target cell will reflect any changes in the original cell by creating a **link** between the two cells. Rather than enter a value into the target cell by typing or pasting, you create a type of formula that identifies the source from which Excel will derive the target cell's value.

Ex2002-4-3

Approved Courseware

To create a link between cells, open both the workbook with the cell from which you want to pull the value and the workbook with the target cell. Then click the target cell, and type an equal sign, signifying you want to create a formula. After you type the equal sign, activate the workbook with the cell from which you want to derive the value and then click that cell.

When you switch back to the workbook with the target cell, you will find that Excel has filled in the formula with a reference to the cell you clicked.

	IF	▾ X ✓ *fx*	=[TotalByHour2001.xls]Sheet1!$D$8					
	A	B	C	D	E	F		(
1								
2								
3		=[TotalByHour2001.xls]Sheet1!$D$8						
4								
5								

The reference from this example, *=[TotalByHour2001.xls]Sheet1!$D$8*, gives three pieces of information: the workbook, the worksheet, and the cell you clicked in the worksheet. The first element of the reference, the name of the workbook, is enclosed in square brackets; the end of the second element is marked with an exclamation point; and the third element, the cell reference, has a dollar sign before both the row and the column identifiers. This type of reference is known as a **3-D reference**, reflecting the three dimensions (workbook, worksheet, and cell) you need to point to a cell in another workbook.

Tip

For references to cells in the same workbook, the workbook information is omitted. Likewise, references to cells in the same worksheet don't use a worksheet identifier.

Whenever you open a workbook with a link to another document, Excel will try to update the information in linked cells. If the program can't find the source, such as when a workbook or worksheet is deleted or renamed, an alert box appears, indicating that there is a broken link. At that point, you can click the **Update** button and then the **Edit Links** button to open the **Edit Links** dialog box and find which link is broken. After you identify the broken link, you can close the **Edit Links** dialog box, click the cell where the problem occurred, and create a new link to the desired data.

If you type a link yourself and you make an error, a #REF! error message will appear in the cell with the link. To fix the link, click the cell, delete its contents, and then either retype the link or create it with the point-and-click method described earlier in this section.

Linking
2001Q1
Y2001Q1

Open

In this exercise, you create a link to another workbook, break the link, and then use the **Edit Links** dialog box to identify the broken link and the **Change Source** dialog box to fix the link.

1 On the Standard toolbar, click the **Open** button.

The **Open** dialog box appears.

2 Hold down the ⌃ key while you click the **Linking.xls** and **2001Q1.xls** files, and then click **Open**.

Linking.xls and 2001Q1.xls open.

3 On the **Window** menu, click **Arrange**.

The **Arrange Windows** dialog box appears.

4   Select the **Cascade** option button, and then click **OK**.

The open Excel documents cascade in the Excel window.

5   Click cell D10, and then type =.

6   Click the 2001Q1.xls title bar.

The 2001Q1.xls file appears.

7   If necessary, click the **January** sheet tab.

8   Click cell Q38.

9   Click the Linking.xls title bar.

Linking.xls appears, with the formula =[2001Q1.xls]January!$Q$38 in cell D10.

8			1999	$ 51,384.00	$ 46,331.00	$ 41,
9			2000	$ 55,972.00	$ 44,899.00	$ 68,
10			=[2001Q1.xls]January!$Q$38		
11			2002		
12			2003		

10   Press [Enter].

The value $97,925 appears in cell D10.

Save

11   On the Standard toolbar, click the **Save** button.

Excel saves your changes.

Close

12   Click the **Close** button.

Linking.xls closes.

13   Click the **Close** button.

2001Q1.xls closes.

14   On the Standard toolbar, click the **Open** button.

The **Open** dialog box appears.

15   Click **2001Q1.xls**, and then press [Del].

2001Q1.xls moves to the **Recycle Bin**.

16   Double-click **Linking.xls**.

Linking.xls opens, with an alert box asking whether you want to update the links in the workbook.

17   In the alert box, click **Update**.

The original alert box disappears, and a second alert box, with a message asking if you want to edit the broken link, appears.

18   Click **Edit Links**.

The **Edit Links** dialog box appears.

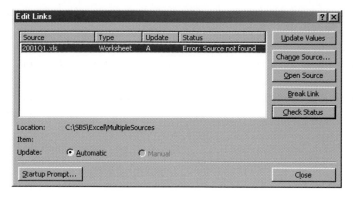

19   Click **Change Source**.

The **Change Source** dialog box appears.

20   Double-click **Y2001Q1.xls**.

The **Change Source** dialog box disappears, and the **Edit Links** dialog box reappears, with an indication that Y2001Q1.xls is a valid source for links.

21   Click **Close**.

The **Edit Links** dialog box disappears, and *$97,925.00* appears in cell D10.

22   Click cell D10.

=[Y2001Q1.xls]January!$Q$38 appears on the formula bar.

23   On the Standard toolbar, click the **Save** button.

Excel saves your changes.

24   Click the **Close** button.

Linking.xls closes.

Summarizing Multiple Sets of Data

When you create a series of worksheets that contain similar data, perhaps by using a template, you build a consistent set of workbooks where data is stored in a predictable place. For example, in the workbook template in the following graphic, sales for the hour 9:00 a.m. to 10:00 a.m. on the first day of the month are always stored in cell D6.

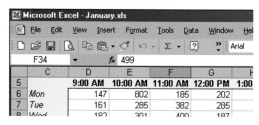

Using links to bring data from one worksheet to another gives you a great deal of power in combining data from several sources in a single spot. For example, you can create a worksheet that lists the total sales just for certain months of a year, use links to draw the values from the worksheets in which the sales were recorded, and then create a formula to perform calculations on the data. However, for large worksheets with hundreds of cells filled with data, creating links from every cell to cells on another worksheet is time-consuming. Also, to calculate a sum or an average for the data, you would need to include links to cells in every workbook.

Ex2002e-2-3

Fortunately, there is an easier way to combine data from multiple worksheets in a single worksheet. This process, called **data consolidation**, lets you define ranges of cells from multiple worksheets and have Excel summarize the data. You define these ranges in the **Consolidate** dialog box.

Approved Courseware

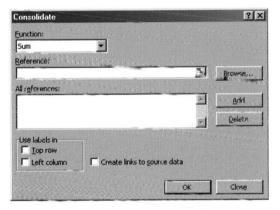

Once you have opened the dialog box, you move to the worksheet with the cells in the first range you want to include in your summary. When you select the cells, the 3-D reference for the cell range appears in the **Consolidate** dialog box.

Clicking **Add** stores the reference, while clicking **Delete** removes a range from the calculation. You can then choose the other cell ranges with data to include in the summary. Cells that are in the same relative position in the ranges will have their contents summarized together. So the cell in the upper left corner of one range will be added to the cell in the upper left corner of another range, even if those ranges are in different areas of the worksheet. After you choose the ranges to be used in your summary, you can choose the calculation to perform on the data (sum, average, and so on). When you're done selecting ranges to use in the calculation, click **OK** to have Excel summarize the data on your target worksheet.

Important

You can define only one data consolidation summary per workbook.

Consolidate
Y2001ByMonth

Open

In this exercise, you define a series of ranges from two workbooks to be included in a data consolidation calculation. You then add the contents of the ranges and show the results in a worksheet.

1 On the Standard toolbar, click the **Open** button.

The **Open** dialog box appears.

2 Hold down the ⌃ key while you click **Consolidate.xls** and **Y2001ByMonth.xls**, and then click **Open**.

Consolidate.xls and Y2001ByMonth.xls open.

3 If necessary, on the **Window** menu, click **Consolidate.xls**.

Conslidate.xls becomes the active document.

4 Click cell D5, and then, on the **Data** menu, click **Consolidate**.

The **Consolidate** dialog box appears.

5 On the **Window** menu, click **Y2001ByMonth.xls**.

Y2001ByMonth.xls becomes the active file.

6 If necessary, click the **January** sheet tab.

7 Click cell D6 and drag to cell O36.

As you drag, the **Conslidate** dialog box rolls up. When you release the mouse button, *[Y2001ByMonth.xls]January!$D$6:$O$36* appears in the **Reference** box of the **Consolidate** dialog box.

8 Click **Add**.

[Y2001ByMonth.xls]January!$D$6:$O$36 appears in the **All references** list of the **Consolidate** dialog box.

9 Click the **February** sheet tab.

Cells in the range D6:O36 are already selected.
[Y2001ByMonth.xls]February!$D$6:$O$36 appears in the **Reference** box of the **Consolidate** dialog box.

10 Click **Add**.

[Y2001ByMonth.xls]February!$D$6:$O$36 appears in the **All references** list of the **Consolidate** dialog box.

11 Click the **March** sheet tab.

Cells in the range D6:O36 are already selected.
[Y2001ByMonth.xls]March!$D$6:$O$36 appears in the **Reference** box of the **Consolidate** dialog box.

12 Click **Add**.

[Y2001ByMonth.xls]March!$D$6:$O$36 appears in the **All references** list of the **Consolidate** dialog box.

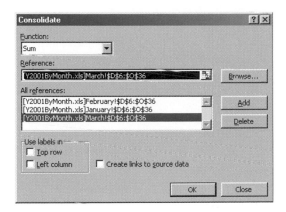

13 On the **Window** menu, click **Consolidate.xls**.

Consolidate.xls becomes the active document.

14 Click cell D5.

15 In the **Consolidate** dialog box, click **OK**.

The **Consolidate** dialog box disappears. The sums of the contents of the cells in the three worksheets named in the **Consolidate** dialog box appear in cells D5:O35.

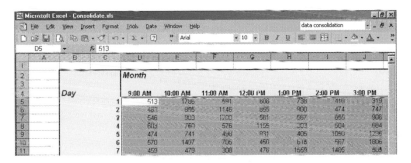

Save

16 On the Standard toolbar, click the **Save** button.

Excel saves your changes.

Close

17 Click the **Close** button.

Consolidate.xls closes, and Y2001ByMonth.xls becomes the active document.

18 Click the **Close** button.

Y2001ByMonth.xls closes.

Grouping Multiple Data Lists

When you work with Excel for a while, you'll find that you often work with a number of the same workbooks at a time. For instance, Catherine Turner, the owner of The Garden Company, might always pull up a yearly sales summary workbook and the sales figures for product categories offered by The Garden Company. She can open the workbooks together through the **Open** dialog box, but she can also group the files together so that she has the option of opening them all simultaneously.

Ex2002e-2-2

Approved Courseware

If you want to open a set of files simultaneously, you can define them as part of a workspace, which uses a single Excel file name to reference several workbooks instead of one. To define a workspace, you open the files you want to include and then open the **Save Workspace** dialog box.

When the **Save Workspace** dialog box is open, clicking **Save** saves references to the Excel files that are currently open. Whenever you open the workspace you create, all of the files that were open when you defined the workspace will appear. Including a file in a workspace doesn't remove it from general circulation; you can still open it by itself.

Y2001ByMonth
TotalByHour2001

In this exercise, you save a workspace that consists of two workbooks, close the included files, and then test the workspace by opening it from the **Open** dialog box.

Open

1 On the Standard toolbar, click the **Open** button.

The **Open** dialog box appears.

2 Hold down the [Ctrl] key while you click the **Y2001ByMonth.xls** and **TotalByHour2001.xls** files, and then click **Open**.

Y2001ByMonth.xls and TotalByHour2001.xls appear.

3 On the **File** menu, click **Save Workspace**.

The **Save Workspace** dialog box appears, with the file type in the **Save as type** box set to *Workspaces (*.xlw)*.

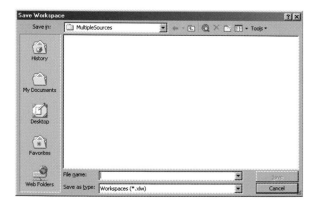

4 In the **File name** box, type **Y2001Summary** and then click **Save**.

Excel saves your workspace.

Close

5 Click the **Close** button.

Y2001ByMonth.xls closes, and TotalByHour2001.xls becomes the active document.

6 Click the **Close** button.

TotalByHour2001.xls closes.

7 On the Standard toolbar, click the **Open** button.

The **Open** dialog box appears.

8 Double-click **Y2001Summary.xlw**.

The TotalByHour2001.xls and Y2001ByMonth.xls workbooks open.

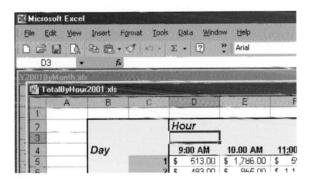

9 Click the **Close** button.

TotalByHour2001.xls closes, and Y2001ByMonth.xls becomes the active document.

10 Click the **Close** button.

Y2001ByMonth.xls closes.

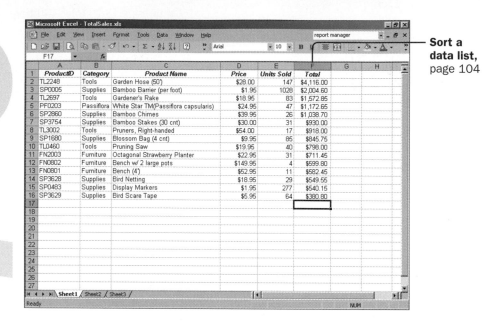

Sort a data list, page 104

Organize data into levels, page 108

Chapter 7
Reordering and Summarizing Data

In this chapter, you will learn how to:

✔ Sort a data list.
✔ Organize data into levels.

Most of the time, when you enter data in a Microsoft Excel worksheet, you will enter the data in chronological order. For instance, you would probably enter hourly sales data in a worksheet at the end of each day, starting with the first hour your store was open and moving to closing time. The data would naturally be displayed in the order in which you entered it, but that may not always be the best order to answer your questions. For instance, you might want to sort your data so that the top row in your worksheet shows the best sales day for the month, with subsequent rows displaying the remaining days of the month arranged by total sales. You can also sort based on the contents of more than one column. A good example would be sorting sales data by week, day, and then hour of the day.

Once you have sorted your data into the desired order, Excel lets you find partial totals, or **subtotals**, for groups of cells within a given range. Yes, you can create formulas to find the sum, average, or standard deviation of data in a cell range, but you can do the same thing much more quickly by having Excel calculate the total for cells with the same value in a column. If your worksheet held sales data for a list of products, you could calculate subtotals for each product category.

When you calculate subtotals in a worksheet, Excel creates an outline that marks the cell ranges used in each subtotal. For example, if the first ten rows of a worksheet have furniture sales data and the second ten rows have tool sales data, Excel will divide the rows into two units. You can use the markers on the worksheet to hide or display the rows used to calculate a subtotal; in this case, you can hide all of the rows with tool data, hide all of the rows with furniture data, hide both, or show both.

In this chapter, you'll learn how to sort your data using one or more criteria, calculate subtotals, and organize your data into levels.

This chapter uses the practice files Sorting and Levels that you installed from this book's CD-ROM. For details about installing the practice files, see "Using the Book's CD-ROM" at the beginning of this book.

Sorting a Data List

While Excel makes it easy to enter your business data and to manage it after you've saved it in a worksheet, it's rare that your data will answer every question you want to ask it. For example, you might want to discover which of your products has the highest total sales, which product has the next highest, and so on. You can discover that information by sorting your data.

When you **sort** data in a worksheet, you rearrange the worksheet rows based on the contents of cells in a particular column. Sorting a worksheet to find your highest-selling products in terms of units sold, for instance, might show the results displayed in the following graphic.

	A	B	C	D	E	F
1	ProductID	Category	Product Name	Price	Units Sold	Total
2	SP0005	Supplies	Bamboo Barrier (per foot)	$1.95	1028	$2,004.60
3	SP0483	Supplies	Display Markers	$1.95	277	$540.15
4	TL2248	Tools	Garden Hose (50')	$28.00	147	$4,116.00
5	SP1680	Supplies	Blossom Bag (4 cnt)	$9.95	85	$845.75
6	TL2697	Tools	Gardener's Rake	$18.95	83	$1,572.85
7	SP3629	Supplies	Bird Scare Tape	$5.95	64	$380.80

Sort Descending

There are a number of ways you can sort a group of rows in a worksheet, but the first step is identifying the column that will provide the values by which the rows should be sorted. In the above graphic, you could find the highest sales totals by choosing the cells in the Total column and then clicking the **Sort Descending** toolbar button. Clicking the **Sort Descending** button has Excel put the row with the highest value in the Total column at the top of the worksheet and continue down to the lowest value.

Sort Ascending

If you wanted to sort the rows in the opposite order, from the lowest sales to the highest, you would select the cells in the Total column and then click the **Sort Ascending** toolbar button.

The **Sort Ascending** and **Sort Descending** toolbar buttons let you sort rows in a worksheet quickly, but you can use them only to sort the worksheet based on the contents of one column. For example, you might want to order the worksheet rows by product category and then by total so that you can see the highest-selling items in each category. You can sort rows in a worksheet by the contents of more than one column through the **Sort** dialog box, where you can pick up to three columns to use as sort criteria and choose whether to sort the rows in ascending or descending order.

The default setting for Excel is to sort numbers according to their values and to sort words in alphabetical order, but that pattern doesn't work for some sets of values. One example of where sorting a list of values in alphabetical order would yield incorrect results is with the months of the year. In an "alphabetical" calendar, April is the first month and September the last! Fortunately, Excel recognizes a number of special lists, such as days of the week and months of the year. You can have Excel sort the contents of a worksheet based on values in a known list; if needed, you can create your own list of values using the tools on the **Custom Lists** tab page of the **Options** dialog box.

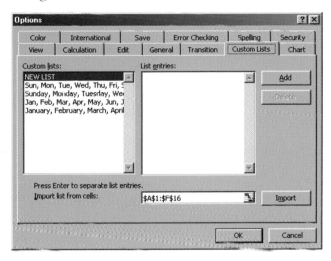

The default lists of weekdays in Excel both start with Sunday. If you keep your business records based on a Monday–Sunday week, you can create a new list with Monday as the first day and Sunday as the last.

Important

If you sort using a custom list, the custom list must be the primary sorting criterion.

Sorting

In this exercise, you sort your worksheet using the **Sort Ascending** toolbar button, use the **Sort** dialog box to sort your worksheet based on the contents of more than one row, create a custom sort order, and then apply that custom sort order to your worksheet.

Open

1   On the Standard toolbar, click the **Open** button.

The **Open** dialog box appears.

2   Navigate to the ReorderingAndSummarizing folder, and double-click the **Sorting.xls** file.

Sorting.xls opens.

3   If necessary, click the **Sales** tab to display the Sales worksheet.

4   Click cell A1 and drag to cell A32.

5   On the Standard toolbar, click the **Sort Ascending** button.

The data in the selected range of cells is sorted in ascending order. Note that the first cell, which contains a data label, is not included in the sort.

6 Click the **AllInfo** tab.

The AllInfo worksheet appears.

7 Click cell A1 and drag to cell D32.

8 On the **Data** menu, click **Sort**.

The **Sort** dialog box appears.

9 If necessary, click the **Sort by** down arrow and then, from the list that appears, click **Sales**.

Sales appears in the **Sort by** box.

10 Click the **Then by** down arrow, and then, from the list that appears, click **Weekday**.

Weekday appears in the **Then by** box.

11 Click **OK**.

The contents of the selected cells appear in sorted order.

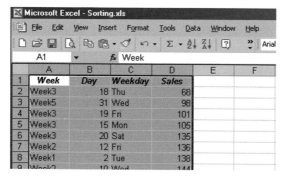

12 On the Standard toolbar, click the **Undo** button.

The contents of the selected cells appear in their original order.

13 Click cell G2 and drag to cell G8.

Undo

14 On the **Tools** menu, click **Options**.

The **Options** dialog box appears.

15 Click the **Custom Lists** tab.

The **Custom Lists** tab page appears, with *$G$2:$G$8* in the **Import list from cells** box.

16 Click **Import**.

The items in the cells appear in the **List entries** list, while the series appears in the **Custom lists** list.

17 Click **OK**.

The **Options** dialog box closes.

18 Click cell A1 and drag to cell D32.

19 On the **Data** menu, click **Sort**.

The **Sort** dialog box appears.

20 Click the **Sort by** down arrow, and then, from the list that appears, click **Weekday**.

Weekday appears in the **Sort by** box.

21 Click the **Options** button.

The **Sort Options** dialog box appears.

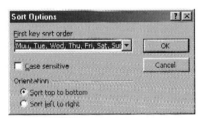

22 Click the **First key sort order** down arrow, and then, from the list that appears, click **Mon, Tue, Wed, Thu, Fri, Sat, Sun**.

Mon, Tue, Wed, Thu, Fri, Sat, Sun appears in the **First key sort order** box.

23 Click **OK**.

The **Sort Options** dialog box disappears.

24 Click the **Then by** down arrow, and then, from the list that appears, click **Sales**.

Sales appears in the **Then by** box.

25 Click **OK**.

The selected data appears in sorted order.

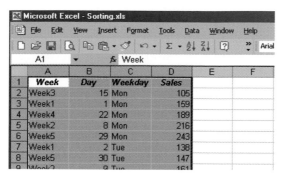

26   On the Standard toolbar, click the **Save** button to save your changes.

Close

27   Click the **Close** button to close Sorting.xls.

Organizing Data into Levels

Ex2002e-7-1

Approved Courseware

After you have sorted the rows in an Excel worksheet or entered the data in such a way that it doesn't need to be sorted, you can have Excel calculate subtotals, or totals for a portion of the data. In a worksheet with sales data for three different product categories, for example, you can sort the products by category, select all of the cells with data, and then open the **Subtotal** dialog box.

In the **Subtotal** dialog box, you can choose the column on which to base your subtotals (such as every change of value in the Category column), the summary calculation you want to perform, and the column or columns with values to be summarized. In the worksheet in the preceding graphic, for example, you could also calculate subtotals for the number of units sold in each category. After you define your subtotals, they appear in your worksheet.

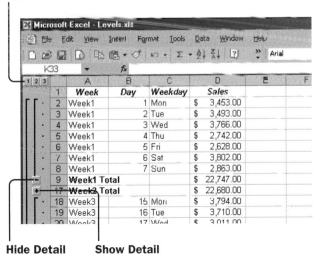

Ex2002e-7-3

Approved Courseware

As the graphic shows, when you add subtotals to a worksheet, Excel also defines groups based on the rows used to calculate a subtotal. The groupings form an outline of your worksheet based on the criteria you used to create the subtotals. In the above example, all of the rows with furniture products are in one group, rows with tools are in another, and so on. The outline section at the left of your worksheet holds controls you can use to hide or display groups of rows in your worksheet.

There are three types of controls in the outline section: **Hide Detail** buttons, **Show Detail** buttons, and level buttons.

Level buttons

Hide Detail   **Show Detail**

109

Hide Detail

The **Hide Detail** button beside a group can be clicked to hide the rows in that group. In the previous graphic, clicking the **Hide Detail** button next to row 9 would hide rows 2 through 8 but leave the row holding the subtotal for that group, row 9, visible.

Show Detail

When you hide a group of rows, the button next to the group changes to a **Show Detail** button. Clicking a group's **Show Detail** button restores the rows in the group to the worksheet.

Level

The other set of buttons in the outline section of a worksheet with subtotals is the level buttons. Each button represents a level of organization in a worksheet; clicking a level button hides all levels of detail below that of the button you clicked. The following table identifies the three levels of organization in the previous graphic.

Level	Description
1	The grand total
2	Subtotals for each group
3	Individual rows in the worksheet

Level 2

Clicking the **Level 2** button in the worksheet shown in the previous illustration would hide the rows with data on the sales of individual products but would leave the row with the grand total (Level 1) and all rows with the subtotals for each product (Level 2) visible in the worksheet.

		A	B	C	D	E	F
	1	Week	Day	Weekday	Sales		
+	9	Week1 Total			$ 22,747.00		
+	17	Week2 Total			$ 22,680.00		
+	25	Week3 Total			$ 22,090.00		
+	33	Week4 Total			$ 21,279.00		
+	37	Week5 Total			$ 9,129.00		
-	38	Grand Total			$ 97,925.00		
	39						
	40						

If you like, you can add levels of detail to the outline Excel creates. For instance, you might want to be able to hide sales of bamboo barrier, bamboo chimes, and bamboo stakes (which you know sell well) to see how other products sell in comparison. To create a new outline group within an existing group, select the rows you want to group and then open the **Data** menu, point to **Group and Outline**, and click **Group**. Excel will create a new group on a new level.

	A	B	C	D	
1	**ProductID**	**Category**	**Product Name**	**Price**	**Units**
2	TL2248	Tools	Garden Hose (50')	$28.00	
3	TL2697	Tools	Gardener's Rake	$18.95	
4	TL3002	Tools	Pruners, Right-handed	$54.00	
5	TL0460	Tools	Pruning Saw	$19.95	
6		**Tools Total**			
7	SP0005	Supplies	Bamboo Barrier (per foot)	$1.95	
8	SP2860	Supplies	Bamboo Chimes	$39.95	
9	SP3754	Supplies	Bamboo Stakes (30 cnt)	$30.00	
10	SP3628	Supplies	Bird Netting	$18.95	
11	SP3629	Supplies	Bird Scare Tape	$5.95	
12	SP1680	Supplies	Blossom Bag (4 cnt)	$9.95	
13	SP0483	Supplies	Display Markers	$1.95	
14		**Supplies Total**			

You can remove a group by selecting the rows in the group and clicking **Ungroup** from the same submenu.

Tip

If you want to remove all subtotals from a worksheet, open the **Subtotal** dialog box and click the **Remove All** button.

Levels

Open

In this exercise, you add subtotals to a worksheet and then use the outline that appears to show and hide different groups of data in your worksheet.

1 On the Standard toolbar, click the **Open** button.

The **Open** dialog box appears.

2 Double-click **Levels.xls**.

Levels.xls opens.

3 Click the row head of row 1 and drag to the row head of row 32.

Rows 1 through 32 are highlighted.

4 On the **Data** menu, click **Subtotals**

The **Subtotal** dialog box appears, with the default options to add a subtotal at every change in the Week column, to return the sum of the values in the subtotaled rows, and to add a row with the subtotal of values in the Sales column below the final selected row.

5   Click **OK**.

The **Subtotal** dialog box disappears. In Levels.xls, new rows appear with subtotals for sales during each week represented in the worksheet. The new rows are numbered 9, 17, 25, 33, and 37. A row with the grand total of all rows also appears; that row is row 38. A new section with outline bars and group-level indicators appears to the left of column A.

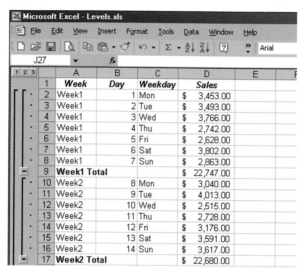

6   Click the row head of row 2 and drag to the row head of row 6.

Rows 2 through 6 are highlighted.

7   On the **Data** menu, point to **Group and Outline**, and then click **Group**.

Rows 2 through 6 are made into a new group. An outline bar appears on a new level in the outline section, and a corresponding **Level 4** button appears at the top of the outline section.

8   In the outline section, click the **Hide Detail** button next to row 7.

Rows 2 through 6 are hidden, and the **Hide Detail** button you clicked changes to a **Show Detail** button.

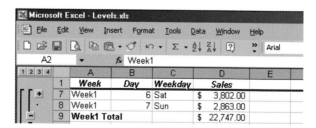

9   In the outline section, click the **Show Detail** button next to row 7.

Rows 2 through 6 reappear.

Level 1

10   In the outline section, click the **Level 1** button.

All rows except row 1, with the column headings, and row 38, with the grand total, are hidden.

Level 2

11   In the outline section, click the **Level 2** button.

The rows with the subtotal for each week appear.

Level 3

12   In the outline section, click the **Level 3** button.

All rows except rows 2 through 6 appear.

Level 4

13   In the outline section, click the **Level 4** button.

Rows 2 through 6 reappear.

14   On the Standard toolbar, click the **Save** button to save your work.

Close

15   Click the **Close** button to close Levels.xls.

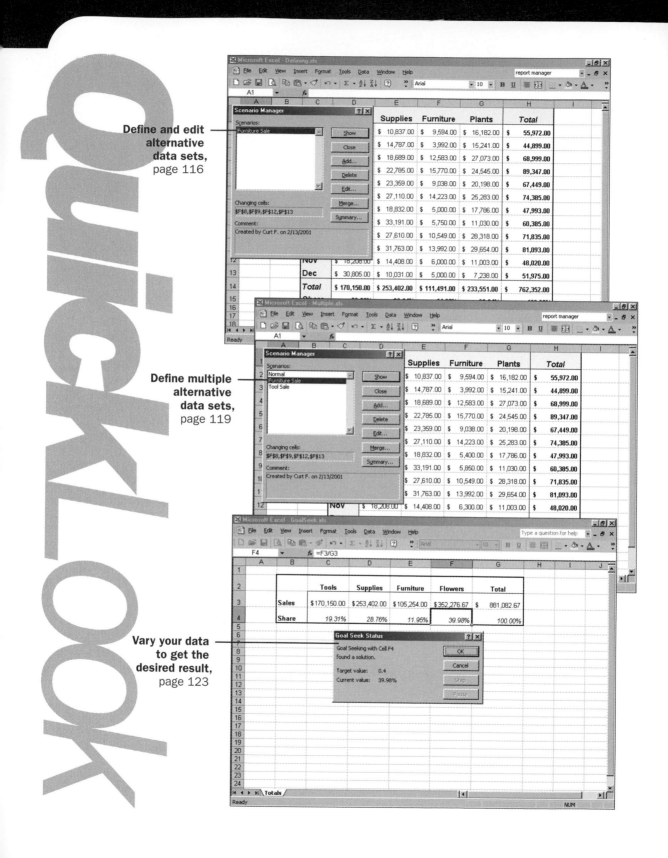

Define and edit alternative data sets, page 116

Define multiple alternative data sets, page 119

Vary your data to get the desired result, page 123

Chapter 8
Analyzing Alternative Data Sets

After completing this chapter, you will be able to:

✔ Define and edit an alternative data set.

✔ Define multiple alternative data sets.

✔ Vary your data to get a desired result.

When you store data in a Microsoft Excel workbook, you can use that data, either by itself or as part of a calculation, to discover important information about your business. When you track total sales on an hourly basis, you can find your best and worst sales periods and correlate them with outside events. For businesses like The Garden Company, sales of all products pick up during the early spring as gardeners get ready for the coming year. During the winter holidays, tool sales pick up as customers purchase gifts for friends and family members who garden.

The data in your worksheets is great for asking, "What happened?" but is less useful for asking "what if" questions, such as, "How would our total revenue be affected if we increased furniture sales by 20 percent?" You can always save an alternative version of a workbook and create formulas that calculate the effects of your changes, but you can do the same thing in your workbook by defining one or more alternative data sets and switching between the original data and the new sets you create.

Excel also provides the tools to determine the inputs that would be required for a formula to produce a given result. For example, the owner of The Garden Company could find out to what level tool sales would need to rise for that category to account for 25 percent of total sales.

In this chapter, you'll learn how to define alternative data sets and determine the necessary inputs to make a calculation produce a particular result.

This chapter uses the practice files Defining, Multiple, and GoalSeek that you installed from this book's CD-ROM. For details about installing the practice files, see "Using the Book's CD-ROM" at the beginning of this book.

Defining and Editing Alternative Data Sets

When you save data in an Excel worksheet, you create a record that reflects the characteristics of an event or object. That data could represent an hour of sales on a particular day, the price of an item you just began offering for sale, or the percentage of total sales accounted for by a category of products. Once the data is in place, you can create formulas to generate totals, find averages, and sort the rows in a worksheet based on the contents of one or more columns. However, if you want to perform **what-if analysis**, or explore the impact that changes in your data would have on any of the calculations in your workbooks, you will need to change your data.

Ex2002e-8-3

Approved Courseware

The problem of working with data that reflects an event or item is that changing any data to affect a calculation runs the risk of destroying the original data if you accidentally save your changes. You can avoid ruining your original data by creating a duplicate workbook and making your changes to it, but you can also create alternative data sets, or **scenarios**, within an existing workbook.

When you create a scenario, you give Excel alternative values for a list of cells in a worksheet. You can add, delete, and edit scenarios using the **Scenario Manager**.

Clicking the **Add** button causes the **Add Scenario** dialog box to appear.

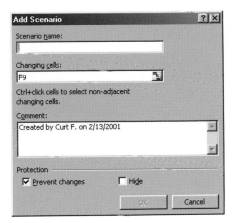

From within this dialog box, you can identify the cells that will hold alternative values, and after you click **OK**, a new dialog box with spaces for you to enter the new values will appear.

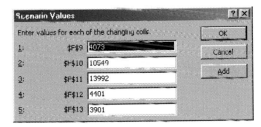

Clicking **OK** returns you to the **Scenario Manager** dialog box. From there, clicking the **Show** button will replace the values in the original worksheet with the alternative values you just defined. Any formulas using cells with changed values will recalculate their results.

In this exercise, you create a scenario to measure the projected impact of a furniture sale on total revenue for The Garden Company.

Defining

Open

1   On the Standard toolbar, click the **Open** button.

The **Open** dialog box appears.

2   Navigate to the AnalyzingAlternativeDataSets folder, and double-click the **Defining.xls** file.

Defining.xls opens.

3   Click cell A1.

4   On the **Tools** menu, click **Scenarios**.

The **Scenario Manager** dialog box appears.

5   Click **Add**.

The **Add Scenario** dialog box appears.

6   In the **Scenario name** box, type **Furniture Sale**.

Collapse Dialog
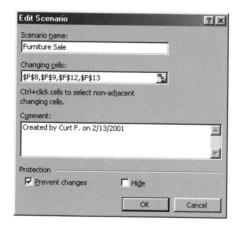

7   At the right edge of the **Changing cells** box, click the **Collapse Dialog** button.

The **Add Scenario** dialog box collapses, and its title bar changes to *Add Scenario - Changing Cells*.

8   Delete the contents of the **Add Scenario** dialog box, and then hold down Ctrl while you click cells F8, F9, F12, and F13.

$F$8,$F$9,$F$12,$F$13 appears in the **Changing cells** box.

Expand Dialog

9   At the right edge of the **Changing cells** box, click the **Expand Dialog** button.

The **Edit Scenario** dialog box appears.

10   Click **OK**.

The **Edit Scenario** dialog box disappears, and the **Scenario Values** dialog box appears.

11   In the **1: $F$8** box, type **5000**.

12   In the **2: $F$9** box, type **5750**.

13   In the **3: $F$12** box, type **6000**.

14   In the **4: $F$13** box, type **5000**.

15   Click **OK**.

The **Scenario Manager** dialog box reappears.

16   Click **Show**.

The contents of your worksheet change to reflect the values in your scenario.

17 Click **Close**.

The **Scenario Manager** dialog box closes.

18 On the Standard toolbar, click the **Save** button to save your changes.

Close

19 Click the **Close** button to close Defining.xls.

Defining Multiple Alternative Data Sets

Ex2002e-8-3

Approved Courseware

One great feature of Excel scenarios is that you're not limited to creating one alternative data set—you can create as many as you like and switch between them at will with the **Scenario Manager**. To change from one scenario to another in the **Scenario Manager**, click the name of the scenario to which you want to change and then click the **Show** button. The values you defined as part of that scenario will appear in your worksheet, and Excel will update any calculations involving the changed cells.

Tip

If you apply a scenario to a worksheet and then apply another scenario to the same worksheet, both sets of changes will appear. If the second scenario changes a cell changed by the first scenario, the cell will reflect the value in the second scenario.

Changing from one scenario to another gives you an overview of how the scenarios affect your calculations, but Excel also gives you a way to view the results of all of your scenarios in a single worksheet. To create a worksheet in your current workbook that summarizes the changes caused by your scenarios, open the **Scenario Manager** and then click the **Summary** button. When you do, the **Scenario Summary** dialog box appears.

Collapse Dialog

From within the **Scenario Summary** dialog box, you can choose the type of summary worksheet you want to create and the cells you want to appear in the summary worksheet. To choose the cells to appear in the summary, click the **Collapse Dialog** button in the **Result cells** box, select the cells you want to appear, and then expand the dialog box. After you verify that the range in the **Result cells** box represents the cells you want included on the summary sheet, click **OK** to create the new worksheet.

It's a good idea to create an "undo" scenario named *Normal* with the original values of every cell changed in other scenarios. For example, if you create a scenario named *No rain* that changes the sales figures in three cells, your *Normal* scenario will restore those cells to their original values. That way, even if you accidentally modify your worksheet, you can apply the *Normal* scenario and won't have to reconstruct the worksheet from scratch.

Tip

Each scenario can change a maximum of 32 cells, so you may need to create more than one scenario to restore a worksheet.

Multiple

In this exercise, you create scenarios to represent projected revenue increases from two sales, view the two scenarios, and then summarize the scenario results in a new worksheet.

Open

1   On the Standard toolbar, click the **Open** button.

The **Open** dialog box appears.

2   Double-click **Multiple.xls**.

Multiple.xls opens.

3   Click cell A1.

4   On the **Tools** menu, click **Scenarios**.

The **Scenario Manager** dialog box appears.

5   Click **Add**.

The **Add Scenario** dialog box appears, with A1 in the **Changing cells** box.

6   In the **Scenario name** box, type **Furniture Sale**.

7   In the **Changing cells** box, click the **Collapse Dialog** button.

The **Add Scenario** dialog box collapses, and its title bar changes to *Add Scenario - Changing Cells*.

8   Delete the contents of the **Add Scenario** dialog box, and then hold down Ctrl while you click cells F8, F9, F12, and F13.

$F$8,$F$9,$F$12,$F$13 appears in the **Changing cells** box.

Expand Dialog

9   At the right edge of the **Changing cells** box, click the **Expand Dialog** button.

The **Edit Scenario** dialog box appears.

10   Click **OK**.

The **Edit Scenario** dialog box disappears, and the **Scenario Values** dialog box appears.

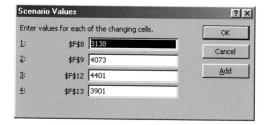

11 In the **1: $F$8** box, type **5400**.

12 In the **2: $F$9** box, type **5850**.

13 In the **3: $F$12** box, type **6300**.

14 In the **4: $F$13** box, type **7000**.

15 Click **OK**.

The **Scenario Values** dialog box disappears, and the **Scenario Manager** dialog box appears.

16 Click **Add**.

The **Add Scenario** dialog box appears.

17 In the **Scenario name** box, type **Tool Sale**.

18 In the **Changing cells** box, click the **Collapse Dialog** button.

The **Add Scenario** dialog box collapses, and its title bar changes to *Add Scenario - Changing Cells*.

19 Delete the contents of the **Add Scenario** dialog box, click cell D7, and drag to cell D11.

$D$7:$D$11 appears in the **Changing cells** box.

20 At the right edge of the **Changing cells** box, click the **Expand Dialog** button.

The **Edit Scenario** dialog box appears.

21 Click **OK**.

The **Edit Scenario** dialog box disappears, and the **Scenario Values** dialog box appears.

22 In the **1: $D$7** box, type **8500**.

23 In the **2: $D$8** box, type **9000**.

24 In the **3: $D$9** box, type **12091**.

25 In the **4: $D$10** box, type **7500**.

26 In the **5: $D$11** box, type **7500**.

27 Click **OK**.

The **Scenario Manager** dialog box appears.

28 In the **Scenarios** list, click **Furniture Sale** and then click **Show**.

The values in your worksheet change to reflect the values in the Furniture Sale scenario.

29 In the **Scenarios** list, click **Tool Sale** and then click **Show**.

The values in your worksheet change to reflect the values in the Tool Sale scenario.

30 Click **Summary**.

The **Scenario Summary** dialog box appears.

31 In the **Result cells** box, click the **Collapse Dialog** button.

The **Scenario Summary** dialog box is minimized.

32 Click cell C14 and drag to cell H15.

=$C$14:$H$15 appears in the **Result cells** box.

33 In the **Result cells** box, click the **Expand Dialog** button.

The **Scenario Summary** dialog box is maximized.

34 Click **OK**.

Excel adds a new worksheet named *Scenario Summary* to your workbook and displays that worksheet.

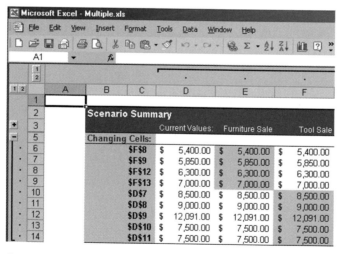

35 On the Standard toolbar, click the **Save** button to save your work.

Close

36 Click the **Close** button to close Multiple.xls.

Varying Your Data to Get a Desired Result

An important aspect of running a business is knowing how every department and product is performing, both in absolute terms and in relation to other departments or products in the company. Just as you might want to reward your employees for maintaining a perfect safety record and keeping down your insurance rates, you would also want to stop carrying products you were unable to sell.

When you plan how you want to grow your business, you should have specific goals in mind for each department or product category. For example, Catherine Turner, the owner of The Garden Company, might have the goal of increasing the total revenue generated from flower sales by 10 percent a year. Finding the sales amount that represents the 10 percent increase is simple, but expressing goals in other ways may make finding the solution more challenging. Rather than grow flower sales by 10 percent a year, Catherine might want to increase the sales so that flower sales represent 40 percent of the total sales for The Garden Company.

As an example, consider the following worksheet, which holds sales figures for the four categories of products offered by The Garden Company and uses those figures to calculate both total sales and the share each category has of that total.

		Tools	Supplies	Furniture	Flowers	Total
Sales		$170,150.00	$253,402.00	$105,254.00	$233,551.00	$ 762,357.00
Share		22.32%	33.24%	13.81%	30.64%	100.00%

Important

In this worksheet, the values in the Share row are displayed as percentages, but the underlying values are decimals. For example, 0.3064 is represented as 30.64%.

While it would certainly be possible to figure the sales target that would make flower sales represent 40 percent of the total, there is an easier way to do it in Excel: **Goal Seek**. To use **Goal Seek**, you choose **Goal Seek** from the **Tools** menu to open the **Goal Seek** dialog box.

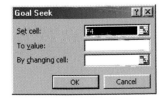

In the **Set cell** box, you identify the cell with the target value; in this case, that would be cell F4, which has the percentage of sales accounted for by the Flowers category. The **To value** box has the target value (*.4*, which is equivalent to *40%*), and the **By changing cell** box identifies the cell with the value Excel should change to generate the target value of *40%* in cell F4. In this example, the cell to be changed is F3.

Clicking **OK** tells Excel to find a solution for the goal you set. When Excel finishes its work, the new values appear in the designated cells and the **Goal Seek Status** dialog box appears.

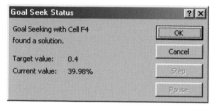

Tip

Goal Seek finds the closest solution it can without exceeding the target value. In this case, the closest percentage it could find was *39.98%*.

GoalSeek

In this exercise, you use **Goal Seek** to determine how much total revenue from tool sales would be required to make the Tools category account for 25 percent of total sales for The Garden Company.

Open

1   On the Standard toolbar, click the **Open** button.

The **Open** dialog box appears.

2   Double-click the **GoalSeek.xls** file.

GoalSeek.xls opens.

3   Click cell C4.

4   On the **Tools** menu, click **Goal Seek**.

The **Goal Seek** dialog box appears with C4 in the **Set cell** box.

5   In the **To value** box, type **.25**.

Tip

You type *.25*, not *25*, because cells C4:G4 are formatted to show percentages. With the Percentage format, *.25* is displayed as *25%*.

6   In the **By changing cell** box, type **C3**.

7 Click **OK**.

The **Goal Seek Status** dialog box appears, announcing that Excel has found a solution. The new values appear in your worksheet.

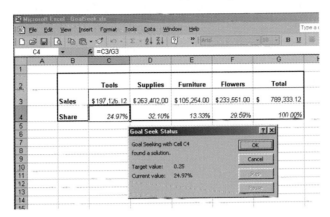

8 Click **OK**.

The **Goal Seek Status** dialog box disappears.

Undo

9 On the Standard toolbar, click the **Undo** button.

The contents of the cells in your workbook revert to their original values.

10 On the Standard toolbar, click the **Save** button to save your changes.

Close

11 Click the **Close** button to close GoalSeek.xls.

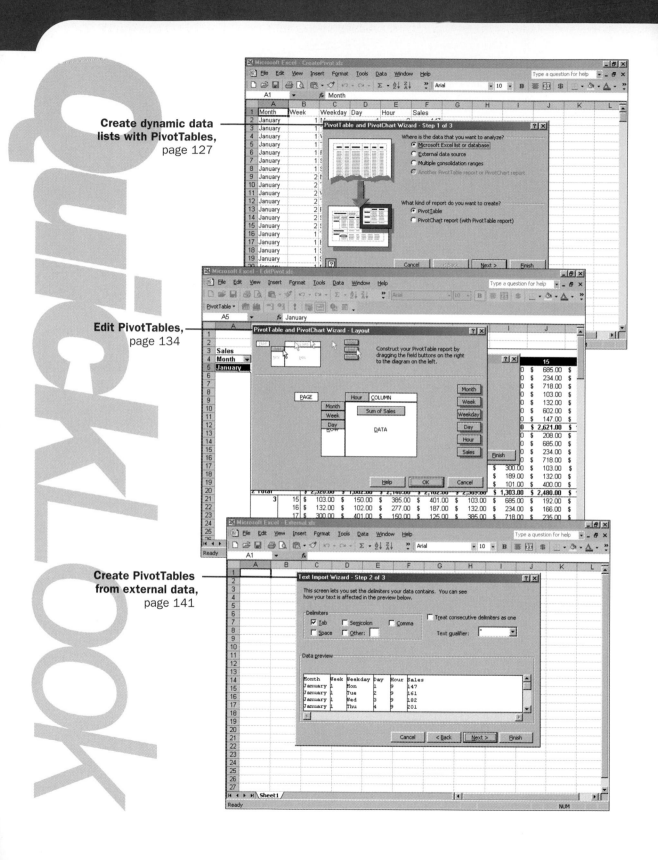

Chapter 9
Creating Dynamic Lists with PivotTables

After completing this chapter, you will be able to:

✔ **Create dynamic data lists with PivotTables.**

✔ **Edit PivotTables.**

✔ **Create PivotTables from external data.**

An important consideration when you create your Microsoft Excel worksheets is how you want the data to appear when you show it to your colleagues. You can change your data's formatting to emphasize the contents of specific cells, sort and filter your worksheets based on the contents of specific columns, or hide rows with data that doesn't help illustrate whatever point you're trying to make.

One limitation of the standard Excel worksheet is that you can't change how the data is organized on the page. For example, in a worksheet in which each column represents an hour in the day, each row represents a day in a month, and the body of the worksheet contains the total sales for every hourly period of the month, you can't easily change the worksheet so it displays only sales on Tuesdays during the afternoon.

There is an Excel tool that lets you create worksheets that can be sorted, filtered, and rearranged dynamically to emphasize different aspects of your data. That tool is the PivotTable.

In this chapter, you'll learn how to create and edit PivotTables from an existing worksheet, and how to create a PivotTable with data imported from a text file.

 This chapter uses the practice files CreatePivot, EditPivot, Export, and External that you installed from this book's CD-ROM. For details about installing the practice files, see "Using the Book's CD-ROM" at the beginning of this book.

Creating Dynamic Lists with PivotTables

Excel worksheets let you gather and present important data, but the standard worksheet can't be changed from its original configuration easily. As an example, consider the worksheet in the following graphic.

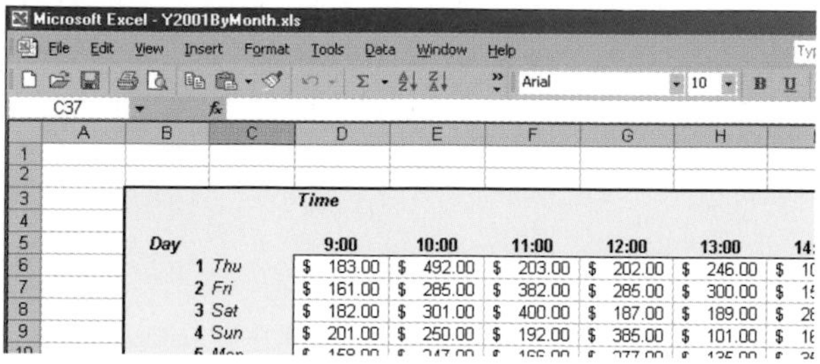

This worksheet records hourly sales for The Garden Company. The data in the worksheet is organized so that each row represents a day of sales, while the columns in the body of the worksheet represent an hour of each day. When presented in this arrangement, the monthly sales totals for an hourly period (calculated at the bottom of the worksheet) and the daily sales totals (calculated at the right edge of the worksheet) are given equal billing: neither set of totals stands out.

Such a neutral presentation of your data is versatile, but it has limitations. First, while you can use sorting and filtering to restrict the rows or columns shown, it's difficult to change the worksheet's organization. For example, in a standard worksheet you can't reorganize the contents of your worksheet so that the hours are assigned to the rows and the days to the columns.

Ex2002e-8-1

There is an Excel tool you can use to reorganize and redisplay your data dynamically. You can create a **PivotTable**, or dynamic worksheet, that lets you reorganize and filter your data on the fly. For instance, you can create a PivotTable with the same layout as the worksheet shown above and then change the PivotTable layout to have the rows represent the month, week, and day and the columns represent hours in a day, as shown in the following graphic.

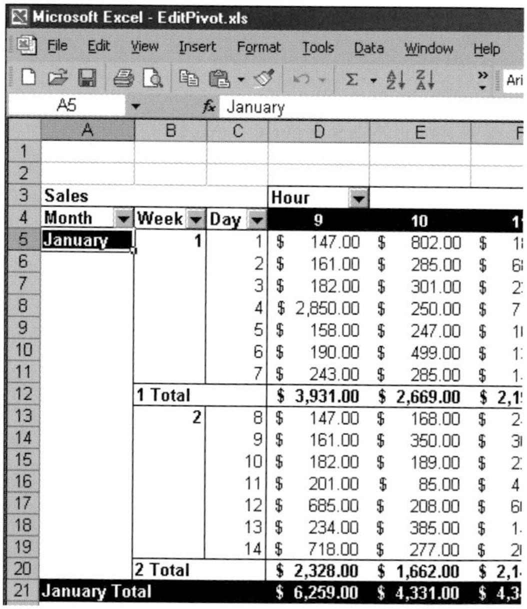

To create a PivotTable, you must have collected your data in a list in which every row represents a cell in the body of the finished PivotTable. The following graphic shows the first few lines of the list used to create the PivotTable just shown.

	A	B	C	D	E	F
1	Month	Week	Weekday	Day	Hour	Sales
2	January	1	Mon	1	9	147
3	January	1	Tue	2	9	161
4	January	1	Wed	3	9	182
5	January	1	Thu	4	9	201
6	January	1	Fri	5	9	158
7	January	1	Sat	6	9	190
8	January	1	Sun	7	9	243
9	January	2	Mon	8	9	147

Notice that every line of the list holds the Month, Week, Weekday, Day, Hour, and Sales for every hour in the month. Excel needs that data when it creates the PivotTable so that it can maintain relationships among the data. If you want to filter your Pivot-Table so that it shows all sales from 5:00 p.m. to 8:00 p.m. on Thursdays in January, Excel must be able to identify January 11 as a Thursday and find the entries in the list representing sales for the hours beginning at 5:00 p.m., 6:00 p.m., and 7:00 p.m.

Once you have created a list, you can click any cell in that list, open the **Data** menu, and click **PivotTable and PivotChart Report** to launch the **PivotTable and Pivot-Chart Wizard**.

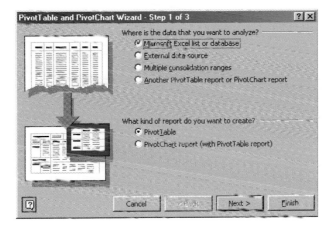

On this wizard page, you identify the data source for your PivotTable and whether you want to create a PivotTable by itself or a PivotTable and a PivotChart. Clicking **Next** accepts the default choices and moves you to the second wizard screen.

129

Collapse Dialog

On this screen, you verify that the wizard has correctly identified the cells with the data for your PivotTable. If not, you can click the **Collapse Dialog** button in the **Range** box, select the cells that contain your data, and then expand the dialog box to continue. Once the proper cell range is listed in the **Range** box, click **Next** to move to the final wizard screen.

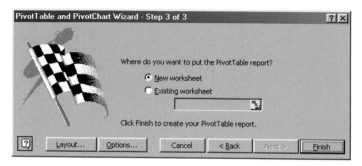

This wizard screen asks whether you want to create your PivotTable in a new or an existing worksheet. Because the data lists used to create PivotTables are usually quite long, it is often best to create the PivotTable in a new worksheet. Clicking **Finish** closes the wizard, creates a new worksheet in your workbook, and adds a PivotTable, the **PivotTable** toolbar, and the **Pivot Table Field List** dialog box to that worksheet.

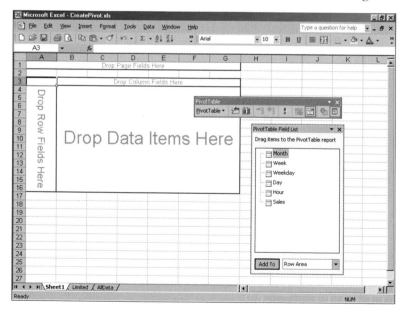

PivotTables
new for
OfficeXP

The **Pivot Table Field List** dialog box is new in Excel, and the **PivotTable** toolbar has been redesigned to make finding the toolbar buttons and functions you want easier.

To assign a **field**, or column in a data list, to an area of the PivotTable, you drag the field head to the desired area on the PivotTable outline. For example, you can drag the **Week** field head to the **Drop Row Fields Here** box, drag the **Day** field head to the **Drop Row Fields Here** box, drag the **Hour** field head to the **Drop Column Fields Here** box, and then drag the **Sales** field head to the **Drop Data Items Here** box to populate the body of the PivotTable with data. After you drop a field head in the **Drop Data Items Here** box, the PivotTable fills with data.

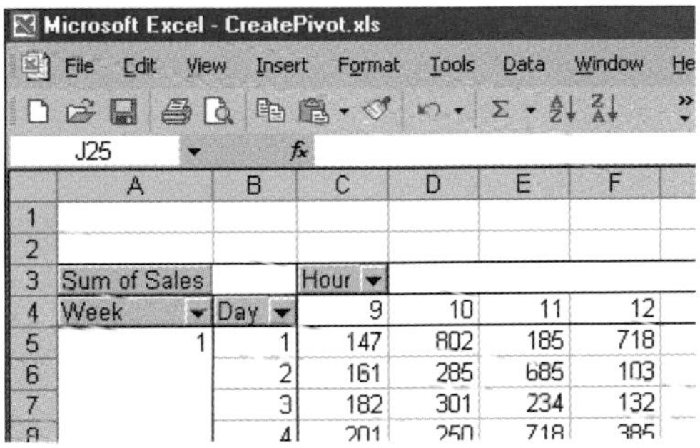

Tip

You can also move a field head to an area of the PivotTable by clicking the field head, clicking the **Add To** down arrow in the **Pivot Table Field List** dialog box, clicking the area to which you want to move the field, and then clicking the **Add To** button in the **Pivot Table Field List** dialog box.

Note that the order in which you enter the fields in the row and column areas affects how the data in the PivotTable is grouped. In the example above, the rows show all of the days in the first week before showing all of the days in the second week, while the columns show all of the hours in a business day at The Garden Company. You could change how the data in the PivotTable is grouped by moving the **Hour** field head to the left of the **Week** field head in the **Drop Row Fields Here** box. Doing so would cause Excel to group the data in the PivotTable as shown in the following graphic.

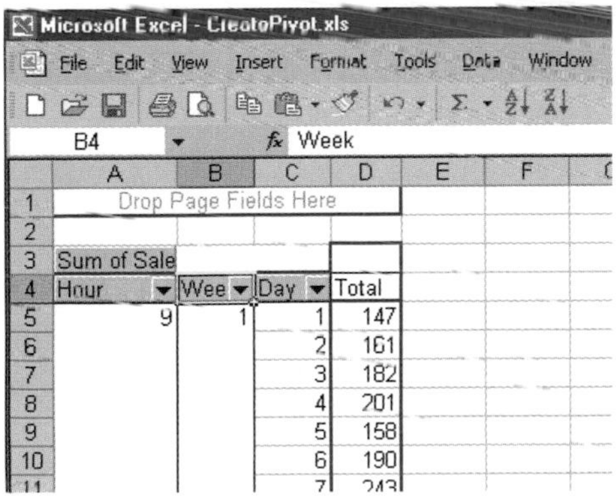

Tip

The **Drop Page Fields Here** box is used to filter the contents of the worksheet based on the values in a column from the original data list. You'll work with the Page area in the next section of this chapter.

Currency Style

Once you have created a PivotTable, you can change the formatting of its cells as on any other Excel worksheet. Because the data in the sample PivotTable is sales data, you can apply the Currency style to those cells by selecting them and then clicking the **Currency Style** button on the Formatting toolbar. You can also distinguish cells with headings, subtotals, and totals by formatting the contents of those cells in bold type, italics, or a larger type size.

Ex2002-3-5

Approved Courseware

Although you can apply your own formats to a PivotTable, Excel comes with a set of **AutoFormats**, or predefined formats that you can apply to your PivotTable. To view the AutoFormats available in Excel and apply one to your PivotTable, click any cell in the PivotTable, and then, on the **PivotTable** toolbar, click the **Format Report** button to display the **AutoFormat** dialog box.

To assign an AutoFormat to a PivotTable, pick the AutoFormat you like the best from the list in the **AutoFormat** dialog box and then click **OK**.

Tip

To return a PivotTable to its default formatting, choose the **PivotTable Classic** AutoFormat, which can be found at the bottom of the list in the **AutoFormat** dialog box.

CreatePivot

In this exercise, you create a PivotTable on a new worksheet, arrange its data, format the cells in the body of the PivotTable, and then apply an AutoFormat to the PivotTable.

Open

1 On the Standard toolbar, click the **Open** button.

The **Open** dialog box appears.

2 Navigate to the PivotTable folder, and double-click the **CreatePivot.xls** file.

CreatePivot.xls opens.

3 Click cell A1, and then, on the **Data** menu, click **PivotTable and PivotChart Report**.

The **PivotTable and PivotChart Wizard** appears with the **Microsoft Excel list or database** option button selected in the top pane, identifying your worksheet as the data source, and the **PivotTable** option button selected in the bottom pane, indicating that you want to create a PivotTable only.

4 Click **Next** to move to the next page of the wizard.

The next page of the wizard appears, with the range $A$1:$F$169 in the **Range** box.

5   Click **Next** to move to the next page of the wizard.

The final page of the wizard appears, with the **New worksheet** option but-ton selected, which tells the wizard to create a new worksheet to hold the PivotTable.

6   Click **Finish**.

The wizard closes, and the **PivotTable** toolbar, the **PivotTable Field List** dia-log box, and your new PivotTable appear in a new worksheet.

7   From the **PivotTable Field List** dialog box, drag **Month** to the **Drop Row Fields Here** box.

Month appears in the **Drop Row Fields Here** box.

8   From the **PivotTable Field List** dialog box, drag **Week** to the **Drop Row Fields Here** box.

Tip

A large gray insertion point will appear to the right of the **Month** field head when the mouse pointer is in the correct position.

Week appears in the **Drop Row Fields Here** box.

9   From the **PivotTable Field List** dialog box, drag **Day** to the **Drop Row Fields Here** box and drop it to the right of the **Week** field head.

The PivotTable is updated to reflect the added field.

10   From the **PivotTable Field List** dialog box, drag **Hour** to the **Drop Column Fields Here** box.

The PivotTable is updated to reflect the added field.

11   From the **PivotTable Field List** dialog box, drag **Sales** to the **Drop Data Items Here** box.

The PivotTable is updated to reflect the added field.

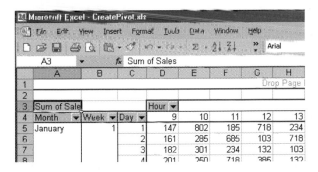

Hide Field List

12   On the **PivotTable** toolbar, click the **Hide Field List** button to hide the **Pivot-Table Field List** dialog box.

13 Select cells in the range D5:P22, and then, on the Formatting toolbar, click the **Currency Style** button.

Excel applies the Currency style to the selected cells.

Format Report

14 On the **PivotTable** toolbar, click the **Format Report** button.

The **AutoFormat** dialog box appears.

15 Click the **Table 1** format, and then click **OK**.

Excel applies the AutoFormat to your PivotTable.

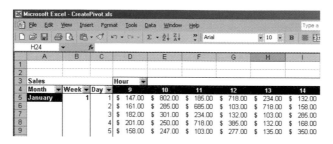

16 On the Standard toolbar, click the **Save** button to save your work.

Close

17 Click the **Close** button to close CreatePivot.xls.

Editing PivotTables

After you have created a PivotTable, you can edit it to affect how your data is displayed. As an example, consider the following PivotTable.

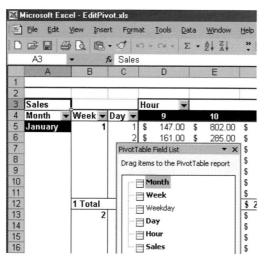

In this example, two fields require editing: **Month** and **Weekday**. Because all of the data in the list used to create the PivotTable is from the month of January, no information is imparted by including the **Month** field. The unused **Weekday** field, however, can be used to limit the data shown in the body of the PivotTable to sales occurring on one weekday, such as Wednesday.

Tip

Fields used in the PivotTable appear bold in the **Pivot Table Field List** dialog box, while fields not used in the PivotTable appear in normal type.

Show Field List

To open a PivotTable for editing, you click any cell in the PivotTable and then, if necessary, display the fields available for the PivotTable by clicking the **Show Field List** button on the **PivotTable** toolbar.

While the **PivotTable Field List** dialog box is open, you can drag any field name from the dialog box to the active PivotTable. Dragging a field name to the **Drop Page Fields Here** box doesn't change how the data in your PivotTable is arranged, but it does let you filter your PivotTable based on the contents of the field. As an example, consider the following graphic, in which the **Weekday** field has been added to the **Drop Page Fields Here** box and its down arrow clicked.

Clicking a field head's down arrow displays a list of values in the field (in this case, the days of the week). Clicking any of these values and then clicking **OK** limits the data shown in the PivotTable to data gathered on the selected weekday.

To remove a filter from a PivotTable, click the down arrow of the field head used to filter the PivotTable, click **(All)**, and then click **OK**.

You can filter a PivotTable based on the contents of fields in either the **Drop Row Fields Here** or the **Drop Column Fields Here** box as well. To do so, click the down arrow of the field head holding the values with which you want to filter the PivotTable and then clear the check box next to any value you don't want displayed. To limit the hours shown to 9:00 a.m. to 11:00 a.m., for example, you would click the **Hour** down arrow and then clear the check boxes next to every entry in the list except *9*, *10*, and *11*.

Another way to modify the contents of your PivotTable is to **pivot** the table by changing the arrangement of field heads while the PivotTable is open. To pivot a PivotTable, you drag a field head to a new position on the PivotTable. For example, in the following graphic, the PivotTable rows are grouped by week and then by day, while the columns are grouped by hour.

	A	B	C	D	E	F
1	Weekday	(All) ▼				
2						
3	Sales		Hour ▼			
4	Week ▼	Day ▼	9	10	11	12
5	1	1	$ 462.00	$ 1,786.00	$ 1,073.00	$ 1,122.00
6		2	$ 483.00	$ 855.00	$ 1,301.00	$ 673.00
7		3	$ 546.00	$ 903.00	$ 1,352.00	$ 506.00
8		4	$ 3,252.00	$ 750.00	$ 1,013.00	$ 1,155.00
9		5	$ 474.00	$ 741.00	$ 401.00	$ 831.00
10		6	$ 570.00	$ 1,497.00	$ 602.00	$ 450.00
11		7	$ 459.00	$ 479.00	$ 909.00	$ 476.00
12	1 Total		$ 6,246.00	$ 7,011.00	$ 6,651.00	$ 5,213.00
13						
14	2	8	$ 979.00	$ 504.00	$ 732.00	$ 1,203.00
15		9	$ 556.00	$ 1,050.00	$ 1,705.00	$ 897.00
16		10	$ 1,082.00	$ 1,063.00	$ 565.00	$ 1,146.00
17		11	$ 505.00	$ 404.00	$ 1,262.00	$ 1,200.00
18		12	$ 1,502.00	$ 1,134.00	$ 1,307.00	$ 1,528.00
19		13	$ 658.00	$ 873.00	$ 426.00	$ 657.00
20		14	$ 1,679.00	$ 1,094.00	$ 624.00	$ 1,769.00
21	2 Total		$ 6,961.00	$ 6,122.00	$ 6,621.00	$ 8,400.00
22						

To pivot the PivotTable, drag the **Hour** field head to the right of the **Day** field head in the **Drop Row Fields Here** box. When you release the mouse button, Excel updates the PivotTable to reflect the new organization.

	A	B	C	D
1	Weekday	(All) ▼		
2				
3	Week ▼	Day ▼	Hour ▼	Sales
4	1	1	9	$ 462.00
5			10	$ 1,786.00
6			11	$ 1,073.00
7			12	$ 1,122.00
8			13	$ 1,198.00
9			14	$ 348.00
10			15	$ 914.00
11			16	$ 402.00
12			17	$ 593.00
13			18	$ 1,502.00
14			19	$ 1,785.00
15			20	$ 1,080.00
16		1 Total		$ 12,265.00
17		2	9	$ 483.00

Tip

When you drag a field name over an area where the field can be dropped, a large gray insertion point will appear on the PivotTable, indicating where the field name you are dragging will be dropped when you release the mouse button.

If you have trouble dropping field names at the right place in your PivotTable, you can use the **Layout** screen of the **PivotTable and PivotChart Wizard** to help you. To open the **Layout** screen, click any cell in the PivotTable and then, on the **PivotTable** toolbar, click **PivotTable** and then click **Wizard** to display the final page of the **Pivot-Table and PivotChart Wizard**.

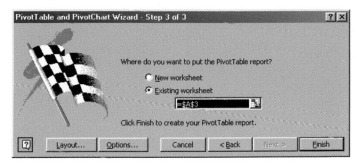

In this screen, click the **Layout** button to display a slightly friendlier version of the PivotTable template.

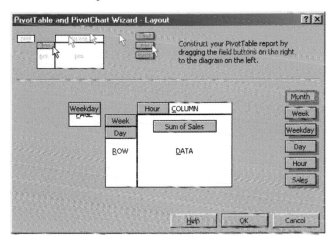

Refresh Data

One nice aspect of PivotTables is that you can update them to reflect any changes in the data list used to create them. For example, the general manager of The Garden Company might have received a large phone order from a client and, rather than routing it through a cash register at the retail store, instead added the total to the company's books directly. Updating the PivotTable's data list to reflect the sale will change the values in the PivotTable, but you don't need to re-create the PivotTable to account for the change. Instead, you can click any cell in the PivotTable and then, on the **PivotTable** toolbar, click the **Refresh Data** button to have Excel reexamine the data list and update the PivotTable.

Another way to manipulate the contents of a PivotTable is to show or hide its detail rows. For example, the PivotTable in the following graphic displays its rows organized by month, then by week, and then by day.

	A	B	C	D	E
1	Weekday	(All) ▼			
2					
3	Sales			Hour ▼	
4	Month ▼	Wee ▼	Day ▼	9	10
5	January	1	1	$ 147.00	$ 802.00
6			2	$ 161.00	$ 285.00
7			3	$ 182.00	$ 301.00
8			4	$ 2,850.00	$ 250.00
9			5	$ 158.00	$ 247.00
10			6	$ 190.00	$ 499.00
11			7	$ 243.00	$ 285.00
12		1 Total		$ 3,931.00	$ 2,669.00
13		2	8	$ 147.00	$ 168.00
14			9	$ 161.00	$ 350.00
15			10	$ 182.00	$ 189.00
16			11	$ 201.00	$ 85.00
17			12	$ 685.00	$ 208.00
18			13	$ 234.00	$ 385.00
19			14	$ 718.00	$ 277.00
20		2 Total		$ 2,328.00	$ 1,662.00
21	January Total			$ 6,259.00	$ 4,331.00

Double-clicking cell A5, which holds the *January* value for the **Month** field, hides the detail of all sales in January, leaving only the Total row for the month.

	A	B	C	D	E
1	Weekday	(All) ▼			
2					
3	Sales			Hour ▼	
4	Month ▼	Wee ▼	Day ▼	9	10
5	January			$ 6,259.00	$ 4,331.00
6					
7	February	1	1	$ 132.00	$ 492.00
8			2	$ 161.00	$ 285.00
9			3	$ 182.00	$ 301.00

To show the detail rows for the month of January, double-click cell A5 again.

Link to PivotTable Cell
new for
OfficeXP

In this version of Excel, you now have the ability to create a link from a cell in another workbook to a cell in your PivotTable. To create a link, you click the cell to link to your PivotTable, type an equal sign, and then click the cell in the PivotTable with the data to which you want to link. When you click the PivotTable cell, a *GET-PIVOTDATA* formula appears in the formula bar of the worksheet with the PivotTable. When you press Enter, the contents of the PivotTable cell will appear in the linked cell.

EditPivot

In this exercise, you add a field to a PivotTable, filter the contents of a PivotTable, change a PivotTable's layout, refresh PivotTable data, show and hide PivotTable detail, and create a link to a PivotTable field.

Open

1 On the Standard toolbar, click the **Open** button.

The **Open** dialog box appears.

2 Double-click **EditPivot.xls**.

EditPivot.xls opens.

3   If necessary, click the **PivotTable** sheet tab on the tab bar to display the PivotTable worksheet.

4   If necessary, right-click the Standard toolbar, and then, from the shortcut menu that appears, click **PivotTable** to show the **PivotTable** toolbar.

5   Click any cell in the PivotTable, and then, on the **PivotTable** toolbar, click the **Show Field List** button.

The **PivotTable Field List** dialog box appears.

6   From the **PivotTable Field List** dialog box, drag the **Weekday** field to the **Drop Page Fields Here** box.

The **Weekday** field head appears in the **Drop Page Fields Here** box.

Hide Field List

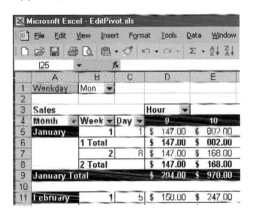

7   On the **PivotTable** toolbar, click the **Hide Field List** button.

The **PivotTable Field List** dialog box disappears.

8   Drag the **PivotTable** toolbar to the top of the workbook window.

The **PivotTable** toolbar docks below the Standard toolbar.

9   Click the **Weekday** down arrow, click **Mon**, and then click **OK**.

Excel filters the PivotTable so that only data representing sales on Mondays appears in the PivotTable.

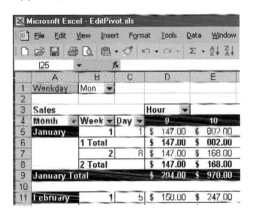

10   Click the **Weekday** down arrow, click **(All)**, and then click **OK**.

The PivotTable displays data from all weekdays.

11   Click the **Week** down arrow, and clear the check boxes next to 3, 4, and 5. Click **OK** to apply the filter.

Excel filters the PivotTable so that only data representing sales during the first two weeks of a month appears in the PivotTable.

12   Click the **Week** down arrow, and select the **(Show All)** check box. Click **OK** to apply the filter.

The PivotTable displays data from all weeks.

13 On the **PivotTable** toolbar, click **PivotTable** and then click **Wizard**.

The **PivotTable and PivotChart Wizard** appears.

14 Click **Layout**.

The **Layout** page of the **PivotTable and PivotChart Wizard** appears.

15 Drag **Hour** from the **Column** box to the **Page** box.

16 Drag **Weekday** from the **Page** box to the **Column** box, and click **OK**.

The **Layout** page disappears.

17 Click **Finish**.

Your PivotTable changes to reflect the new layout.

	A	B	C	D	E	F
1	Hour	(All)				
2						
3	Sales			Weekday		
4	Month	Week	Day	Sun	Mon	Tue
5	January	1	1		$ 4,657.00	
6			2			$ 4,251.00
7			3			
8			4			
9			5			
10			6			
11			7	$ 2,863.00		
12		1 Total		$ 2,863.00	$ 4,657.00	$ 4,251.00
13		2	8		$ 3,040.00	
14			9			$ 3,970.00
15			10			
16			11			
17			12			
18			13			
19			14	$ 4,733.00		
20		2 Total		$ 4,733.00	$ 3,040.00	$ 3,970.00

18 Drag the **Hour** field head to the **Drop Column Fields Here** box.

Your PivotTable changes in response to the pivot.

19 Drag the **Weekday** field head to the **Drop Page Fields Here** box.

Your PivotTable changes in response to the pivot.

20 On the tab bar, click the **AllData** sheet tab to display the AllData worksheet.

21 Click cell F5, type **2850**, and then press ⏎ Enter.

22 On the tab bar, click the **PivotTable** sheet tab to display the PivotTable worksheet.

23 On the **PivotTable** toolbar, click the **Refresh Data** button.

Excel updates the data in your PivotTable to reflect the change in the source data list.

24 Double-click cell A5.

The detail rows of the January section of the PivotTable are hidden, leaving only the January Total data displayed.

25 Double-click cell A5.

The detail rows of the January section of the PivotTable are unhidden.

26 On the tab bar, click the **Link** sheet tab to move to the Link worksheet.

27 Click cell C5, type **=**, and then, on the tab bar, click the **PivotTable** sheet tab.

The PivotTable worksheet appears.

28 Click cell P115.

=GETPIVOTDATA("Sales",PivotTable!$A$3) appears on the formula bar.

29 Press [Enter].

Excel switches back to the Link worksheet, and *$330,896.00*, the value in the cell linked to, appears in cell C5.

Tip

Cell C5 had the Currency style applied to it when the worksheet was created. If cell C5 were formatted with the General style, the value would be displayed as *330896*.

30 On the Standard toolbar, click the **Save** button to save your work.

Close

31 Click the **Close** button to close EditPivot.xls.

Creating PivotTables from External Data

While most of the time you will create PivotTables from data stored in Excel worksheets, you can also bring data from outside sources into Excel. For example, you might need to work with data created in another spreadsheet program with a file format Excel can't read directly. Fortunately, you can transfer worksheets from one program to another by exporting the data from the original program into a text file, which Excel then translates into a worksheet.

Spreadsheet programs store data in cells, so the goal of representing spreadsheet data in a text file is to indicate where the contents of one cell end and those of the next cell begin. The character that marks the end of a cell is a delimiter, in that it marks the end (or "limit") of a cell. The most common cell delimiter is the comma, so the delimited sequence *15, 18, 24, 28* would represent data in four cells. The problem with using commas to delimit financial data is that larger values, such as *52,802*, may be written with commas as thousands markers. To avoid confusion when importing a text file, the most commonly used delimiter for financial data is the Tab character.

To import data from a text file, you open the **Data** menu, point to **Import External Data**, and then click **Import Data** to open the **Select Data Source** dialog box.

From within the **Select Data Source** dialog box, you navigate to the directory with the text file you want to import. Double-clicking the file launches the **Text Import Wizard**.

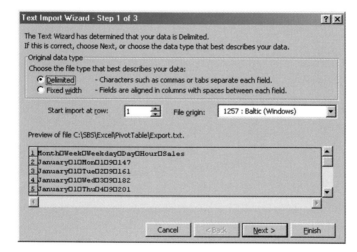

The first page of the **Text Import Wizard** lets you indicate whether the data file you are importing is delimited or fixed-width, meaning that each cell value will fall within a specific position in the file. Clicking **Next** to accept the default choice, **Delimited** (which Excel assigns after examining the data source you selected), advances you to the next wizard screen.

This screen lets you choose the delimiter for the file (in this case, Excel detected tabs in the file and selected the **Tab** check box for you) and gives you a preview of what the text file will look like when imported. Clicking **Next** advances you to the final wizard screen.

This screen lets you change the data type and formatting of the columns in your data list. Because you will assign formats and AutoFormats after you create the PivotTable from the data, you can click **Finish** to import the data into your worksheet. Once the data is in Excel, you can work with it normally.

External
Export

In this exercise, you import a data list into Excel from a text file and then create a PivotTable based on that list.

Open

1 On the Standard toolbar, click the **Open** button.

The **Open** dialog box appears.

2 Double-click the **External.xls** file.

External.xls opens.

3 On the **Data** menu, point to **Import External Data** and then click **Import Data**.

The **Select Data Source** dialog box appears.

4 Navigate to the PivotTable directory, and double-click **Export.txt**.

The **Text Import Wizard** appears, with the **Delimited** option button selected, *1* in the **Start import at row** box, and a preview of the file's contents in the **Preview** box.

5 Click **Next**.

The second page of the **Text Import Wizard** appears. In the Delimiters pane, the **Tab** check box is selected. A preview of your data as it will appear when imported appears in the **Data Preview** box.

6 Click **Next**.

The next screen of the **Text Import Wizard** appears. The data type for each column is set to General.

7 Click **Finish** to accept the values and data types as assigned by the wizard.

The **Import Data** dialog box appears with the **Existing worksheet** option button selected and *=$A$1* in the **Existing worksheet** box.

8 Click **OK** to paste the imported data into the active worksheet, beginning at cell A1.

The data appears in your workbook, and the **External Data** toolbar appears.

Close

9 Click the **Close** button to hide the **External Data** toolbar.

10 Click cell A1, and then, on the **Data** menu, click **PivotTable and PivotChart Report**.

The **PivotTable and PivotChart Wizard** appears with the **Microsoft Excel list or database** option button selected in the top pane, identifying your worksheet as the data source, and the **PivotTable** option button selected in the bottom pane, indicating that you want to create a PivotTable only.

11 Click **Next** to move to the next page of the wizard.

The next page of the wizard appears, with the range *$A$1:$F$169* in the **Range** box.

12 Click **Next** to move to the next page of the wizard.

The final page of the **PivotTable and PivotChart Wizard** appears, with the **New worksheet** option button selected, which tells the wizard to create a new worksheet to hold the PivotTable.

13 Click **Finish**.

The wizard closes, and the **PivotTable** toolbar, the **PivotTable Field List** dialog box, and your new PivotTable appear in a new worksheet.

14 From the **PivotTable Field List** dialog box, drag **Week** to the **Drop Row Fields Here** box.

Week appears in the **Drop Row Fields Here** box.

15 From the **PivotTable Field List** dialog box, drag **Day** to the **Drop Row Fields Here** box and drop it to the right of the **Week** field head.

Tip

A large gray insertion point will appear to the right of the **Week** field head when the mouse pointer is in the correct position.

The PivotTable is updated to reflect the added field.

16 From the **PivotTable Field List** dialog box, drag **Hour** to the **Drop Column Fields Here** box.

The PivotTable is updated to reflect the added field.

17 From the **PivotTable Field List** dialog box, drag **Sales** to the **Drop Data Items Here** box.

The PivotTable is updated to reflect the added field.

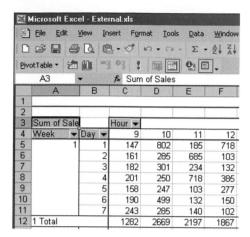

18 On the Standard toolbar, click the **Save** button to save your work.

19 Click the **Close** button to close External.xls.

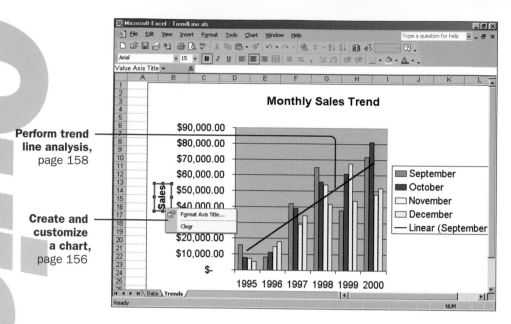

Perform trend line analysis, page 158

Create and customize a chart, page 156

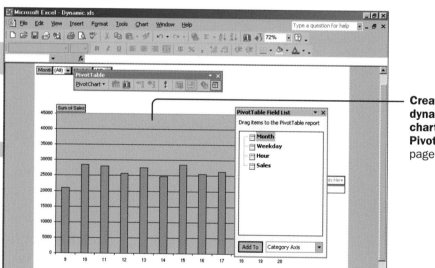

Create a dynamic chart using PivotCharts, page 161

Chapter 10
Creating Charts

After completing this chapter, you will be able to:

✔ Create and customize a chart.
✔ Perform trend line analysis.
✔ Create a dynamic chart using PivotCharts.

When you enter data into a Microsoft Excel worksheet, you create a record of important events, whether they are individual sales, sales for an hour of a day, or the price of a product. What a list of values in cells can't communicate easily, however, are the overall trends in the data. The best way to communicate trends in a large collection of data is through **charts** and **graphs**, which summarize data visually.

You have a great deal of control over your charts' appearance—you can change the color of any chart element, modify a chart's type to better summarize the underlying data, and change the display properties of text and numbers in a chart. If the data in the worksheet used to create a chart represents a progression through time, such as sales over a number of months, you can have Excel extrapolate future sales and add a **trend line** to the graph representing that prediction.

Finally, just as you can create PivotTables to reorganize a data list dynamically, you can create a **PivotChart** that reflects the contents and organization of the associated PivotTable.

In this chapter, you'll learn how to create a chart and customize its elements, find trends in your overall data, and create dynamic charts.

 This chapter uses the practice files CreateChart, Customize, TrendLine, and Dynamic that you installed from this book's CD-ROM. For details about installing the practice files, see "Using the Book's CD-ROM" at the beginning of this book.

Creating a Chart

Chart Wizard

To present your Excel data graphically, you select the cells you want to represent graphically and then click the **Chart Wizard** button on the Standard toolbar to launch the **Chart Wizard**.

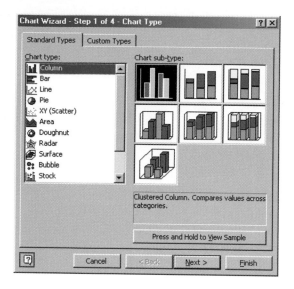

Ex2002-6-1

Approved Courseware

On the first page of the **Chart Wizard**, you choose the type and subtype of chart you want to create. When you click a chart type, the subtypes for that type appear in the **Chart sub-type** section, and a description of the default subtype for that type appears in the description box. You can go beyond those descriptions and get a preview of how your data would appear in a specific chart subtype by selecting the subtype and using the **Press and Hold to View Sample** button. When you've selected the type and subtype for your chart, click **Next** to move to the next wizard page.

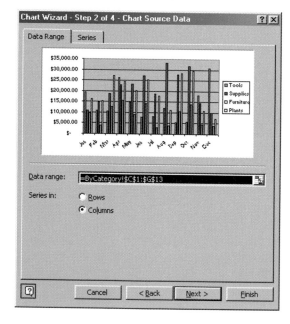

On this wizard page, you ensure that the **Data range** box has the reference for the cells to be used to create the chart, and you tell the wizard whether the data to be used to create the chart is arranged in columns or rows.

Tip

Excel does a good job of guessing whether the cells are arranged in columns or rows, but you should check the preview of the chart that appears in the wizard and select the other option button if necessary.

Once you have ensured that the correct cells and their arrangement have been selected, you can click the **Series** tab to name the data series, or set of values used to define the contents of the chart.

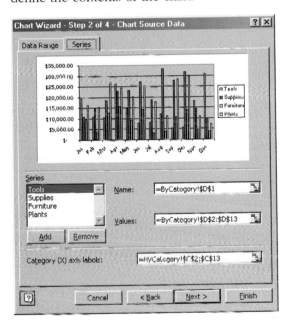

The cell range used to create this chart has the data labels included, so the correct labels appear in the wizard. You should verify that the series labels are indeed correct and then click **Next**.

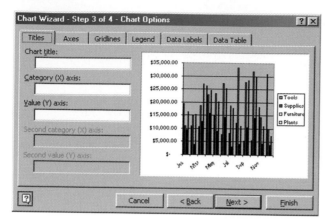

This wizard page lets you set the appearance of your chart, such as by adding a chart title and labels for both the horizontal (X) and vertical (Y) axes. After you type a label or a title in a box, the preview of the chart will change to reflect that addition. The other tab pages available on this wizard screen let you change the appearance of the chart, such as by adding gridlines to reflect changes in value, changing the position of or hiding the legend, or labeling the columns or points on your chart. When you're satisfied with the chart's appearance, click **Next** to move to the final **Chart Wizard** page.

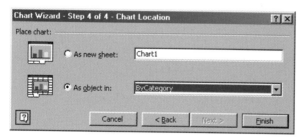

On this wizard page, you can choose to create your chart on a new page by selecting the **As new sheet** option button or as part of an existing worksheet. The name of the worksheet with the data used to create the chart appears in the **As object in** box, but you can choose another worksheet by clicking the down arrow at the right edge of the **As object in** box and clicking the name of another worksheet from the list that appears. If you plan to use the chart as an independent exhibit, or if you are printing the entire contents of the worksheet on a single page and the chart would obscure the underlying data, you can create the chart in a new worksheet. If you want the chart to be associated with its data whenever you or your colleagues open the worksheet with the data, or if you want to group all charts you create on a single worksheet, you should create the chart in an existing worksheet. When you click **Finish**, the chart appears in the selected worksheet.

Tip

Notice that the cells with the chart data are outlined in blue, the cells with the series names are outlined in green, and the cells with the categories are outlined in purple.

As with most other objects in an Excel worksheet, you can customize the chart's appearance. For example, you can resize the chart by dragging one of the sizing handles at the edges of the chart. You can also change the chart's fill effect, or background, by opening the **Format Chart Area** dialog box. To open that dialog box, you right-click the chart's Chart Area and then choose **Format Chart Area** from the shortcut menu that appears.

You can change the chart's background color by clicking any of the color squares on the palette in the **Area** section of the dialog box. To change the chart's fill effect, click the **Fill Effects** button.

You can use the controls in the **Fill Effects** dialog box to choose the color scheme, texture, pattern, or picture to serve as the background for the active chart.

CreateChart

In this exercise, you create a chart using the **Chart Wizard**, resize the chart, customize the chart's appearance, and then change the chart's fill effect.

Open

1   On the Standard toolbar, click the **Open** button.

The **Open** dialog box appears.

2   Navigate to the Charts folder, and double-click **CreateChart.xls**.

CreateChart.xls opens.

3   Select cells C1:G13, and then, on the Standard toolbar, click the **Chart Wizard** button.

The **Chart Wizard** appears.

4   If necessary, in the **Chart type** list click **Column** and then, in the **Chart subtype** section, click the first subtype.

5   Click **Next** to move to the next wizard page.

The next wizard page appears.

6   Verify that the Category (X) axis is labeled with the months of the year and that the four series are named *Tools*, *Supplies*, *Furniture*, and *Plants*.

7   Click **Next**.

The next wizard page appears.

8   In the **Chart title** box, type **Monthly Sales by Category** and then press Tab.

The chart preview is updated to reflect the new chart title.

9 In the **Category (X) axis** box, type **Month** and then press `Tab`.

The chart preview is updated to reflect the value in the **Category (X) axis** box.

10 In the **Value (Y) axis** box, type **Sales** and then click **Next**.

The next wizard page appears.

11 Click **Finish** to accept the default choice to create the chart as part of the ByCategory worksheet.

The chart appears in the ByCategory worksheet.

C	D	E	F	G	H
	Tools	**Supplies**	**Furniture**	**Plants**	**Total**
Jan	$ 19,359.00	$ 10,837.00	$ 9,594.00	$ 16,182.00	$ 55,972.00
Feb	$ 10,879.00	$ 14,787.00	$ 3,992.00	$ 15,241.00	$ 44,899.00
Mar	$ 10,654.00	$ 18,689.00	$ 12,583.00	$ 27,073.00	$ 68,999.00
Apr					89,347.00
May					67,449.00
Jun					74,385.00
Jul					47,993.00
Aug					60,385.00
Sep					71,835.00
Oct					81,093.00
Nov					48,020.00
Dec	$ 30,805.00	$ 10,031.00	$ 3,901.00	$ 7,238.00	51,975.00
Total	$ 170,150.00	$ 253,402.00	$ 105,254.00	$ 233,551.00	$ 762,352.00
Share	22.32%	33.24%	13.81%	30.64%	100.00%

(Chart overlaid on the data above: "Monthly Sales by Category" — a column chart with Sales ($-, $10,000.00, $20,000.00, $30,000.00, $40,000.00) on the Y axis and Month (Jan, Mar, May, Jul, Sep, Nov) on the X axis, with a legend for Tools, Supplies, Furniture, Plants.)

12 Drag the chart until it covers cells C17:G30.

13 Grab the sizing handle at the lower right corner of the chart, and drag it to the lower right corner of cell H33.

The chart becomes larger, giving you more room to add other information in the chart.

14 Right-click anywhere in the Chart Area of the chart, and then, from the short-cut menu that appears, click **Format Chart Area**.

The **Format Chart Area** dialog box appears.

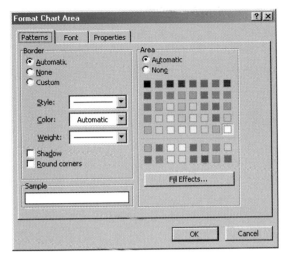

15 In the **Border** section of the dialog box, select the **Custom** option button.

16 Click the **Weight** down arrow, and then, from the list that appears, click the item at the bottom of the list.

17 Select the **Shadow** check box.

18 In the **Area** section, click the **Fill Effects** button.

The **Fill Effects** dialog box appears.

19 Click the **Texture** tab to display the **Texture** tab page.

20 In the upper left corner of the **Texture** section, click the **Newsprint** texture.

A preview of the Newsprint texture appears in the Sample pane, in the lower right corner of the dialog box.

21 Click **OK**.

The **Format Chart Area** dialog box reappears.

22 Click **OK**.

The **Format Chart Area** dialog box disappears, and the chart takes on the characteristics you applied to it.

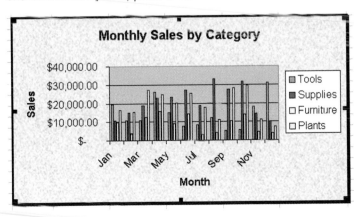

23 On the Standard toolbar, click the **Save** button to save your work.

Close

24 Click the **Close** button to close CreateChart.xls.

Customizing Chart Labels and Numbers

After you create a chart, you can customize its elements to conform to a particular color scheme, fill effect, or border pattern. You can also change the appearance of the labels and numbers in your chart.

Ex2002-6-1

Approved Courseware

To change the display characteristics of a chart label, double-click the label to open a formatting dialog box. You can use the controls in the dialog box to format the label.

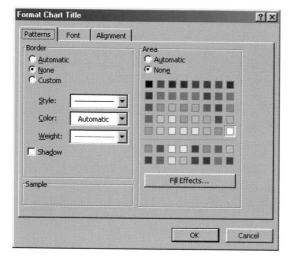

Tip

If you want to change the text of a label, click the label to activate it and then click in the box that appears around the label. When you're done editing the text, click outside the box around the label.

You can also change the display characteristics of the format used to display numeric values in your charts. For example, the sales values on the vertical axis of the chart in the following graphic are formatted with the Accounting format.

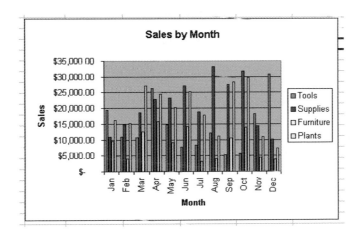

The default setting for the Accounting format has a thousands separator, a currency symbol, and two digits to the right of the decimal point. In the chart above, the vertical axis measures sales in $5,000 increments, so the digits to the right of the decimal point are superfluous. You can change the format of the numbers displayed on the vertical axis by double-clicking the axis and then clicking the **Number** tab in the dialog box that appears.

To change the number of digits to the right of the decimal point, type the new number in the **Decimal places** box. When you click **OK**, the chart will change to reflect your choice.

In this exercise, you create a line graph, change the formatting of the chart title, and then change the display characteristics of the numbers on the chart's vertical axis.

Customize

Open

1   On the Standard toolbar, click the **Open** button.

The **Open** dialog box appears.

2   Double-click **Customize.xls**.

Customize.xls opens.

Chart Wizard

3   Select the cells in the range C1:G13, and then, on the Standard toolbar, click the **Chart Wizard** button.

The **Chart type** page of the **Chart Wizard** appears.

4   In the **Chart type** list, click **Line** and then click **Next**.

The next **Chart Wizard** page appears.

5   Click **Next** to move to the next wizard page.

6   In the **Chart title** box, type **Sales by Month** and then press `Tab`.

Sales by Month appears as the chart title in the preview box.

7   In the **Category (X) axis** box, type **Month** and then press `Tab`.

Month appears as the Category (x) axis label.

8 In the **Value (Y) axis** box, type **Sales** and then press [Enter].

The next wizard page appears.

9 Click **Finish**.

The chart appears in the active worksheet.

10 Drag the chart so that it covers cells in the range C17:G30.

11 Double-click **Sales by Month**.

The **Format Chart Title** dialog box appears.

12 Click the **Font** tab.

The **Font** tab page appears.

13 In the **Size** box, click **14** and then click **OK**.

The chart title appears in 14-point type.

14 Double-click the Value (Y) axis area of the chart.

The **Format Axis** dialog box appears.

15 If necessary, click the **Number** tab to display the **Number** tab page.

16 In the **Decimal places** box, type **0** and then click **OK**.

The values on the Value (Y) axis appear with the formatting changes applied.

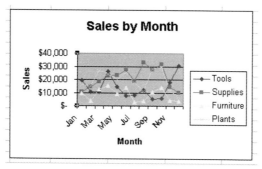

17 On the Standard toolbar, click the **Save** button to save your changes.

18 Click the **Close** button to close Customize.xls.

Close

X

Finding Trends in Your Data

You can use the data in Excel workbooks to discover how your business has performed in the past, but you can also have Excel make its best guess as to future sales if the current trend continues. As an example, consider the following graph for The Garden Company.

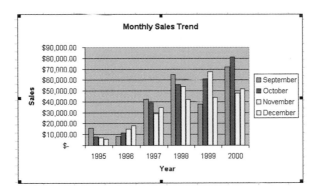

This graph shows the September to December sales totals for the years 1995 through 2000. The total for each month has grown from 1995 to 2000, but the growth hasn't been uniform, so guessing how much sales would increase if the overall trend continued would require math you might not know.

Fortunately, Excel knows that math. To have Excel project future sales for one of the data series in the chart, right-click the first column for that data series and then, from the shortcut menu that appears, click **Add Trendline** to open the **Add Trendline** dialog box.

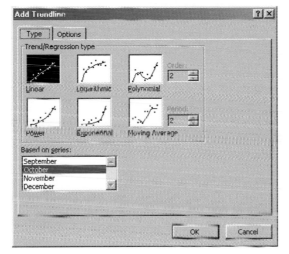

The **Type** tab page of the **Add Trendline** dialog box lets you choose the data distribution that Excel should expect when it makes its projection. The right choice for most business data is Linear—the other distributions (such as Exponential, Logarithmic, and Polynomial) are used for scientific and operations research applications.

Tip

Basically, if you don't know what distribution to choose, choose Linear.

After you pick the distribution type, click the **Options** tab to display the **Options** tab page.

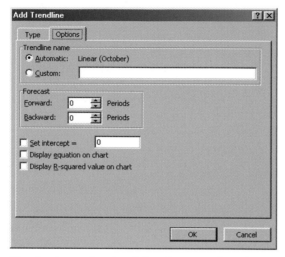

The horizontal axis of the chart used in this example shows sales by year from 1995 to 2000. To tell Excel how far in the future to look, you type a number in the **Forecast** section's **Forward** box. In this case, to look ahead two years you would type **2** in the **Forward** box and then click **OK** to add the trend line to the chart.

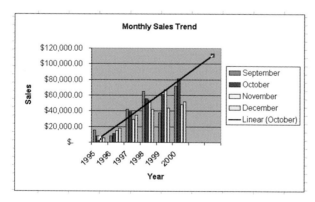

TrendLine

As with other chart elements, you can double-click the trend line to open a formatting dialog box.

In this exercise, you add a trend line to a chart.

1   On the Standard toolbar, click the **Open** button.

The **Open** dialog box appears.

2   Double-click **TrendLine.xls**.

TrendLine.xls opens.

3   If necessary, on the tab bar, click the **Trends** tab.

The Trends worksheet appears.

4   In the embedded chart, right-click the **September** column above the **1995** label and then, from the shortcut menu that appears, click **Add Trendline**.

The **Type** tab page of the **Add Trendline** dialog box appears.

5   If necessary, in the **Trend/Regression type** section, click **Linear**.

6   Click the **Options** tab.

The **Options** tab page appears.

7   In the **Forecast** section, type **2** in the **Forward** box and then click **OK**.

The **Add Trendline** dialog box disappears, and the trend line you created appears on the chart.

8   On the Standard toolbar, click the **Save** button to save your work.

Close

9   Click the **Close** button to close TrendLine.xls.

Creating a Dynamic Chart Using PivotCharts

Fx2002e-8-1

Approved Courseware

Just as you can create tables that you can reorganize on the fly to emphasize different aspects of the data in a list, you can also create dynamic charts, or PivotCharts, to reflect the contents and organization of a PivotTable.

There are two ways to create a PivotChart: by clicking a cell in an existing PivotTable and then clicking the **Chart Wizard** button on the Standard toolbar, or by selecting the appropriate option button on the last page of the **PivotTable and PivotChart Wizard**.

Chart Wizard

The first method of creating a PivotChart is fairly straightforward. In a worksheet with an existing PivotTable, click a cell in the PivotTable and then click the **Chart Wizard** button. When you do, a PivotChart appears in a new worksheet.

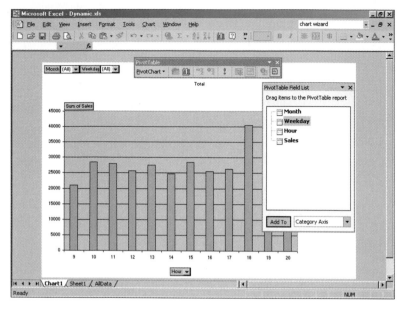

Refresh Data

Any changes to the PivotTable on which the PivotChart is based will be reflected in the PivotChart. For example, if the data in an underlying data list changes, clicking the **Refresh Data** button on the **PivotTable** toolbar will change the PivotChart to reflect the new data. Also, you can filter the contents of the PivotTable by clicking the **Weekday** down arrow, clicking **Wed** from the list that appears, and then clicking **OK**. The PivotTable will then show sales on Wednesdays. The PivotChart will also reflect the filter.

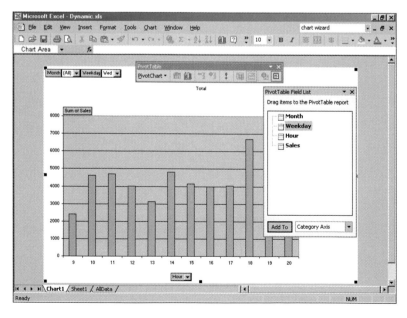

The PivotChart has controls with which you can filter the data in the PivotChart and PivotTable. Clicking the **Weekday** down arrow, clicking **(All)** from the list that appears, and then clicking **OK** will restore the PivotChart to its original configuration.

Once you have created a PivotChart, you can save it as a chart type that will be available in the **Chart Wizard**. To save the PivotChart as a user-defined chart type, click the chart, and on the **Chart** menu, click **Chart Type** to display the **Chart Type** dialog box. Once the **Chart Type** dialog box appears, click the **Custom Types** tab.

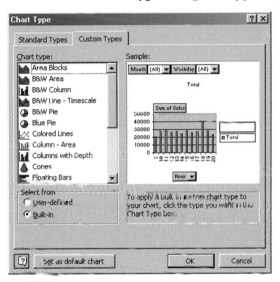

On the **Custom Types** tab page, click the **User-defined** option button in the **Select From** section to display the available user-defined chart types. The list of types in the **Chart type** list has one entry; **Default**. To add a new type, click the **Add** button.

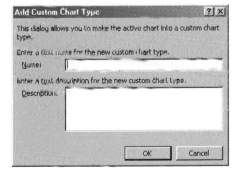

Type a name and a description for the new type, and then click **OK**. The new chart type will appear in the **Chart Type** dialog box.

If you ever want to change the chart type of an existing chart, you can do so by opening the **Chart Type** dialog box and clicking a new type for the chart. When you click **OK**, your data will be represented by the new chart.

Tip

If your data is of the wrong type to be represented by the chart type you select, an error message will appear.

Dynamic

Open

In this exercise, you create a PivotTable and associated PivotChart, change the underlying data and update the PivotChart to reflect that change, save the PivotChart as a custom chart type, and then change the PivotChart's type.

1 On the Standard toolbar, click the **Open** button.

The **Open** dialog box appears.

2 Double-click **Dynamic.xls**.

Dynamic.xls opens.

3 Click cell A1, and then on the **Data** menu, click **PivotTable and PivotChart Report**.

The first page of the **PivotTable and PivotChart Wizard** appears.

4 Select the **PivotChart report (with PivotTable report)** option button, and then click **Next**.

The next wizard page appears with *$A$1:$D$1117* in the **Range** box.

5 Click **Next**.

The final wizard page appears.

6 Be sure that the **New worksheet** option button is selected, and then click **Finish**.

Two new worksheets appear in the active workbook, one with the new Pivot-Table and the other with the new PivotChart. The worksheet with the Pivot-Chart is active and has the **PivotTable Field List** dialog box and the **PivotTable** toolbar displayed.

7 From the **PivotTable Field List** dialog box, drag the **Hour** field to the **Drop Category Fields Here** box.

The PivotChart changes to reflect the assignment.

8 From the **PivotTable Field List** dialog box, drag the **Month** field to the **Drop Page Fields Here** box.

The PivotChart changes to reflect the assignment.

9 From the **PivotTable Field List** dialog box, drag the **Weekday** field to the right of the **Month** field head in the **Drop Page Fields Here** box.

The PivotChart changes to reflect the assignment.

10 From the **PivotTable Field List** dialog box, drag the **Sales** field to the **Drop Data Items Here** box.

The body of the PivotChart fills with data from the **Sales** field, organized by the contents of the **Hour** field.

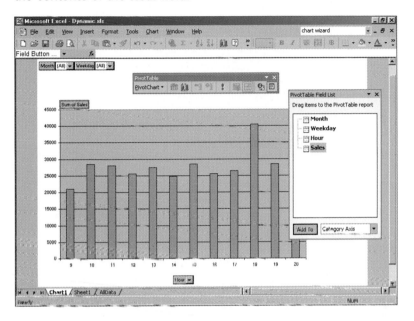

Close

11 In the **PivotTable Field List** dialog box, click the **Close** button.

The **PivotTable Field List** dialog box disappears.

12 On the tab bar, in the lower left corner of the workbook, click the **AllData** sheet tab.

The AllData worksheet appears.

13 In cell D9, type **4140**.

14 On the tab bar, click the **Chart1** sheet tab.

The Chart1 worksheet appears.

15 On the **PivotTable** toolbar, click the **Refresh Data** button.

The bar representing total sales for hour 9 changes to reflect the new total.

16 On the **Chart** menu, click **Chart Type**.

The **Chart Type** dialog box appears.

17 If necessary, click the **Custom Types** tab to display the **Custom Types** tab page.

18 In the **Select from** section, select the **User-defined** option button and then click **Add**.

The **Add Custom Chart Type** dialog box appears.

19 In the **Name** box, type **Sales PivotChart**.

20 In the **Description** box, type **PivotChart created with Month, Weekday, Hour, and Sales fields** and then click **OK**.

The **Add Custom Chart Type** dialog box disappears, and the new chart type appears in the **Chart Type** dialog box.

21 Click the **Standard Types** tab.

The **Standard Types** tab page of the **Chart Type** dialog box appears.

22 In the **Chart type** list, click **Area** and then click **OK**.

The chart changes to reflect its new type.

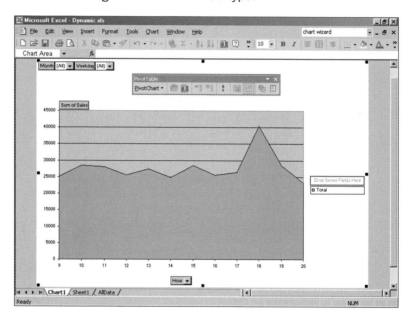

Save

23 On the Standard toolbar, click the **Save** button to save your work.

24 Click the **Close** button to close Dynamic.xls.

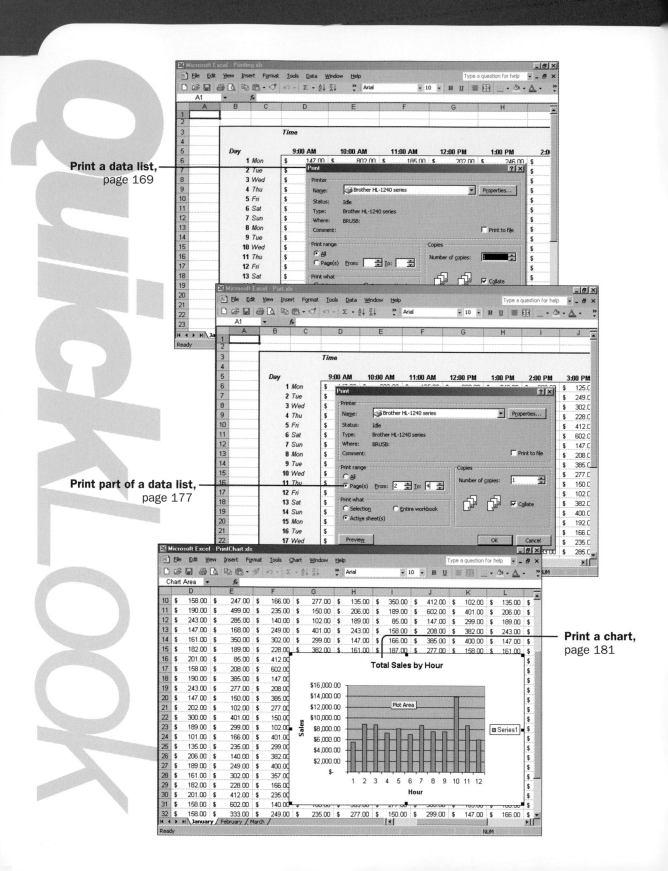

Print a data list,
page 169

Print part of a data list,
page 177

Print a chart,
page 181

Chapter 11
Printing

After completing this chapter, you will be able to:

✔ **Print data lists.**

✔ **Print part of a data list.**

✔ **Print a chart.**

Excel gives you a wide range of tools to create and manipulate your data lists. By using filters, by sorting, and by creating PivotTables and charts, you can change your worksheets so that they convey the greatest possible amount of information. Once you have configured your worksheet so that it shows your data to best advantage, you can print your Excel documents to use in a presentation or include in a report. You can choose to print all or part of any of your worksheets, change how your data and charts appear on the printed page, and even suppress any error messages that might appear in your worksheets.

In this chapter, you'll learn how to print all or part of a data list and how to print charts.

This chapter uses the practice files Printing, Part, and PrintChart that you installed from this book's CD-ROM. For details about installing the practice files, see "Using the Book's CD-ROM" at the beginning of this book.

Printing Data Lists

One of the most important considerations in creating a paper copy of an Excel document is determining how you want your data to appear on the printed page. For example, you can decide how far from the edge of the page you want your data to start, change the order in which Excel prints the pages in your worksheet, and even change where Excel ends one printed page and begins the next.

Tip

Print

If you want to print the active worksheet without changing any settings, click the **Print** button on the Standard toolbar.

Preview a Worksheet Before Printing

You can view your Excel worksheet as it would be printed by clicking the **Print Preview** button on the Standard toolbar. When you do, Excel displays the active worksheet in the Print Preview window.

When the Print Preview window opens, it shows the active worksheet as it would be printed with its current settings. In the lower left corner of the Print Preview window, Excel indicates how many pages the worksheet will require when printed and the number of the page you are viewing.

Tip

You can view the next printed page by pressing the [Page Down] key; to move to the previous page, press the [Page Up] key.

Change Your Printer Setup

Ex2002-3-6

Approved Courseware

While you have your worksheet open in the Print Preview window, you can use the buttons at the top of the window to change how your worksheet will appear when printed. Clicking the **Setup** button, for example, opens the **Page Setup** dialog box.

Important

Any page setup or other changes you make to a worksheet are confined to that worksheet.

You can use the controls in the **Page Setup** dialog box to change the orientation of the printed page between portrait mode, which has the short edge of the paper at the top, and landscape mode, which has the long edge of the paper at the top. Clicking the **Margins** tab displays a tab page with controls for changing the amount of space to be left at the edges of the paper (and the amount of space dedicated to headers and footers) when Excel prints your worksheet.

Important

The remaining controls on the **Page** tab page are discussed in the next section of this chapter, "Printing Part of a Data List."

You can also change the margins allotted to each area of your worksheet in the Print Preview window. When you click the **Margins** button, Excel draws lines on your worksheet to indicate where the sections of your document begin and end. To change a margin, you just drag its line to the desired position.

Tip

When you drag a margin to a new position, the distance the margin is from the nearest edge appears in the lower left corner of the Print Preview window.

Zoom In on Part of a Page

While you are viewing a worksheet in the Print Preview window, you can view the details of any section of the worksheet by clicking the **Zoom** button. Clicking the **Zoom** button doubles the size of the document in the window; clicking it again returns the document to its normal display size.

Change the Page Breaks in a Worksheet

Another way you can change how your worksheet will appear on the printed page is to change where Excel assigns its page breaks, or the point where Excel prints all subsequent data on a new sheet of paper. You can do that indirectly by changing a worksheet's margins, but you can do it directly by displaying your document in Page Break Preview mode. To display your worksheet in Page Break Preview mode from the Print Preview window, click the **Page Break Preview** button.

The blue lines in the window represent the page breaks. To move a page break, you drag the line representing the break to its new position. Excel will change the worksheet's properties so that the area you defined will be printed on a single page. You exit Page Break Preview mode by clicking **Normal** on the **View** menu.

Tip

You can view your worksheet in Page Break Preview mode at any time by clicking **Page Break Preview** on the **View** menu.

Change the Page Printing Order for a Worksheet

When you view a document in Page Break Preview mode, Excel indicates the order in which the pages will be printed with light gray words on the worksheet pages. (These indicators appear only in Page Break Preview mode; they won't show up when the document is printed.) You can change the order in which the pages are printed by opening the **Page Setup** dialog box to the **Sheet** page.

On the **Sheet** page, selecting the **Over, then down** option button will change the order in which the worksheets will be printed from the default **Down, then over**. You might want to change the order in which your worksheets are printed to keep certain information together on consecutive printed pages. For example, suppose you have a worksheet that holds hourly sales information; the columns represent hours of the day and the rows represent days of the month. If you want to print out consecutive days for each hour, you use **Down, then over**, as shown in the following graphic. Pages 1 and 2 let you see the 9:00 a.m. to 12:00 p.m. sales for the entire month, pages 3 and 4 let you see the 1:00 p.m. to 7:00 p.m. sales for the entire month, and so on.

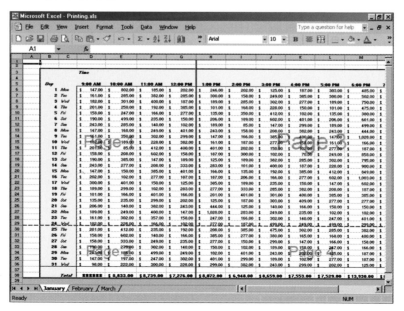

As the next graphic shows, changing the print order to **Over, then down** prints consecutive hours for each day. Pages 1, 2, and 3 let you see the 9:00 a.m. to 7:00 p.m.

sales for the first 24 days of the month, and pages 4, 5, and 6 let you see the 9:00 a.m. to 7:00 p.m. sales for the last 7 days of the month.

Suppress Errors in a Worksheet

A new option on the **Sheet** tab page of the **Page Setup** dialog box is the **Cell errors as** down arrow, which lets you define how Excel will print any errors in your worksheet. You can print the error as it normally appears in the worksheet, print a blank cell in place of the error, or choose one of two other indicators that are not standard Excel error messages.

Once you have prepared your worksheet for printing, you can print it by opening the **Print** dialog box. In the **Print** dialog box, you can choose the pages of the worksheet you want to print. To print every page in the worksheet, select the **All** option button in the **Print range** section and then click **OK**. To print every worksheet in the active workbook, select the **Entire workbook** option button in the **Print what** section.

Print Nonadjacent Sheets from a Workbook

If you want to print more than one worksheet from the active workbook, but not every worksheet in the workbook, you can select the worksheets to print from the tab bar. To select the worksheets to print, hold down the [Ctrl] key while you click the sheet tabs of the worksheets you want to print and then click the **Print** toolbar button.

Tip

The worksheets you select for printing do not need to be next to one another in the workbook.

Printing

In this exercise, you preview a worksheet before printing, change your printer setup, change the document's margins, zoom in on part of a page, preview and change your worksheet's page breaks, change the page printing order for a worksheet, suppress errors in a worksheet, and then print nonadjacent worksheets in your workbook.

Open

1 On the Standard toolbar, click the **Open** button.

The **Open** dialog box appears.

2 Navigate to the Printing folder, and double-click **Printing.xls**.

Printing.xls opens.

3 If necessary, click the **January** sheet tab.

4 On the Standard toolbar, click the **Print Preview** button.

The worksheet appears in preview mode.

5 Click **Setup**.

The **Page Setup** dialog box appears.

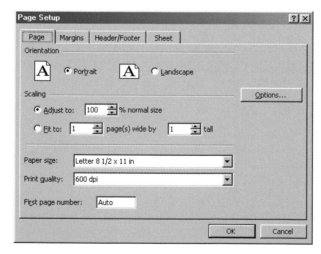

6 In the **Orientation** section, select the **Landscape** option button and then click **OK**.

The **Page Setup** dialog box closes, and the active worksheet reappears in preview mode.

7 Click **Margins**.

Margin lines appear on your worksheet.

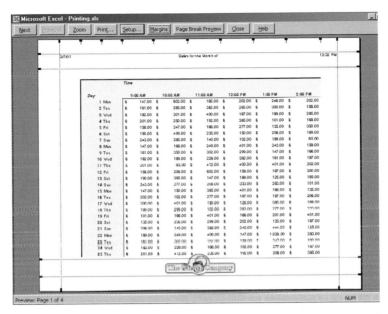

8 Move the mouse pointer over the second margin line from the bottom, and then, when the mouse pointer changes to a vertical double-headed arrow, drag the margin line until it is above the logo.

Excel adjusts the margins to reflect your change.

9 Click the **Zoom** button.

Excel increases the display size of the document.

10 Click the **Zoom** button.

Excel decreases the display size of the document.

11 Click **Page Break Preview**.

12 Click **OK** to clear the message box that appears.

The Print Preview window closes. The active worksheet appears, with the page breaks indicated by blue lines and the printing order of the worksheet sections indicated by gray text on the background of the pages.

13 Drag the page break line on the border of columns I and J to the border of columns G and H.

Excel repaginates your document to reflect the new page break position.

14 On the **View** menu, click **Normal**.

Excel changes the document view from Page Break Preview mode to Normal.

15 On the **File** menu, click **Page Setup**.

The **Page Setup** dialog box appears.

16 Click the **Sheet** tab to display the **Sheet** tab page.

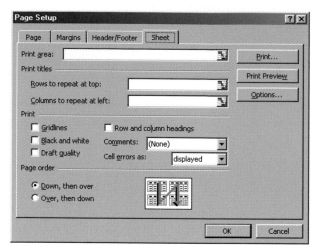

17 In the **Page order** section, select the **Over, then down** option button.

The graphic in the **Page order** section changes to reflect your choice.

18 In the **Print** section, click the **Cell errors as** down arrow and then, from the list that appears, click **<blank>**.

19 Click the **Page** tab to display the **Page** tab page.

20 If necessary, select the **Adjust to** option button and then, in the **Adjust to** box, type **100**.

Tip

The **Adjust to** value might have changed from *100%* to *78%* when you moved the page break earlier in this exercise.

21 Click **OK**.

The **Page Setup** dialog box closes.

22 Hold down the ⎇ key while you click the **March** tab on the tab bar.

The January and March worksheets are now active.

23 On the **File** menu, click **Print**.

The **Print** dialog box appears.

24 In the **Print what** section, ensure that the **Active sheet(s)** option button is selected.

25 Click **OK** to print the selected worksheets, or click **Cancel** to avoid printing the selected worksheets.

26 On the Standard toolbar, click the **Save** button to save your changes.

Close

27 Click the **Close** button to close Printing.xls.

Printing Part of a Data List

Ex2002-3-7

Approved Courseware

Excel gives you a great deal of control over what your worksheets look like when you print them, but you also have a lot of control over what parts of your worksheets will be printed. For example, you can use the **Print** dialog box to choose which pages of a multipage worksheet you want to print.

Selecting the **Page(s)** option button in the **Print range** section of the dialog box lets you fill in the page numbers you want to print in the **From** and **To** boxes.

Tip

You can use the Page Break Preview window to determine which pages you want to print, and if the pages aren't in an order you like, you can use the controls on the **Sheet** tab page of the **Page Setup** dialog box to change the order in which they will be printed.

Another way you can modify how a worksheet will be printed is to have Excel fit the entire worksheet on a specified number of pages. For example, you can have Excel resize a worksheet so that it will fit on a single printed page. Fitting a worksheet onto a single page is a handy tool when you need to add a sales or other summary to a report and don't want to spread important information across more than one page.

To have Excel fit a worksheet on a set number of pages, you open the **Page Setup** dialog box to the **Page** tab and select the **Fit to** option button. The default selection is to fit the worksheet to a print area one page high by one page wide, but you can type different values in the boxes to change the total pages on which the worksheet will be printed.

If you want to print a portion of a worksheet rather than the entire worksheet, you can define the area or areas you want to have printed. To identify the area of the worksheet you want to print, select the cells with the data you want to print, and on the **File** menu, point to **Print Area**, and then click **Set Print Area**. Excel marks the area with a dotted line around the border of the selected cells and will print only the cells you selected. To remove the selection, open the same submenu and click **Clear Print Area**.

Tip

You can include noncontiguous groups of cells in the area to be printed by holding down the [Ctrl] key as you select the cells.

Once you have defined a print area, you can use the **Page Setup** dialog box to position the print area on the page. Specifically, you can have Excel center the print area on the page by selecting the **Horizontally** and **Vertically** check boxes on the **Margins** tab page.

Another option at your disposal when printing an Excel worksheet is to hide specific rows or columns during the printing. For example, if a salesperson were giving a presentation on how different product lines sold at The Garden Company, he or she might want to show every row in a worksheet except the totals by category, saving that information for the next slide.

You can hide rows or columns by selecting the rows or columns, and then on the **Format** menu, pointing to **Row** or **Column**, and then clicking **Hide**. The rows or columns will be hidden until you point to **Row** or **Column** on the **Format** menu and click **Unhide**, but they are still there! They would be erased only if you selected the rows or columns and then clicked **Delete** on the **Edit** menu.

Ex2002-3-6

Approved Courseware

If the contents of a worksheet will take up more than one printed page, you can have Excel repeat one or more rows at the top of the page or columns at the left of the page. For example, if you wanted to print a lengthy data list containing the mailing addresses of customers signed up to receive your company's monthly newsletter, you could repeat the column headings Name, Address, City, and so forth at the top of the page. To repeat rows at the top of each printed page, on the **File** menu, click **Page Setup**. In the **Page Setup** dialog box, click the **Sheet** tab to move to the **Sheet** tab page.

Collapse Dialog

On the **Sheet** tab page, you can use the controls in the **Print titles** section of the dialog box to select the rows or columns to repeat. To choose rows to repeat at the top of the page, click the **Collapse Dialog** button next to the **Rows to repeat at top** box, select the rows, and then click the **Expand Dialog** button. The rows you selected appear in the **Rows to repeat at top** box.

Expand Dialog

Similarly, to have a set of columns appear at the left of every printed page, click the **Collapse Dialog** button next to the **Columns to repeat at left** box, select the columns, and then click the **Expand Dialog** button. When you're done, click **OK** to accept the settings.

Intelliprint
new for
OfficeXP

A final feature that comes in handy when you print Excel worksheets is Intelliprint, which prevents any blank pages from being printed at the end of a document. For example, if you have a 15-page worksheet and you set your print area to include all of those pages, Excel will print them. If, however, you delete enough data to reduce the worksheet's size to 10 pages but don't resize the print area, the print area will have 5 pages of blank cells at the end. Rather than print those blank pages, Intelliprint recognizes that the pages will be blank and stops printing after the last page with data in the body of the worksheet.

Part

In this exercise, you print selected pages from a multipage worksheet, print an entire worksheet on a single page, define a print area and center it on a page, hide rows for printing, and then unhide the rows.

Open

1 On the Standard toolbar, click the **Open** button.

The **Open** dialog box appears.

2 Double-click **Part.xls**.

Part.xls opens.

3 If necessary, click the **January** tab.

4 On the **File** menu, click **Print**.

The **Print** dialog box appears.

5 In the **Print range** section, select the **Page(s)** option button.

6 In the **From** box, type **2**.

7 In the **To** box, type **3**.

8 Click **OK** to print pages 2 and 3 of the worksheet.

Important

If your computer is not connected to a printer, click **Cancel**.

9 On the **File** menu, click **Page Setup**.

The **Page Setup** dialog box appears.

10 If necessary, click the **Page** tab.

11 In the **Scaling** section, select the **Fit to** option button and then, if necessary, type **1** in both the **page(s) wide by** and **tall** boxes.

12 Click **OK**.

Excel resizes your worksheet so it will fit on one printed page.

13 Click cell A1 and drag to cell G12.

14 On the **File** menu, point to **Print Area**, and then click **Set Print Area**.

A dotted line appears on the borders of the cells defined as the print area.

15 On the Standard toolbar, click the **Print Preview** button.

A preview of the selected print area appears.

16 Click the **Setup** button.

The **Page Setup** dialog box appears.

17 Click the **Margins** tab to display the **Margins** tab page.

18 In the **Center on page** section, select the **Horizontally** check box and the **Vertically** check box.

19 Click **OK**.

The Print Preview window reappears, with the selected print area centered on the page.

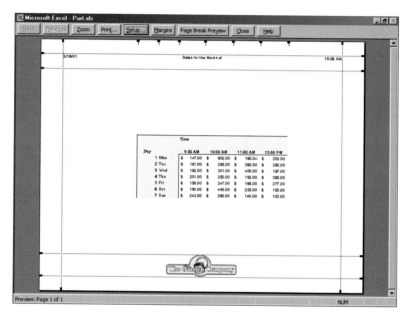

20 In the Print Preview window, click **Close**.

The Print Preview window closes.

21 On the **File** menu, point to **Print Area** and then click **Clear Print Area**.

Excel removes the print area you defined earlier.

22 Select columns D through G, and then, on the **Format** menu, point to **Column** and then click **Hide**.

Columns D through G are hidden.

23 On the Standard toolbar, click the **Print Preview** button.

A preview of your worksheet as it will be printed appears.

24 In the Print Preview window, click **Close** to close the Print Preview window.

25 On the **Format** menu, point to **Column** and then click **Unhide**.

The hidden columns reappear.

26 On the Standard toolbar, click the **Save** button to save your work.

Close

27 Click the **Close** button to close Part.xls.

Printing a Chart

Ex2002-6-1

Approved Courseware

Charts, which are graphic representations of your Excel data, let you communicate lots of information with a picture. Depending on your data and the type of chart you make, you can show trends across time, indicate the revenue share for various departments in a company for a month, or project future sales using trend line analysis. Once you have created a chart, you can print it to include in a report or use in a presentation.

If you embed a chart in a worksheet, however, the chart will probably obscure some of your data unless you move the chart to a second page in the worksheet. That's one way to handle printing a chart or the underlying worksheet, but there are other ways that don't involve changing the layout of your worksheets.

You can print a worksheet without printing an embedded chart by setting the chart's properties so that it remains hidden when the worksheet in which the chart is embedded is printed. You can find this option, which is directly analogous to hiding rows or columns when you print a worksheet, by opening the **Format Chart Area** dialog box to the **Properties** tab page.

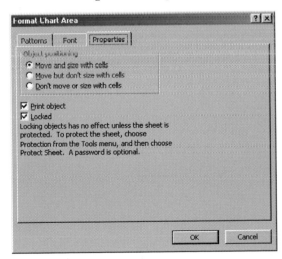

Selecting the **Print object** check box causes Excel to print the chart when the worksheet is printed, while clearing the check box hides the chart.

To print a chart, click the chart and then on the **File** menu, click **Print** to display the **Print** dialog box. In the **Print what** section, the **Selected Chart** option button is the only one available. If you were to click anywhere on the worksheet outside the chart, the **Print what** section would appear with the **Active sheet(s)** option button selected, meaning that the chart and underlying worksheet would be printed as they appear on the screen.

When you print a chart by itself, the default behavior is to resize the chart so that it takes up an entire printed page. If you want to print the chart at its actual size, such as when a full-page slide would be too large for your projection equipment, you can do so by opening the **Page Setup** dialog box to the **Chart** tab page. Selecting the **Custom** option button in the **Printed chart size** section tells Excel to print the chart at its actual size.

Tip

You can resize a chart by selecting it in the workbook window and dragging one of the corner handles until the outline of the chart is the desired size.

PrintChart

In this exercise, you print a chart by itself, print the underlying worksheet without the chart, and then set the chart's Page Setup properties so that it is printed at its actual size.

Open

1 On the Standard toolbar, click the **Open** button.

The **Open** dialog box appears.

2 Double-click **PrintChart.xls**.

PrintChart.xls opens.

3 Click the chart, and then, on the **File** menu, click **Print**.

The **Print** dialog box appears.

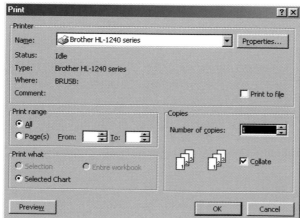

4   In the **Print what** section, ensure that the **Selected Chart** option button is selected.

5   Click **OK** to print your chart, or click **Cancel** to continue without printing.

The **Print** dialog box disappears. If you printed the chart, notice that the chart expanded to fit the entire page.

6   Right-click the **Chart Area** of the chart, and then, from the shortcut menu that appears, click **Format Chart Area**.

The **Format Chart Area** dialog box appears.

7   Click the **Properties** tab.

The **Properties** tab page appears.

8   Clear the **Print object** check box, and then click **OK**.

The **Format Chart Area** dialog box disappears.

Print

9   If your computer is connected to a printer, on the Standard toolbar, click the **Print** button.

Important

If your computer is not connected to a printer, continue to the next step without printing.

Excel prints the worksheet without the chart.

10   Right-click the **Chart Area** of the chart, and then, from the shortcut menu that appears, click **Format Chart Area**.

The **Format Chart Area** dialog box appears.

11   Click the **Properties** tab.

The **Properties** tab page appears.

12   Select the **Print object** check box, and then click **OK**.

Print Preview

13   On the Standard toolbar, click the **Print Preview** button.

The Print Preview window appears. Notice that the chart has been resized to fit the entire page.

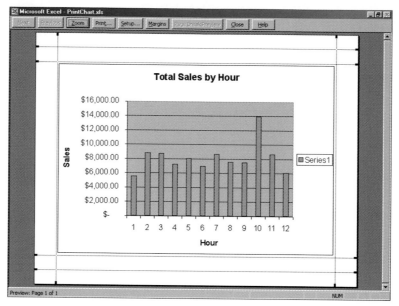

14 Click the **Setup** button.

The **Page Setup** dialog box appears.

15 Click the **Chart** tab.

The **Chart** tab page appears.

16 Select the **Custom** option button, and then click **OK**.

The Print Preview window reappears, with the chart shown at its original size.

17 Click **Print**.

The **Print** dialog box appears.

18 Click **OK** to print your chart, or click **Cancel** to continue without printing.

The worksheet with the chart reappears.

19 On the Standard toolbar, click the **Save** button to save your work.

Close

20 Click the **Close** button to close PrintChart.xls.

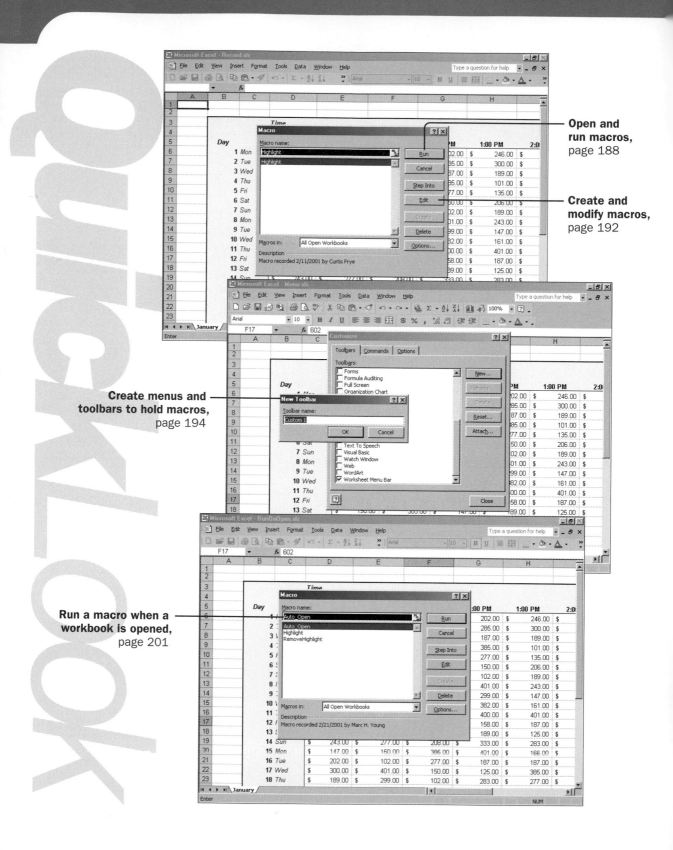

Open and run macros, page 188

Create and modify macros, page 192

Create menus and toolbars to hold macros, page 194

Run a macro when a workbook is opened, page 201

Chapter 12
Automating Repetitive Tasks with Macros

After completing this chapter, you will be able to:

✔ Open and run macros.

✔ Create and modify macros.

✔ Create toolbars and menus to hold macros.

✔ Run a macro when a workbook is opened.

Many tasks you perform in Excel, such as entering sales data for a particular day or adding formulas to a worksheet, either are done once or, like changing the format of a cell range, can be repeated quickly using available tools in Excel. However, you will often have one or two tasks that you perform frequently and that require a lot of steps to accomplish. For example, you might have a number of cells in a worksheet that contain important data you use quite often in presentations to your colleagues.

Rather than go through a lengthy series of steps to highlight the cells with the important information, you can create a **macro**, or series of recorded actions, to perform the steps for you. Once you have created a macro, you can run, edit, or delete it as needed.

Under the standard Excel interface, you run and edit macros using the items on the **Tools** menu. You can make your macros easier to access by creating new toolbars or menus with buttons or menu items to which you can assign macros. If you run a macro to highlight specific cells in a worksheet every time you show that worksheet to a colleague, you can save time by adding a toolbar button that runs a macro to highlight the cells for you.

Another handy feature of Excel macros is that you can create macros that run when a workbook is opened. For example, you might want to ensure that no cells in a worksheet are highlighted when the worksheet opens. You can create a macro that removes any special formatting from your worksheet cells when its workbook opens, allowing you to emphasize the data you want as you present the information to your colleagues.

In this chapter, you'll learn how to open, run, create, and modify macros; create tool-bars and menus to hold macros; and run a macro when a workbook is opened.

This chapter uses the practice files View, Record, Toolbar, Menu, and RunOnOpen that you installed from this book's CD-ROM. For details about installing the practice files, see "Using the Book's CD-ROM" at the beginning of this book.

Introducing Macros

After you have worked with your Excel documents for a while, you will probably discover some series of actions you perform repeatedly. While many of these actions, such as saving your changes or printing, can be accomplished quickly, some sequences involve many steps and take time to accomplish by hand. For example, you may want to highlight a number of cells in a worksheet to emphasize an aspect of your data. Rather than highlight the cells by hand every time you present your findings, you can create a macro, or series of automated actions, to do the highlighting for you.

Ex2002e-5-2

The best way to get an idea of how macros work is to examine an existing macro. To do that, on the **Tools** menu, point to **Macro**, and click **Macros** to open the **Macro** dialog box.

Approved Courseware

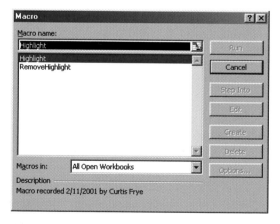

Tip

You can also open the **Macro** dialog box by pressing Alt + F8.

Troubleshooting

If you have trouble running macros in your workbooks because of your security settings, you can change the settings by opening the **Tools** menu and clicking **Options** to display the **Options** dialog box. In the **Options** dialog box, click the **Security** tab and then, on the **Security** tab page, click the **Macro Security** button. On the page that appears, click the **Medium** option button and then click **OK**.

The **Macro** dialog box has a list of macros in your workbook. To view the code behind a macro, you click the macro's name and then click **Edit**.

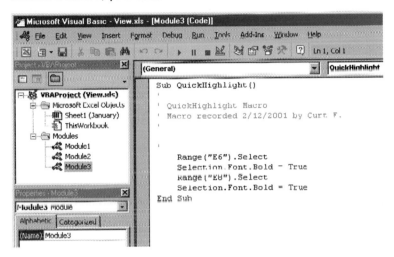

Excel macros are recorded using the Visual Basic for Applications programming language (VBA). The preceding graphic shows the code for a macro that highlights cell E6, changes the cell's formatting to bold, and then repeats the process for cell E8. After introductory information about the macro (its name and when created), the first line of the macro identifies the cell range to be selected (in this case, cell E6). After the cell is selected, the next line of the macro changes the formatting of the selected cell to bold, which is the same as you clicking a cell and then clicking the **Bold** button on the Formatting toolbar. The next two lines of the macro repeat the process for cell E8.

To see how the macro works, you can open the **Macro** dialog box, click the name of the macro you want to examine, and then click **Step Into**. The Microsoft Visual Basic editor appears, with a highlight around the instruction that will be executed next. To execute an instruction, you press F8. The highlight moves to the next instruction, and your worksheet changes to reflect the action that was taken.

Effect of previous instruction

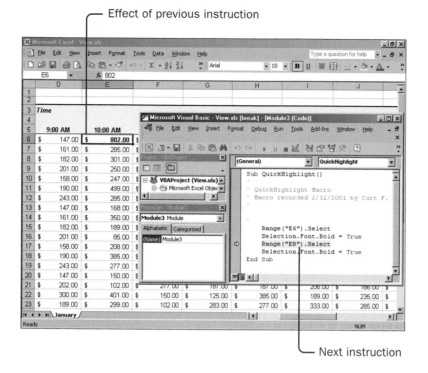

Next instruction

You can run a macro without stopping after each instruction by opening the **Macro** dialog box, clicking the macro to run, and then clicking **Run**.

In this exercise, you examine a macro in the Microsoft Visual Basic editor, move through the macro one step at a time, and then run the macro without stopping.

View

Open

1 On the Standard toolbar, click the **Open** button.

The **Open** dialog box appears.

2 Navigate to the Macros folder, and double-click **View.xls**. If a warning dialog box appears, click **Enable Macros**.

View.xls opens.

3 On the **Tools** menu, point to **Macro** and then click **Macros**.

The **Macro** dialog box appears.

4 In the **Macro name** section, click **Highlight** and then click **Edit**.

The Microsoft Visual Basic editor opens, with the code for the **Highlight** macro displayed in the Module1 (Code) window.

5 Click the **Close** button.

The Microsoft Visual Basic editor closes, and View.xls reappears.

6 On the **Tools** menu, point to **Macro** and then click **Macros**.

The **Macro** dialog box appears.

7 In the **Macro name** section, click **Highlight** and then click **Step Into**.

The Microsoft Visual Basic editor opens, with the first line of the macro highlighted.

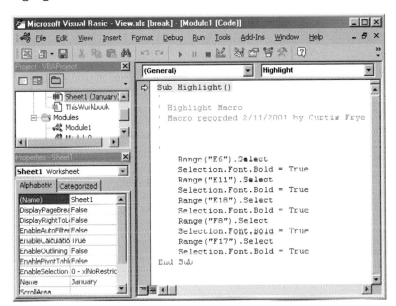

8 Right-click the taskbar, and then, from the shortcut menu that appears, click **Tile Windows Vertically**.

The Excel and Microsoft Visual Basic editor windows appear.

9 Click the Microsoft Visual Basic editor title bar, and then press [F8].

In the Microsoft Visual Basic editor, the next step in the macro is highlighted.

10 Press [F8].

In the Microsoft Visual Basic editor, the next step in the macro is highlighted. In the Excel window, cell E6 is highlighted.

11 Press [F8].

In the Microsoft Visual Basic editor, the next step in the macro is highlighted. In the Excel window, the value in cell E6 appears in bold.

Close
12 In the Microsoft Visual Basic editor, click the **Close** button. Click **OK** to close the dialog box that appears.

The editor closes.

13 On the **Tools** menu, point to **Macro** and then click **Macros**.

The **Macro** dialog box appears.

14 If necessary, in the **Macro name** section, click **Highlight**.

15 Click **Run**.

The **Macro** dialog box disappears, and Excel runs the macro. The contents of cells E6, E11, E18, F8, and F17 appear in bold type.

Save

16 On the Standard toolbar, click the **Save** button to save your work.

17 Click the Close button to close View.xls.

Creating and Modifying Macros

The first step in creating a macro is to plan every step of the process you want to automate. Computers today are quite fast, so adding an extra step that doesn't affect the outcome of a process won't slow you down noticeably, but leaving out a step means you will need to rerecord a macro.

Ex2002e-5-2

Approved Courseware

Once you have planned your process, you can create a macro by pointing to **Macro** on the **Tools** menu and then clicking **Record New Macro**. When you do, the **Record Macro** dialog box appears.

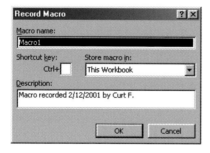

After you type the name of your macro in the **Macro name** box, click **OK**. The **Record Macro** dialog box disappears, and the Stop Recording toolbar appears.

Stop Recording

You can now perform the actions you want Excel to repeat later; when you're done, click the **Stop Recording** button. The Stop Recording toolbar disappears, and your macro is added to the list of macros available in your workbook.

To modify an existing macro, you can open it in the Microsoft Visual Basic editor and add to or change the macro's instructions. If you're not sure how to write the necessary VBA code, you can simply delete the macro and rerecord it. To delete a macro, you open the **Macro** dialog box, click the macro you want to delete, and then click **Delete**.

Record

In this exercise, you record a macro that removes the bold formatting from four cells and then modify the macro to remove the bold formatting from a fifth cell.

Open

1 On the Standard toolbar, click the **Open** button.

The **Open** dialog box appears.

2 Double-click **Record.xls**. If a warning dialog box appears, click **Enable Macros**.

Record.xls opens.

3 On the **Tools** menu, point to **Macro** and then click **Record New Macro**.

The **Record Macro** dialog box appears.

4 In the **Macro name** box, delete the existing name, and then type **RemoveHighlight**.

5 Click **OK**.

The Stop Recording toolbar appears.

Bold

6 Click cell E6, and then, on the Formatting toolbar, click the **Bold** button.

7 Click cell E11, and then, on the Formatting toolbar, click the **Bold** button.

8 Click cell E18, and then, on the Formatting toolbar, click the **Bold** button.

9 Click cell F8, and then, on the Formatting toolbar, click the **Bold** button.

10 On the Stop Recording toolbar, click the **Stop Recording** button.

The Stop Recording toolbar disappears.

11 On the **Tools** menu, point to **Macro** and then click **Macros**.

The **Macro** dialog box appears.

12 In the **Macro name** section, click **RemoveHighlight** and then click **Edit**.

The Microsoft Visual Basic editor appears.

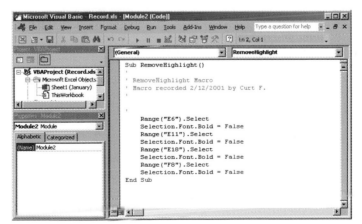

13 Click to the left of *End Sub*, type **Range("F17").Select**, and then press Enter .

This macro statement selects cell F17.

Tip

To get more information about Visual Basic for Applications, type **VBA** in the Ask A Question box on the Standard toolbar and click **Get Help for Visual Basic for Applications** from the list of help topics that appears.

14 Type **Selection.Font.Bold = False**, and then press ⌷Enter⌷.

This macro statement removes bold formatting from the selected cell (F17).

15 On the Standard toolbar, click the **Save** button to save your change.

Close

16 Click the **Close** button.

The Microsoft Visual Basic editor disappears, and Record.xls appears.

17 On the **Tools** menu, point to **Macro** and then click **Macros**.

The **Macro** dialog box appears.

18 Click **Highlight**, and then click **Run**.

The contents of cells E6, E11, E18, F8, and F17 appear in bold type.

19 On the **Tools** menu, point to **Macro** and then click **Macros**.

The **Macro** dialog box appears.

20 Click **RemoveHighlight**, and then click **Run**.

The contents of cells E6, E11, E18, F8, and F17 appear in regular type.

21 On the Standard toolbar, click the **Save** button to save your changes.

22 Click the **Close** button to close Record.xls.

Creating a Toolbar to Hold Macros

Ex2002e-5-1

Approved Courseware

Although you can run any of your macros from the **Macro** dialog box, the ability to run a macro by clicking a toolbar button makes your worksheets much easier to use, especially for colleagues with relatively little experience using Excel. To create a toolbar to host your macros, on the **Tools** menu, click **Customize** to open the **Customize** dialog box.

Important

The **Customize** dialog box must be open for you to be able to change any of your toolbars or menus.

To create a toolbar in the **Customize** dialog box, you display the **Toolbars** tab page and then click **New**. The **New Toolbar** dialog box appears; type a name for your new toolbar in the space provided, and then click **OK**. Your new toolbar appears next to the **Customize** dialog box.

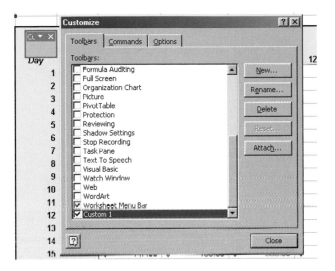

Once you have created the new toolbar, you can assign your macros to it. To do so, you display the **Commands** tab page of the **Customize** dialog box.

On the **Commands** tab page, you pick **Macros** from the list of options in the **Categories** list. Two items will appear in the **Commands** list: **Custom Menu Item** and **Custom Button**. To add a button to your new toolbar, drag the **Custom Button** item to it.

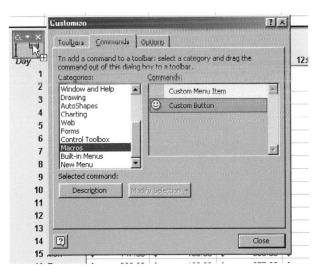

Tip

When your button is over a place where it can be dropped, the indicator at the lower right of your mouse pointer will change to a plus sign.

After you have added the button to your toolbar, you can assign the macro that the button will run by right-clicking the button and then, from the shortcut menu that appears, clicking **Assign Macro**. The **Assign Macro** dialog box appears; click the macro you want to run when the toolbar button is clicked, and then click **OK**.

After you create a toolbar, Excel will display it whenever you open the workbook in which it was created. If you want, you can hide your toolbar so that only you and colleagues who know the toolbar exists can use it. Right-clicking any toolbar shows a shortcut menu with the names of toolbars available in the active workbook—toolbars currently displayed have a check next their name. To hide a toolbar, click its name to remove the check mark. You can always redisplay the toolbar by right-clicking any toolbar and clicking the toolbar's name from the list that appears.

If you remove the macros you've created from your workbook, or if you don't want to make the macros available on a toolbar, you can delete the toolbar from the **Customize** dialog box. To do so, click the toolbar you want to delete in the **Toolbars** list and then click **Delete**.

Important

Be careful! You can delete any Excel toolbar. If you accidentally delete a toolbar from the default set, you will have to reinstall Excel to restore it.

If you like, you can customize the button you use to represent your macro. To change the appearance of a toolbar button, you open the **Customize** dialog box, right-click the button you want to change, and then, from the shortcut menu that appears, point to **Change Button Image** to display a set of images you can use for your button.

Toolbar

In this exercise, you create a toolbar to hold your macro, create a button to represent the macro on the toolbar, run the macro from the toolbar, and then delete the toolbar.

Open

1 On the Standard toolbar, click the **Open** button.

The **Open** dialog box appears.

2 Double-click **Toolbar.xls**. If a warning dialog box appears, click **Enable Macros**.

Toolbar.xls opens.

3 On the **Tools** menu, click **Customize**.

The **Customize** dialog box appears.

4 If necessary, click the **Toolbars** tab to display the **Toolbars** tab page.

5 Click **New**.

The **New Toolbar** dialog box appears.

6 In the **Toolbar name** box, type **Custom Macros** and then click **OK**.

A new toolbar named Custom Macros appears in the workbook window; the toolbar is also listed in the **Toolbars** list of the **Customize** dialog box.

7 In the **Customize** dialog box, click the **Commands** tab.

The **Commands** tab page appears.

8 In the **Categories** list, click **Macros**.

The **Commands** list changes to reflect your choice.

9 Drag the **Custom Button** command to the Custom Macros toolbar.

The **Custom** button appears on the Custom Macros toolbar.

10 On the Custom Macros toolbar, right-click the **Custom** button and then, from the shortcut menu that appears, click **Name**.

The text next to the **Name** menu item is highlighted.

11 Type **Highlight**, and then press ⏎.

The menu disappears, and your button is now named Highlight.

12 On the Custom Macros toolbar, right-click the **Highlight** button, point to **Change button image** on the shortcut menu that appears, and then click the Up Arrow button image.

The Highlight button image changes to an up arrow.

13 On the Custom Macros toolbar, right-click the **Highlight** button and then, from the shortcut menu that appears, click **Assign Macro**.

The **Assign Macro** dialog box appears.

14 Click **Highlight** and then click **OK**.

The **Assign Macro** dialog box disappears. Clicking the **Highlight** button on the Custom Macros toolbar when the **Customize** dialog box is closed will now run the Highlight macro.

15 In the **Customize** dialog box, click **Close**.

The **Customize** dialog box disappears.

16 On the Custom Macros toolbar, click the **Highlight** button.

The **Highlight** macro runs. The contents of cells E6, E11, E18, F8, and F17 appear in bold type.

17 Right-click the title bar of the Custom Macros toolbar, and then, from the shortcut menu that appears, click **Custom Macros**.

The Custom Macros toolbar disappears.

18 On the **Tools** menu, click **Customize**.

The **Customize** dialog box appears.

19 If necessary, click the **Toolbars** tab.

20 In the **Toolbars** list, click **Custom Macros**, click **Delete**, and then click **OK** in the warning dialog box that appears.

Important

You should click the name of the toolbar, not select the check box next to the toolbar name.

The toolbar is deleted.

21 Click **Close** to close the **Customize** dialog box.

22 On the Standard toolbar, click the **Save** button to save your work.

Close

23 Click the **Close** button to close Toolbar.xls.

Creating a Menu to Hold Macros

Ex2002e-5-1

Approved Courseware

As with toolbars, you can create custom menus to hold your macros. To create a custom menu, you open the **Customize** dialog box to the **Commands** page and then, in the **Categories** list, click **New Menu**. The **New Menu** option appears in the **Commands** list.

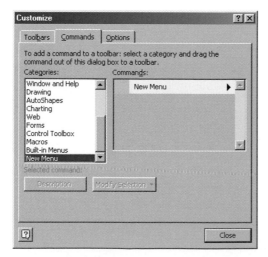

To add the new menu to an existing menu bar or toolbar, you drag the **New Menu** command from the **Customize** dialog box to the desired spot.

Tip

When your menu is over a place where it can be dropped, the indicator at the lower right of your mouse pointer will change to a plus sign.

Once the menu is in place, you can rename it and add items to it. You can rename a menu by right-clicking the menu head and choosing **Name** from the shortcut menu that appears. The shortcut menu will stay open, and the menu's name will be highlighted. Just type the new name and press [Enter] to rename your menu.

To add a macro to a menu, click the **Macros** item in the **Categories** list of the **Customize** dialog box to display the macros available in the current workbook. When you add a macro to a menu, you need to create a new menu item and then assign the macro to the new item. You can add a new menu item to a menu by clicking the **Macros** item in the **Categories** list and then, from the **Commands** list, dragging **Custom Menu Item** to your menu.

When you get **Custom Menu Item** to the menu, hold the mouse pointer over the menu head until a small gray box appears below the menu head.

Drag the mouse pointer to that gray box to add the item to the menu. Once you have added the item to the menu, you can rename it by right-clicking it, choosing **Name** from the shortcut menu that appears, and then typing the name in the space provided. To assign a macro to the menu item, right-click the menu item, choose **Assign Macro** from the shortcut menu that appears, and then choose the macro in the **Assign Macro** dialog box.

Whether you create a toolbar or a menu is entirely up to personal preference because there is no functional difference between running a macro by clicking a toolbar button and clicking a menu item. Remember, clicking the **Save** button on the Standard toolbar and clicking **Save** on the **File** menu do the same thing!

If you remove the macros you've created from your workbook, or if you don't want to make the macros available on a menu, you can delete the menu while the **Customize** dialog box is open. To do so, right-click the menu head and then, from the shortcut menu that appears, click **Delete**.

Important

Be careful! You can delete any Excel menu. If you accidentally delete a menu from the default set, you will have to reinstall Excel to restore it.

Menu

In this exercise, you create and name a menu, add an item to that menu and name the item, and then assign a macro to be run when the menu item is clicked. You then delete the custom menu.

Open

1   On the Standard toolbar, click the **Open** button.

The Open dialog box appears.

2   Double-click **Menu.xls**. If a warning dialog box appears, click **Enable Macros**.

Menu.xls opens.

3   On the **Tools** menu, click **Customize**.

The **Customize** dialog box appears.

4   If necessary, click the **Commands** tab to display the **Commands** tab page.

5   In the **Categories** list, click **New Menu**.

New Menu appears in the **Commands** list.

6   Drag **New Menu** to the end of the main menu bar.

An insertion point appears at the position on the main menu bar where the new menu will be inserted. When you release the mouse button, the new menu appears on the main menu bar.

7   Right-click the **New Menu** heading, and then, from the shortcut menu that appears, click **Name**.

The shortcut menu stays open, with the new menu's name highlighted in the shortcut menu.

8   Type **Custom Macros**, and then press ⌷Enter⌷.

The new menu's name changes to Custom Macros.

9   In the Categories pane of the **Customize** dialog box, click **Macros**.

The contents of the **Commands** list change to reflect your choice.

10 In the **Commands** list, drag the **Custom Menu Item** command to the **Custom Macros** menu head. When a box appears under the **Custom Macros** menu head, drag **Custom Menu Item** onto it.

The **Custom Menu Item** command appears on the **Custom Macros** menu.

11 On the **Custom Macros** menu, right-click **Custom Menu Item** and then, from the shortcut menu that appears, click **Name**.

The shortcut menu stays open, with the menu item's name highlighted in the shortcut menu.

12 Type **Highlight**, and then press ⌅ [Enter].

The name of the menu item changes to Highlight.

13 On the **Custom Macros** menu, right-click **Highlight** and then, from the short-cut menu that appears, click **Assign Macro**.

The **Assign Macro** dialog box appears.

14 In the **Macro name** box, click **Highlight** and then click **OK**.

Excel assigns the **Highlight** macro to the selected menu item and closes the **Assign Macro** dialog box.

15 Click **Close** to close the **Customize** dialog box.

16 On the **Custom Macros** menu, click **Highlight**.

The **Highlight** macro runs. The contents of cells E6, F11, E18, F8, and F17 appear in bold type.

17 On the **Tools** menu, click **Customize**

The **Customize** dialog box appears.

18 Right-click the **Custom Macros** menu head, and then, from the shortcut menu that appears, click **Delete**.

The **Custom Macros** menu is deleted.

19 In the **Customize** dialog box, click **Close**.

The **Customize** dialog box disappears.

20 On the Standard toolbar, click the **Save** button to save your work.

Close

21 Click the **Close** button to close Menu.xls.

Running a Macro When a Workbook Is Opened

One advantage of writing Excel macros in the Visual Basic for Applications language is that you can have Excel run a macro whenever a workbook is opened. For example, if you use a worksheet for presentations, you can create macros that render the contents of selected cells in bold type, italics, or different typefaces to set the data apart from data in neighboring cells. If you should close a workbook without removing that formatting, however, the contents of your workbook will have highlights when you open it. While this is not a catastrophe, returning the workbook to its original formatting will take a few seconds to accomplish.

Rather than run a macro by hand, or even from a toolbar button or a menu, you can have Excel run a macro whenever a workbook is opened. The trick to making that happen is in the name you give the macro. Whenever Excel finds a macro with a name starting with *Auto_* (*Auto* followed by an underscore), it runs the macro when the workbook to which it is attached is opened.

RunOnOpen

In this exercise, you create a macro that will run whenever someone opens the workbook to which it is attached.

Open

1 On the Standard toolbar, click the **Open** button.

The **Open** dialog box appears.

2 Double-click **RunOnOpen.xls**. If a warning dialog box appears, click **Enable Macros**.

RunOnOpen.xls opens. Notice that the contents of cells E6, E11, E18, F8, and F17 appear in bold.

3 On the **Tools** menu, point to **Macro** and then click **Record New Macro**.

The **Record Macro** dialog box appears.

4 In the **Macro name** box, type **Auto_Open** and then click **OK**.

The **Record Macro** dialog box disappears, and the Stop Recording toolbar appears.

5 Select the cell range D6:O36, and then, on the **Format** menu, click **Cells**.

The **Format Cells** dialog box appears.

6 If necessary, click the **Font** tab.

7 In the **Font style** box, click **Regular** and then click **OK**.

The **Format Cells** dialog box disappears, and the contents of cells E6, E11, E18, F8, and F17 appear in regular type.

Stop Recording

8 On the Stop Recording toolbar, click the **Stop Recording** button.

Excel stops recording your macro, and the Stop Recording toolbar disappears.

9 On the **Tools** menu, point to **Macro** and then click **Macros**.

The **Macro** dialog box appears.

10 Click **Highlight**, and then click **Run**.

The contents of cells E6, E11, E18, F8, and F17 appear in bold type.

Save

11 On the Standard toolbar, click the **Save** button to save your work.

Close

12 Click the **Close** button to close RunOnOpen.xls.

13 Open the **File** menu, and then click **RunOnOpen.xls**. If a warning dialog box appears, click **Enable Macros**.

RunOnOpen.xls opens, with the contents of cells E6, E11, E18, F8, and F17 appearing in regular type.

14 On the Standard toolbar, click the **Save** button to save your work.

15 Click the **Close** button to close RunOnOpen.xls.

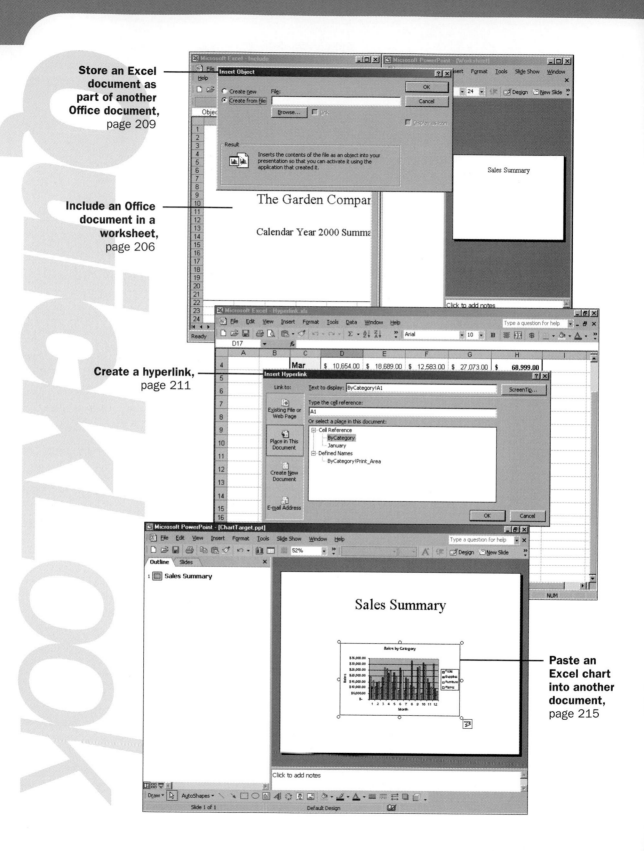

Store an Excel document as part of another Office document, page 209

Include an Office document in a worksheet, page 206

Create a hyperlink, page 211

Paste an Excel chart into another document, page 215

Chapter 13
Working with Other Microsoft Office Programs

After completing this chapter, you will be able to:

✔ Include an Office document in a worksheet.

✔ Store an Excel document as part of another Office document.

✔ Create a hyperlink.

✔ Paste an Excel chart into another document.

By itself, Microsoft Excel is a powerful program that gives you a broad range of tools so you can store, present, and summarize your financial data. Other Microsoft Office XP programs extend your capabilities even further, letting you create databases, presentations, written reports, and custom Web pages through which you can organize and communicate your data in print and over networks.

A tremendous benefit of Excel being part of the Office XP suite is that the programs can interact in many useful ways. For example, you can include a file created with another Office program in an Excel worksheet. If you use Microsoft Word to write a quick note on why tool sales increased significantly in January, you can include the report in your workbook. Similarly, you can include your Excel workbooks in documents created with other Office XP programs. If you want to copy only part of a workbook, such as a chart, to another Office document, you can do that as well.

One of the hallmarks of the World Wide Web is the **hyperlink**, or connection from a document to a place in the same file or to another file anywhere on a network the user's computer can reach. You can create hyperlinks in Excel documents, connecting to other cells or worksheets in the active workbook, to other Office files anywhere on your computer, or to files anywhere else on your company's intranet or the Internet.

In this chapter, you'll learn how to include an Office document in a worksheet, store an Excel workbook as part of another Office document, create hyperlinks, and paste an Excel chart into another document.

This chapter uses the practice files Include, YearEndSummary, Worksheet, SalesBy-Category, Hyperlink, ProductList, PasteChart, and ChartTarget that you installed from this book's CD-ROM. For details about installing the practice files, see "Using the Book's CD-ROM" at the beginning of this book.

Including an Office Document in an Excel Worksheet

A benefit of working with Excel is that, because Excel is part of the Microsoft Office XP program suite, it is possible to combine data from Excel and other Office programs to create informative presentations. Just like combining data from more than one Excel document, combining information from other Office files with an Excel workbook entails either pasting another Office document in an Excel workbook or creating a link between a workbook and the other document.

There are two advantages to creating a link between your Excel workbook and another file. The first benefit is that linking to the other file, as opposed to copying the entire file into your workbook, keeps your Excel workbook small. If the workbook is copied to another drive or computer, you can maintain the link by copying the linked file along with the Excel workbook, re-creating the link if the linked file is on the same network as the Excel workbook. It is also possible to use the workbook without the linked file. The second benefit of linking to another file is that any changes in the file to which you link will be reflected in your Excel workbook.

Tip

Usually, you must close and reopen your Excel workbook for any changes in the linked document to appear in your workbook. The exception to this rule occurs when you open the file for editing from within your Excel workbook (as discussed later in this chapter).

You create a link between an Excel workbook and another Office document by clicking **Object** on the **Insert** menu to display the **Object** dialog box. Once the **Object** dialog box appears, click the **Create from File** tab.

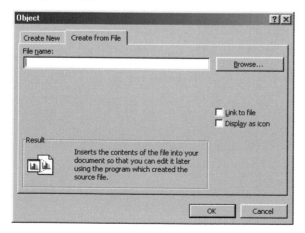

The **Create from File** tab page appears. Clicking the **Browse** button opens the **Browse** dialog box, from which you can navigate to the folder with the file to which you want to link. Once you locate the file, double-clicking it closes the **Browse** dialog box and adds the file's name and path to the **File name** box of the **Object** dialog box. To create a link to the file, select the **Link to file** check box and click **OK**. The file appears in your workbook.

If you want to link a file to your workbook but don't want the file's image to take up much space on the screen, you can select the **Display as icon** check box. After you select the file to embed and click **OK**, the file will be represented by the same icon used to represent it in **My Computer**. Double-clicking the icon opens the linked document in its original application.

Once you have linked a file to your Excel workbook, you can edit the file by right-clicking its image in your workbook and then, from the shortcut menu that appears, pointing to **Presentation Object** and clicking **Edit**. The file will open in its native application (in this case, Microsoft PowerPoint). When you're done editing the file, your changes will be reflected in your workbook.

Troubleshooting

The specific menu item you point to changes to reflect the program used to create the file to which you want to link. For a Word document, for example, the menu item you point to is **Document Object**.

Include
YearEndSummary

In this exercise, you link a PowerPoint presentation showing a yearly business summary to an Excel workbook and then edit the presentation from within Excel.

Important

You must have PowerPoint installed on your computer to complete this exercise.

Open

1 On the Standard toolbar, click the **Open** button.

The **Open** dialog box appears.

2 Navigate to the OtherPrograms folder, and double-click **Include.xls**.

Include.xls opens.

3 On the **Insert** menu, click **Object**.

The **Object** dialog box appears.

4 Click the **Create from File** tab to display the **Create from File** tab page.

5 Click **Browse**.

The **Browse** dialog box appears.

6 Navigate to the OtherPrograms folder, and double-click **YearEnd-Summary.ppt**.

The **Browse** dialog box closes, and the **Object** dialog box reappears.

7 Select the **Link to file** check box, and then click **OK**.

Excel creates a link to the external file, and the file appears in the workbook.

Tip

Adding the link means that changes in the external file will be reflected in the worksheet.

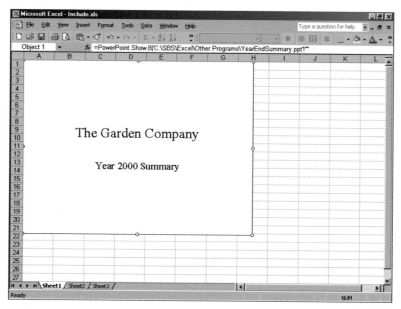

8 Right-click the presentation, and then, from the shortcut menu that appears, point to **Presentation Object** and then click **Edit**.

The presentation opens in a PowerPoint window.

9 Click **Year 2000 Summary**.

The text box containing *Year 2000 Summary* is activated.

10 Click to the left of the text in the box, and type **Calendar**.

Save

11 On the Standard toolbar, click the **Save** button.

PowerPoint saves your changes.

Close

12 Click the **Close** box.

PowerPoint closes, and your change is reflected in Include.xls.

13 On the Standard toolbar, click the **Save** button to save your work.

14 Click the **Close** button to close Include.xls.

Storing an Excel Document
as Part of Another Office Document

In the preceding section of this chapter, you learned how to link to another file from within your Excel workbook. The advantages of linking to another file are that the size of your workbook is kept small and that any changes in the document to which you link will be reflected in your workbook. The disadvantage is that the linked document must be copied along with the workbook, or at least be on a network-accessible computer, to appear in the workbook. If file size isn't an issue and you want to ensure that the other document will always be available, you can **embed** the file in your workbook. Embedding another file in an Excel workbook means that the entirety of the other file is saved as part of your workbook. Wherever your workbook goes, the embedded file goes along with it.

Important

To view the embedded file, you will need to have the program used to create it installed on the computer where you open the workbook.

You can embed a file in an Excel workbook by following the procedure described in the preceding section, with the exception that the **Link to file** check box should remain deselected.

It is also possible to embed your Excel workbooks in other Office documents. In PowerPoint, for example, you can embed an Excel file in a presentation by clicking **Object** on the **Insert** menu to display the **Insert Object** dialog box. When the **Insert Object** dialog box appears, select the **Create from file** option button.

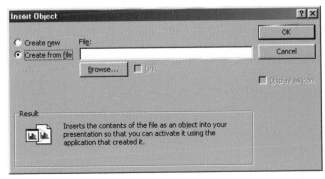

To identify the file you want to embed, click the **Browse** button and then, in the **Browse** dialog box that appears, navigate to the folder where the file is stored and double-click it. The **Browse** dialog box disappears, and the file appears in the **File name** box. Click **OK** to embed your workbook in the presentation.

If you want to embed a workbook in a file created with another program but don't want the worksheet to take up much space on the screen, you can select the **Display as icon** check box. After you select the file to embed and click **OK**, the file will be represented by the same icon used to represent it in **My Computer**. Double-clicking the icon opens the embedded document in its original application.

To edit the embedded Excel workbook, right-click the workbook (or the icon representing it) and then, from the shortcut menu that appears, point to **Worksheet Object** and click **Edit**. The workbook opens for editing. When you are done making your changes, you can click anywhere outside the workbook to return to the presentation.

Worksheet
SalesByCategory

In this exercise, you embed an Excel workbook containing sales data in a Power-Point presentation and then change the formatting of the workbook from within PowerPoint.

Important

You must have PowerPoint installed on your computer to complete this exercise.

1 Double-click **My Computer**, and navigate to the C:\SBS\Excel\Other-Programs directory.

The contents of the C:\SBS\Excel\OtherPrograms directory appear.

2 Double-click **Worksheet.ppt**.

Worksheet.ppt opens.

3 On the **Insert** menu, click **Object**.

The **Insert Object** dialog box appears.

4 Select the **Create from file** option button.

The **Insert Object** dialog box changes to reflect your choice.

5 Click the **Browse** button.

The **Browse** dialog box appears.

6 Navigate to the C:\SBS\Excel\OtherPrograms directory, and then double-click **SalesByCategory.xls**.

The **Browse** dialog box closes, and C:\SBS\Excel\OtherPrograms\SalesBy-Category.xls appears in the **File** box.

7 Click **OK**.

The worksheet that was active when SalesByCategory.xls was last closed appears in the presentation.

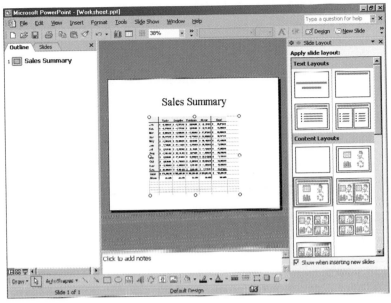

8 Right-click the worksheet, and then, from the shortcut menu that appears, point to **Worksheet Object** and then click **Edit**.

The workbook opens for editing.

9 Select cells D15:H15, and then, on the Formatting toolbar, click the **Bold** button.

The contents of cells D15:H15 appear without bold formatting.

10 Click any blank spot on the presentation to deactivate the included workbook.

11 On the Standard toolbar, click the **Save** button to save your work.

Close

12 Click the **Close** button to close Worksheet.ppt.

Creating a Hyperlink

Ex2002-7-2

Approved Courseware

One of the hallmarks of the World Wide Web is that documents published on the Web can have references, or hyperlinks, to points in the same document or to other Web documents. A hyperlink functions much like a link between two cells or between two files, but hyperlinks can reach any computer on the Web, not just those on a corporate network. Unfollowed hyperlinks usually appear as underlined blue text, and followed hyperlinks appear as underlined purple text, but those settings can be changed by Web users.

Nov	$ 18,208.00	$ 14,408.00	$
Dec	$ 30,805.00	$ 10,031.00	$
Total	$ 170,150.00	$ 253,402.00	$ 1(
Share	22.32%	33.24%	
	Followed	Unfollowed	

To create a hyperlink, right-click the cell in which you want to insert the hyperlink and then, from the shortcut menu that appears, click **Hyperlink**. The **Insert Hyperlink** dialog box appears.

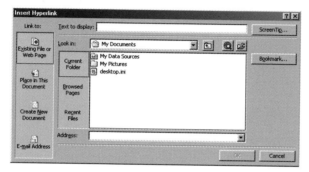

Tip

You can also open the **Insert Hyperlink** dialog box by pressing Ctrl + K.

You can choose one of four types of targets for your hyperlink: an existing file or Web page, a place in the current document, a new document you create on the spot, or an e-mail address.

Tip

The default target for the **Insert Hyperlink** dialog box is an existing file or Web page.

To create a hyperlink to another file or Web page, you can use the **Look in** box's navigation tool to locate the file. If you recently opened the file or Web page to which you want to link, you can click either the **Browsed Pages** or the **Recent Files** button to display the Web pages or files in your History list.

If you want to create a hyperlink to another place in the current Excel workbook, you click the **Place in This Document** button to display a list of available targets in the current workbook.

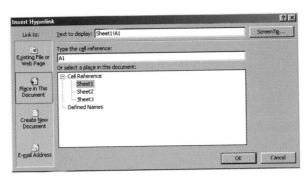

To select the worksheet to which you want to refer, you click the worksheet name in the **Or select a place in this document** box. When you do, a 3-D reference with the name of the worksheet and cell A1 on that worksheet appears in the **Text to display** box.

If you want to refer to a specific cell on a worksheet, click the worksheet's name in the **Or select a place in this document** box, and then change the cell reference in the **Type the cell reference** box.

You can also create hyperlinks that generate e-mail messages to an address of your choice. To create this type of hyperlink, which is called a **mailto** hyperlink, click the **E-mail Address** button.

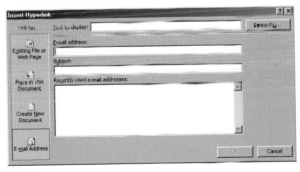

In the dialog box that appears, you can type the recipient's e-mail address in the **E-mail address** box and the subject line for messages sent via this hyperlink in the **Subject** box.

Tip

If you use Outlook or Outlook Express as your e-mail program, a list of recently used addresses will appear in the **Recently used e-mail addresses** box. You can insert any of those addresses in the **E-mail address** box by clicking the address.

When a user clicks the hyperlink you create, their default e-mail program will be launched and will create a message with the recipient's address set to the address in the **E-mail address** box and the subject you typed in the **Subject** box.

Regardless of the type of hyperlink you create, you can specify the text you want to represent the hyperlink in your worksheet. You type that text in the **Text to display** box. When you click **OK**, the text you type there will appear in your worksheet, formatted as a hyperlink.

Tip

If you leave the **Text to display** box empty, the actual link will appear in your worksheet.

You can edit an existing hyperlink by clicking the cell containing the hyperlink and then, from the shortcut menu that appears, clicking **Edit Hyperlink**. You can also click **Open Hyperlink** to go to the target document or create a new e-mail message, or click **Remove Hyperlink** to delete the hyperlink.

Tip

If you delete a hyperlink from a cell, the text in the **Text to display** box remains in the cell.

Hyperlink
ProductList

In this exercise, you create a hyperlink to a place in the same workbook and then a second hyperlink to another document.

Open

1   On the Standard toolbar, click the **Open** button.

The **Open** dialog box appears.

2   Double-click **Hyperlink.xls**.

Hyperlink.xls opens.

3   Right-click cell D17, and then, from the shortcut menu that appears, click **Hyperlink**.

The **Insert Hyperlink** dialog box appears.

4   If necessary, click the **Existing File or Web Page** button.

5   Navigate to the C:\SBS\Excel\OtherPrograms folder.

6   Click **ProductList.xls**.

7   In the **Text to display** box, type **Product List** and then click **OK**.

A hyperlink with the text *Product List* appears in cell D17.

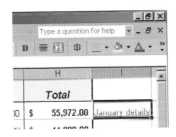

Oct	$ 5,689.00	$ 31,763.00	$ 1:
Nov	$ 18,208.00	$ 14,408.00	$ 4
Dec	$ 30,805.00	$ 10,031.00	$ 3
Total	$ 170,150.00	$ 253,402.00	$ 105
Share	22.32%	33.24%	

Product List

8 Right-click cell I2, and then, from the shortcut menu that appears, click **Hyperlink**.

The **Insert Hyperlink** dialog box appears.

9 Click the **Place in This Document** button.

The **Insert Hyperlink** dialog box changes to reflect your choice.

10 In the **Or select a place in this document** box, click **January**.

11 In the **Text to display box**, type **January details** and then click **OK**.

A hyperlink with the text *January details* appears in cell I2.

	H	I
	Total	
)0	$ 55,972.00	January details

12 In cell I2, click the hyperlink.

The January worksheet in Hyperlink.xls appears.

13 On the Standard toolbar, click the **Save** button to save your work.

Close

14 Click the **Close** button to close Hyperlink.xls.

Pasting a Chart into Another Document

A final way to include objects from one workbook in another workbook is to copy the object you want to share and then paste it into its new location. One object type for which this ability is particularly handy is chart images. You could copy the worksheet with the data used for a chart and then re-create the chart in its new location, but if you just want to copy the image of the chart in its current form to another document, simply right-click the chart image, click **Copy** from the shortcut menu that appears, and then paste the image into the other document.

PasteChart
ChartTarget.ppt

In this exercise, you copy a chart image containing sales information to the Clipboard and paste the image into a PowerPoint presentation.

1 On the Standard toolbar, click the **Open** button.

The **Open** dialog box appears.

2 Double-click **PasteChart.xls**.

PasteChart.xls opens.

3 Right-click a blank spot on the chart, and then, from the shortcut menu that appears, click **Copy** to copy the chart image to the Clipboard.

4 On the Windows desktop, double-click **My Computer**, navigate to the C:\SBS\Excel\OtherPrograms directory, and then double-click **Chart-Target.ppt**.

ChartTarget.ppt opens in PowerPoint.

5 Right-click a blank spot on the active slide, and from the shortcut menu that appears, click **Paste**.

The chart appears on the slide.

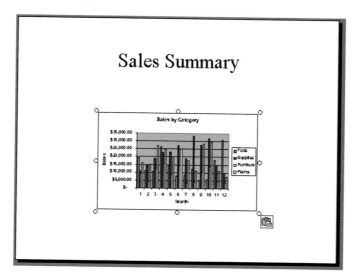

6 On the Standard toolbar, click the **Save** button to save the presentation.

Close

7 Click the **Close** button to close ChartTarget.ppt.

ChartTarget.ppt closes.

8   In PasteChart.xls, on the Standard toolbar, click the **Save** button to save any changes.

9   Click the **Close** button to close PasteChart.xls.

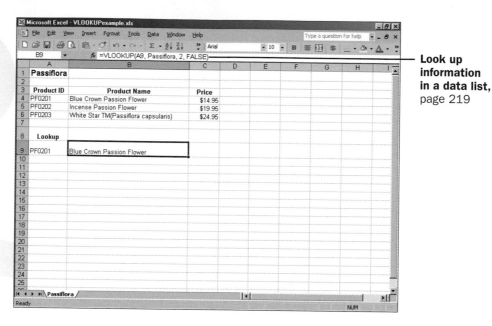

Look up
information
in a data list,
page 219

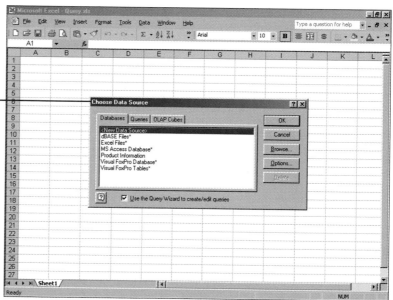

Retrieve data
from a database,
page 223

Chapter 14
Working with Database Data

After completing this chapter, you will be able to:

✔ **Look up information in a data list.**

✔ **Retrieve data from a database.**

All of the programs in the Microsoft Office XP suite work well together, but two programs that have a particularly strong synergy are Microsoft Excel and Microsoft Access. Access, which lets you create and manage databases, and Excel both work with lists of data. In Excel, that data is often stored in complex lists such as Pivot-Tables, but the data used to create PivotTables and other data lists can be represented as a series of rows in a worksheet.

Excel does have a capability you might expect to find only in a database program—the ability to have a user type a value in a cell and have Excel look in a named range to find a corresponding value. For instance, you can have a two-column named range with one column displaying the ISBN of a book and the second column displaying the title of the same book. By using a VLOOKUP formula that references the named range, you can let colleagues using your workbook type an ISBN in a cell and have the name of the book with that ISBN appear in the cell with the formula.

If you have data in a database that you'd like to bring into Excel, you can create a **query**, or statement that locates database records that meet specific criteria, to locate the desired data.

In this chapter, you'll learn how to look up information in a data list and retrieve data from a database.

 This chapter uses the practice files Lookup and Query that you installed from this book's CD-ROM. For details about installing the practice files, see "Using the Book's CD-ROM" at the beginning of this book.

Looking Up Information in a Data List

Ex2002e-4-2

Approved Courseware

Whenever you create a worksheet that holds information about a list of distinct items, such as products offered for sale by a company, you should ensure that at least one column in the list contains a unique value that distinguishes that row (and the item the row represents) from every other row in the list. Assigning each row a column with a unique value means that you can associate data in one worksheet with data in another worksheet. For example, if every customer is assigned a unique identification number, you can store a customer's contact information in one worksheet and all of that customer's orders in another worksheet, and be able to associate the customer's orders and contact information without writing the contact information in a worksheet every time the customer places an order.

In the case of products sold by The Garden Company, the column with those unique values, or **primary key** column, is the Product ID column.

If you know a product's Product ID, it's no trouble to look through a list of twenty or thirty products to find the product represented by a particular ID. If, however, you have a list of several hundred products, looking through the list to find a product would take quite a bit of time. Instead, you can use the VLOOKUP function to let your colleagues type a Product ID in a cell and have the corresponding product information appear in another cell.

The VLOOKUP function finds a value in the leftmost column of a named range and then returns the value from the specified cell to the right of the cell with the found value. A properly formed VLOOKUP function has four arguments (data that is passed to the function), as shown in the following definition: =*VLOOKUP(lookup_value, table_array, col_index_num, range_lookup)*. The following table summarizes the values Excel expects for each of these arguments.

Argument	Expected value
lookup_value	The value to be found in the first column of the named range specified by the table_array argument. The lookup_value argument can be a value, a cell reference, or a text string.
table_array	The multicolumn named range to be searched.
col_index_num	The column in the named range with the value to be returned.
range_lookup	A TRUE or FALSE value, indicating whether the function should find an approximate match (TRUE) or an exact match (FALSE) for the lookup_value. If left blank, the default value for this argument is TRUE.

Important

When range_lookup is left blank or set to TRUE, for VLOOKUP to work properly the rows in the named range specified in the table_array argument must be sorted in ascending order based on the values in the leftmost column of the named range.

The VLOOKUP function works a bit differently depending on whether the range_lookup argument is set to TRUE or FALSE. The following list summarizes how the function works based on the value of range_lookup.

- If the range_lookup argument is left blank or set to TRUE and VLOOKUP doesn't find an exact match for lookup_value, the function returns the largest value that is less than or equal to lookup_value.
- If the range_lookup argument is left blank or set to TRUE and lookup_value is smaller than the smallest value in the named range, an #N/A error is returned.
- If the range_lookup argument is left blank or set to TRUE and lookup_value is larger than all values in the named range, the largest value in the named range is returned.
- If the range_lookup argument is set to FALSE and VLOOKUP doesn't find an exact match for lookup_value, the function returns an #N/A error.

As an example of a VLOOKUP function, consider the following worksheet and the accompanying VLOOKUP formula.

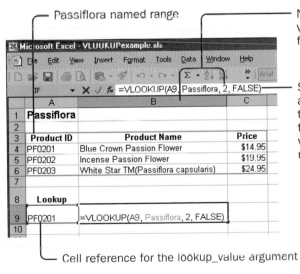

Passiflora named range

Named range column with value to be returned by the function

Setting the range_lookup argument to FALSE requires the VLOOKUP function to find an exact match to the value entered in cell A9 or return an #N/A error.

Cell reference for the lookup_value argument

When you type *PF0202* in cell A9 and press [Enter], the VLOOKUP function searches the first column of the Passiflora named range, finds an exact match, and returns the value *Incense Passion Flower*.

Tip

A related function is HLOOKUP, which finds a value in the first row of a table and returns the specified value in the same column. For more information on using the HLOOKUP function, type **HLOOKUP** in the Ask A Question box.

Lookup

Open

In this exercise, you create a VLOOKUP function to return the names of products with Product IDs typed in a specific cell.

1   On the Standard toolbar, click the **Open** button.

The **Open** dialog box appears.

2   Navigate to the Database folder, and double-click **Lookup.xls**.

Lookup.xls opens.

3   Select the cell range A4:C18.

4   Click in the Name box, type **ToolList**, and then press [Enter].

Excel creates a range, named *ToolList*, that is made up of cells A4:C18.

5   In cell E6, type **=VLOOKUP(E4, ToolList, 2, FALSE)** and press [Enter].

Excel adds the VLOOKUP function to your worksheet. Because there is no value in cell E4, the *#N/A* error code appears in cell E6.

6   In cell E4, type **TL0038** and press [Enter].

Nutcracker appears in cell E6.

7   In cell E4, type **TL3001**.

Pruners, Left-handed appears in cell E6.

	A	B	C	D	E
1	Tools				
2					
3	Product ID	Product Name	Price		Lookup
4	TL2248	Garden Hose (50')	$28.00		TL3001
5	TL2697	Gardener's Rake	$18.95		
6	TL2539	Grafting Knife	$18.95		Pruners, Left-handed
7	TL2538	Grafting/Splicing Tool	$57.95		
8	TL1182	Holster	$10.00		
9	TL0802	Long-handled Loppers	$64.95		
10	TL0038	Nutcracker	$18.00		
11	TL1549	Overhead Loppers	$69.95		
12	TL3001	Pruners, Left-handed	$54.00		
13	TL3002	Pruners, Right-handed	$54.00		

8 On the Standard toolbar, click the **Save** button to save your work.

Close **9** Click the **Close** button to close Lookup.xls.

Retrieving Data from a Database

Ex2002e-1-1
Ex2002e-7-5

Approved Courseware

Just as you can save an Excel workbook as a tab-delimited text file and then open it in other spreadsheet programs, you can also save data lists, or **tables**, that you've created in other database and spreadsheet programs and then import those tables into an Excel worksheet. Excel lets you go one step further, however. In Excel, you can reach directly into an Access, dBASE, Microsoft FoxPro, or Microsoft Visual FoxPro database and retrieve data from that database's tables.

There are three steps to bringing data from a database into Excel: defining a data source, building a query to create a link to that data source, and, if desired, creating a filter to limit the rows that appear in your Excel worksheet.

To define a data source, on the **Data** menu, point to **Import External Data** and then click **New Database Query**. In the **Choose Data Source** dialog box that appears, you click the **<New Data Source>** item and then click **OK** to move to the **Create New Data Source** dialog box. You use the first two controls in the **Create New Data Source** dialog box to name the data source and then pick the **driver** (a program that controls access to a file or device) Excel should use to connect with and open the target database.

Once you have identified the type of database you want to connect with, you click the **Connect** button to open the dialog box from which you select the target database.

Tip

The name of the dialog box that appears after you click the **Connect** button depends on the database driver you chose earlier.

When you choose Access as the database type to which you want to connect, the **ODBC Microsoft Access Setup** dialog box appears. **ODBC**, which is short for **Open DataBase Connectivity**, is a protocol that facilitates data transfer among databases and related programs (such as spreadsheet programs). Clicking the **Select** button opens a navigation dialog box you can use to pick the database from which you want to import table data. Once you have chosen the target database, you can close the navigation dialog box and click **OK** in the **ODBC Microsoft Access Setup** dialog box to return to the **Create New Data Source** dialog box, where the database's path appears. You can then pick the default table to use in the selected database. Clicking **OK** creates the source, which now appears in the **Databases** tab of the **Choose Data Source** dialog box.

Add

>

To create a query to pull information from a data source, click the source and then click **OK** to launch the **Query Wizard**. In the **Choose Columns** page of the **Query Wizard**, you can add a column to the data brought into Excel by clicking the column name and then clicking the **Add** button. The column name appears in the **Columns in your query** box.

Remove

<

You can remove a specific column by clicking the column name in the **Columns in your query** box and then clicking the **Remove** button, or you can reset your selection completely by clicking the **Remove All** button. When you've selected the columns you want included in your query, click **Next** to move to the **Filter Data** wizard page.

Remove All

<<

If you want to import the entire table to which you have linked, just click **Next** to move to the next wizard page. If you want to limit the data returned by the query, especially if the table has hundreds of records or more, you can filter the table based on the contents of one or more columns. To filter the query results, click the first column by which you want to filter, click the down arrow in the first box and click the comparison operator (for example, **is less than or equal to**) for the filter, and then, in the second box, type the value to be used in the comparison. If you select the **Price** column, select **is less than or equal to** in the first box, and then type *50* in the second box, your query will return only products that cost less than $50.00.

Tip

You can filter based on more than one criterion. After you've created the first filter, the second field box will become active.

When you're done setting your criteria, click **Next** to move to the **Sort Order** page. On this page, you can specify a sort order to determine the order in which the table rows are imported into your worksheet. To set the criteria, click the **Sort by** down arrow, click the column by which you want to sort the imported rows, and then select the **Ascending** or **Descending** option button to determine the order in which the rows should be arranged. You can sort the imported rows by the contents of more than one column by entering additional criteria in the **Then by** boxes.

When you're done, click **Next** to move to the **Finish** page of the **Query Wizard**, where you can save your query so that you don't have to re-create it every time you want to run it. Product prices change, for instance, so if The Garden Company published a monthly flyer featuring all products that cost less than $30, an employee could save the query that locates those items in the Products database and rerun it every month. To save your query, click the **Save Query** button and then, in the dialog box that appears, type the name of the query in the **File name** box and click **Save**.

To run an existing query, on the **Data** menu, point to **Import External Data** and then click **New Database Query** to open the **Choose Data Source** dialog box. Clicking the **Queries** tab will display all saved queries. To run a saved query, click its name and then click **Open**.

In this exercise, you define a table in an Access database as a data source and then create a query to import data from that source into Excel.

Query
Products.mdb

Open

1   On the Standard toolbar, click the **Open** button.

The **Open** dialog box appears.

2   Double-click **Query.xls**.

Query.xls opens.

3   On the **Data** menu, point to **Import External Data** and then click **New Database Query**.

Microsoft Query launches, and the **Choose Data Source** dialog box appears.

4   If necessary, click the **Databases** tab.

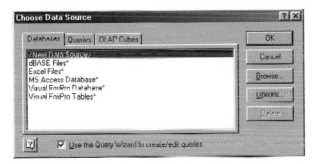

5   Click **<New Data Source>**, and then click **OK**.

The **Create New Data Source** dialog box appears.

6   In the first box, type **Product Information** as the name of the source.

The second box becomes active.

7   In the second box, click the down arrow and then, from the list that appears, click **Microsoft Access Driver (*.mdb)**.

The **Connect** button becomes active.

8   Click **Connect**.

The **ODBC Microsoft Access Setup** dialog box appears.

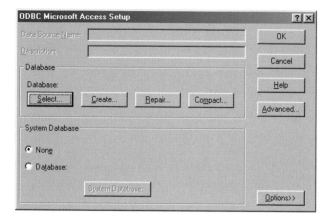

9 Click **Select**.

The **Select Database** dialog box appears.

10 Navigate to the C:\SBS\Excel\Database folder, click **Products.mdb**, and then click **OK**.

The **Select Database** dialog box disappears, and *C:\SBS\Excel\Database \Products.mdb* appears in the **ODBC Microsoft Access Setup** dialog box.

11 Click **OK**.

The **ODBC Microsoft Access Setup** dialog box disappears, and the **Create New Data Source** dialog box reappears.

12 In the fourth box, click the down arrow and then, from the list that appears, click **Products**.

Excel assigns **Products** as the default table for this data source.

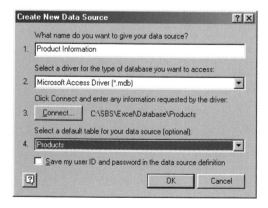

13 Click **OK**.

Product Information is listed as a new data source in the **Choose Data Source** dialog box.

14 Click **Product Information**, and then click **OK**.

The **Query Wizard** appears; the columns in the Products table appear in the **Available tables and columns** box.

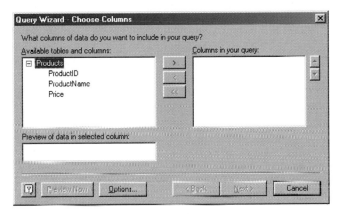

15 Click the **ProductID** column name, and then click the **Add** button.

ProductID appears in the **Columns in your query** box.

16 Click the **ProductName** column name, and then click the **Add** button.

ProductName appears in the **Columns in your query** box.

17 Click the **Price** column name, and then click the **Add** button.

Price appears in the **Columns in your query** box.

18 Click **Next**.

The **Filter Data** page of the **Query Wizard** appears.

19 In the **Column to filter** list, click **Price**.

In the **Only include rows where** section, the first comparison operator box becomes active.

20 In the first comparison operator box, click the down arrow and then, from the list that appears, click **is greater than or equal to**.

The words *is greater than or equal to* appear in the comparison operator box, and the first value box becomes active.

21 In the first value box, type **50** and then click **Next**.

Tip

This filter limits the data brought into the workbook to products that cost $50 or more.

The **Sort Order** page of the **Query Wizard** appears.

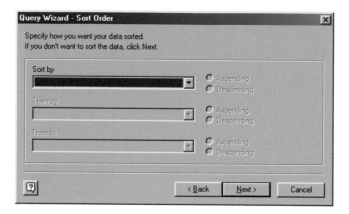

22 In the **Sort by** box, click the down arrow and then, from the list that appears, click **ProductID**.

ProductID appears in the **Sort by** box, and the **Ascending** and **Descending** option buttons become active, with the **Ascending** option button selected. The **Then by** box also becomes active.

23 Click **Next**.

The **Finish** page of the **Query Wizard** appears, with the **Return Data to Microsoft Excel** option button selected.

24 Click **Save Query**.

The **Save As** dialog box appears.

25 In the **File name** box, type **Products50AndOver** and then click **Save**.

Excel saves your query, and the **Save As** dialog box disappears.

26 Click **Finish**.

The **Query Wizard** disappears, and Query.xls reappears with the **Import Data** dialog box open.

27 In the **Import Data** dialog box, click **OK**.

Tip

Clicking **OK** accepts the active workbook cell as the upper left corner cell for the range to hold the query results.

The query results appear in the workbook.

	A	B	C
	ProductID	**ProductName**	**Price**
1	ProductID	ProductName	Price
2	FN0801	Bench (4')	52.95
3	FN0802	Bench w/ 2 large pots	149.95
4	FN0803	Potting Bench/Barbeque Cart	149.95
5	FN1402	Bamboo Night Table	95
6	FN1999	Comfy Chair	119.95
7	FN2002	Cedar Planter Box	59.95
8	FN2004	Picnic Table w/ flip benches	349.95
9	FN3402	Northeastern Arbor	199.95
10	GP0902	Bamboo fencing 8' long x 6' tall	54
11	SP1483	English Fruit Cage	149.95
12	TL0802	Long-handled Loppers	64.95
13	TL1549	Overhead Loppers	69.95
14	TL2538	Grafting/Splicing Tool	67.95
15	TL3001	"Pruners, Left-handed"	54
16	TL3002	"Pruners, Right-handed"	54
17			

28   On the Standard toolbar, click the **Save** button to save your work.

Close

29   Click the **Close** button to close Query.xls.

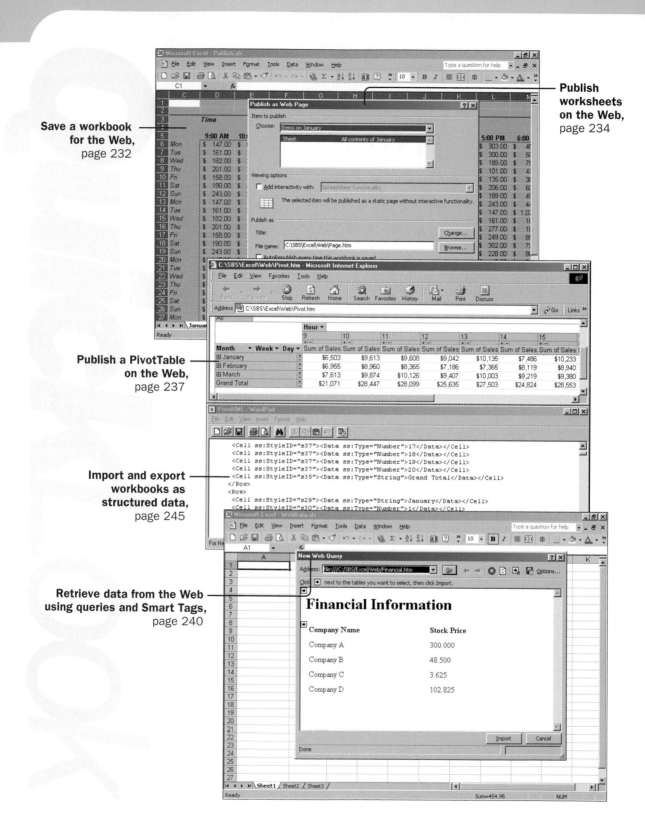

Save a workbook
for the Web,
page 232

Publish
worksheets
on the Web,
page 234

Publish a PivotTable
on the Web,
page 237

Import and export
workbooks as
structured data,
page 245

Retrieve data from the Web
using queries and Smart Tags,
page 240

Chapter 15
Publishing Information on the Web

After completing this chapter, you will be able to:

✔ Save a workbook for the Web.

✔ Publish worksheets on the Web.

✔ Publish a PivotTable on the Web.

✔ Retrieve data from the Web using queries and Smart Tags.

✔ Import and export workbooks as structured data.

One of the hallmarks of Microsoft Excel has been that it lets you save your Excel workbooks and worksheets as files that can be accessed and interacted with via the World Wide Web. Previous versions of Excel also let you bring data from the Web into your workbooks by creating queries.

Excel 2002 extends those capabilities, adding entirely new functions and making existing capabilities easier to use. For example, previous versions of Excel created copies of workbooks or worksheets that had been saved for the Web and that were not connected to the original file, meaning that any updates in the original file would not be reflected in the file published on the Web. In Excel 2002, you can create stand-alone files or create a linked file that is updated whenever the original file is saved.

A new technology that makes its debut in Excel 2002 is **Extensible Markup Language (XML)**. XML is a content markup language, meaning that an XML file has information about the data contained within it (as compared with Hypertext Markup Language, which tells a Web browser how to display a file's contents). Saving Excel workbooks as XML files means that your Excel data will be readable by a wide range of programs, not just those programs listed in the **Save As** dialog box's **Save as type** drop-down list. One application of XML is **Smart Tags**, a technology that recognizes certain types of information, such as stock symbols, and looks up related information on the Web.

In this chapter, you'll learn how to save a workbook for posting on the Web, publish worksheets and PivotTables on the Web, retrieve data from the Web, and move data from one application to another.

This chapter uses the practice files Saving, Publish, Pivot, WebData, Smart, Structured, and PivotXML that you installed from this book's CD-ROM. For details about installing the practice files, see "Using the Book's CD-ROM" at the beginning of this book.

Saving a Workbook for the Web

Ex2002-7-1
Ex2002e-1-3

Approved Courseware

One of the strengths of Excel 2002 is that you can save Excel workbooks as Web documents, allowing you and your colleagues to view workbooks over the Internet or a corporate intranet. For a document to be viewed via the World Wide Web, the document must be saved as a **Hypertext Markup Language (HTML)** file. HTML files, which end with either the .htm or the .html extension, include **tags** that tell a Web **browser** such as Microsoft Internet Explorer how to display the contents of the file.

For example, you might want to set the data labels in a workbook apart from the rest of the data by having the labels displayed with bold text. The HTML tag pair that indicates text to be displayed as bold text is *<B>...</B>*, where the ellipsis points between the tags are replaced by the text to be displayed. So the HTML fragment

```
<B>Excel</B>
```

would be displayed as **Excel**.

You can create HTML files with Microsoft FrontPage, but you can create a file in Excel and then click **Save as Web Page** on the **File** menu to open the **Save As** dialog box.

To save a workbook as an HTML file, verify that the **Entire Workbook** option button is selected, type a name for the file in the **File name** box, and then click **Save** to have Excel create an HTML document for each page in the workbook.

Once you have saved an Excel workbook as a series of HTML documents, you can open it in Internet Explorer 4.01 or later. To open the Excel file, start Internet Explorer, open the **File** menu, and then click **Open** to display the **Open** dialog box. In the **Open** dialog box, clicking the **Browse** button opens the **Microsoft Internet Explorer** dialog box. Use the controls in that box to identify the file you want to open.

Tip

Excel represents the HTML files as a single Microsoft HTML 5 file in the **Microsoft Internet Explorer** dialog box.

When you double-click the file to open, the **Microsoft Internet Explorer** dialog box disappears and the file's name and path appear in the **Open** box. To display the Excel workbook, click **OK**, and the workbook appears in Internet Explorer. You can move between pages in the workbook by clicking the HTML representation of the sheet tabs in the lower left corner of the workbook.

Tip

When you move the mouse pointer over a sheet tab, the address of the HTML page representing that worksheet appears on the status bar.

Saving

In this exercise, you save an Excel workbook as a series of HTML files and then view the files in Internet Explorer.

Open

1 On the Standard toolbar, click the **Open** button.

The **Open** dialog box appears.

2 Navigate to the Web directory, and double-click **Saving.xls**.

Saving.xls opens.

3 On the **File** menu, click **Save as Web Page**.

The **Save As** dialog box appears.

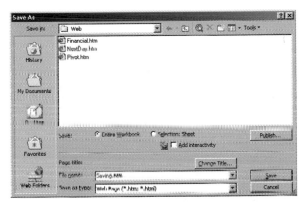

4 If necessary, in the **Save** section, select the **Entire Workbook** option button.

5 Verify that Saving.htm appears in the **File name** box, and then click **Save**.

Excel saves the workbook as a set of HTML documents.

Close

6 Click the **Close** button to close Saving.htm.

7 Start Internet Explorer.

8 In Internet Explorer, on the **File** menu, click **Open**.

The **Open** dialog box appears.

9 Click **Browse**.

The **Browse** dialog box appears.

10 Navigate to the C:\SBS\Excel\Web folder, and then double-click **Saving.htm**.

The **Browse** dialog box disappears, and *C:\SBS\Excel\Web\Saving.htm* appears in the **Open** box.

11 Click **OK**.

Saving.htm appears in Internet Explorer.

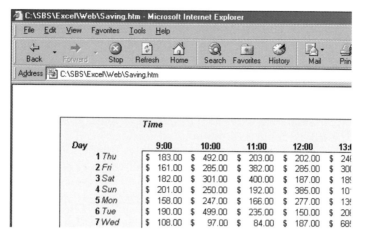

12 Click the **March** sheet tab.

The March worksheet appears.

13 Click the **Close** button to close Internet Explorer.

Publishing Worksheets on the Web

Ex2002e-1-3

Approved Courseware

In addition to the ability to save an Excel workbook as an HTML file, you also have the option of choosing to save individual worksheets as HTML documents. To save a single worksheet as an HTML document, on the **File** menu, click **Save as Web Page** to open the **Save As** dialog box.

Selecting the **Selection: Sheet** option button tells Excel to save the active worksheet as an HTML document. You can also change the title that appears on the title bar of the file when it is opened in a Web browser, allow viewers to interact with the file after it is published on the Web, and have Excel update the Web file whenever the file on which it is based is updated.

Ex2002-2-1

Approved Courseware

If you like, you can store any HTML files in a separate folder. To create a folder in Excel, on the **File** menu, click **Open**. In the **Open** dialog box, click the **Create New Folder** button to create a new folder within the current folder. You can rename the new folder by right-clicking its icon, choosing **Rename** from the shortcut menu that appears, and then typing the folder's new name.

When you open an HTML document in a Web browser, a title appears on the document's title bar. You can set the document's title with an HTML tag; if you don't, the file's name appears on the title bar. In Excel, you can set a title for a workbook or worksheet you save to the Web by clicking the **Publish** button to display the **Publish as Web Page** dialog box. Clicking the **Change** button in the **Publish as** section of the dialog box opens another dialog box, in which you can type a title for the Excel document.

There are several other options you can set in the **Publish as Web Page** dialog box. For example, you can let colleagues interact with a workbook or worksheet you save as an HTML document. To allow interaction, select the **Add interactivity with** check box, select **Spreadsheet functionality** from the adjoining drop-down list, verify that the **Open published web page in browser** check box is selected, and then click **Publish**.

Commands and Options

You and your colleagues can now interact with the worksheet by editing cell values, sorting, filtering, or calculating values with formulas. It's also possible to change cell formatting; to get access to the formatting tools when you view an Excel worksheet via the Web, click the **Commands and Options** button to display the **Commands and Options** dialog box.

AutoRepublish
new for
OfficeXP

AutoRepublish, a new feature in Excel 2002, tells Excel to retain a link to the Web file you create and to update the Web version of that file whenever the original document is saved. You turn on AutoRepublish by opening the **Publish as Web Page** dialog box and selecting the **AutoRepublish every time this workbook is saved** check box.

Publish

In this exercise, you publish a worksheet to the Web, set a title for the worksheet, make the worksheet interactive, change the format of worksheet elements in a Web browser, and turn on AutoRepublish so that any changes in the original document will be reflected in the Web document created from it.

Open

1 On the Standard toolbar, click the **Open** button.

The **Open** dialog box appears.

2 Double-click **Publish.xls**.

Publish.xls opens.

3 If necessary, on the tab bar, click the **January** sheet tab to display the January worksheet.

4 On the **File** menu, click **Save as Web Page**.

The **Save As** dialog box appears.

5 In the **Save** section of the dialog box, select the **Selection: Sheet** option button to publish the active worksheet on the Web.

6 In the **Save** section of the dialog box, select the **Add interactivity** check box and then click **Publish**.

The **Publish as Web Page** dialog box appears.

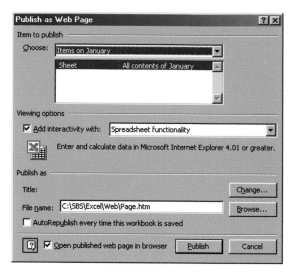

7 In the **Publish as** section of the dialog box, click the **Change** button.

The **Set Title** dialog box appears.

8 In the **Title** box, type **January Sales Data** and then click **OK**.

The **Set Title** dialog box disappears, and *January Sales Data* appears as the title of the Web page.

9 Select the **AutoRepublish every time this workbook is saved** check box.

10 Select the **Open published web page in browser** check box, and then click **Publish**.

The workbook appears in Internet Explorer.

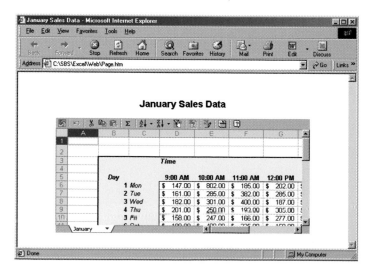

11 Click cell B5, and then, on the Interactivity toolbar, click the **Commands and Options** button.

The **Commands and Options** dialog box appears.

12 If necessary, click the **Format** tab.

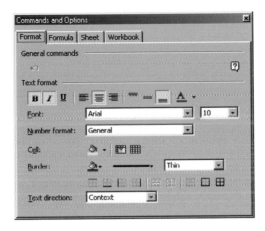

Align Left

13 In the **Text format** section of the dialog box, click the **Align Left** button.

The contents of cell B5 are aligned with the left edge of the cell.

14 In the **Commands and Options** dialog box, click the **Close** box.

The **Commands and Options** dialog box closes.

Close

15 In Internet Explorer, click the **Close** button to close the program.

Publishing a PivotTable on the Web

When you publish an Excel workbook on the Web, you can allow users to interact with the worksheets. The preceding section of this chapter described how to let you and your colleagues interact with an Excel document over the Web. This section continues that theme by demonstrating how to export a PivotTable to the Web. If Catherine Turner, The Garden Company's owner, were on vacation but wanted to participate in a meeting, she could still use her laptop to connect to the company's Web site and use a PivotTable saved there to view any relevant PivotTables.

Once you have created a PivotTable, you can publish it on the Web by clicking any cell in the PivotTable and clicking **Save as Web Page** on the **File** menu to open the **Save As** dialog box. To publish just the worksheet with the PivotTable, select the **Selection: Sheet** option button, select the **Add interactivity** check box, and then click **Publish** to open the **Publish as Web Page** dialog box.

The **Publish as Web Page** dialog box shows the name of the worksheet containing the PivotTable in the **Choose** box, with the items on that worksheet in the lower pane of the box. In the lower pane of the **Choose** box, click the entry beginning with *PivotTable*. The contents of the **Add interactivity with** box in the **Viewing options** section of the dialog box will change to reflect that you are publishing a PivotTable.

Important

If you publish an entire worksheet, rather than just the PivotTable, viewers will not be able to interact with the PivotTable.

To finish publishing the PivotTable on the Web, select the **Open published web page in browser** check box and then click **Publish** to save the PivotTable as a Web document and to show the PivotTable in Internet Explorer.

Show Details

You and your colleagues can now interact with the PivotTable by reorganizing and filtering the PivotTable's contents with Internet Explorer 4.01 or later. To expand the PivotTable so that it shows every cell, and not just the totals and grand totals, click the **Show Details** button.

Pivot

In this exercise, you publish a PivotTable on the Web and then filter the PivotTable's contents using Internet Explorer.

Open

1   On the Standard toolbar, click the **Open** button.

The **Open** dialog box appears.

2   Double-click **Pivot.xls**.

Pivot.xls opens.

3   If necessary, on the tab bar, click the **Pivot** sheet tab and then click any cell in the PivotTable.

4   On the **File** menu, click **Save as Web Page**.

The **Save As** dialog box appears.

5   In the **Save** section of the dialog box, select the **Selection: Sheet** option button.

6   In the **Save** section of the dialog box, select the **Add interactivity** check box and then click **Publish**.

The **Publish as Web Page** dialog box appears.

7   If necessary, click the **Choose** down arrow and then, from the list that appears, click **Items on Pivot**.

Items on Pivot appears in the **Choose** box, and the items on the Pivot worksheet appear in the list below the **Choose** box.

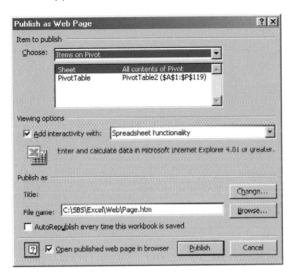

8   In the list below the **Choose** box, click the item beginning with *PivotTable*.

In the **Viewing options** section of the dialog box, the value in the **Add interactivity with** box changes to *PivotTable functionality*.

9   If necessary, in the bottom section of the dialog box, select the **Open published web page in browser** check box.

10 Click **Publish**.

The PivotTable is saved as a Web page and appears in Internet Explorer.

11 Click the **Show Details** button.

The PivotTable expands to show every cell.

12 In the Page Area of the PivotTable, click the **Weekday** down arrow and then, from the list that appears, clear the **Mon**, **Tue**, **Wed**, **Thu**, and **Fri** check boxes.

13 Click **OK**.

The PivotTable is filtered so that only sales for Saturdays and Sundays are shown.

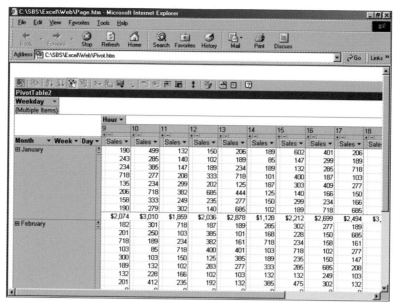

14 In the Page Area of the PivotTable, click the **Weekday** down arrow and then, from the list that appears, select the **All** check box and click **OK**.

Close

The filter is removed.

15 Click the **Close** button to close Internet Explorer.

Save

16 In Excel, on the Standard toolbar, click the **Save** button to save your work.

17 Click the **Close** button to close Pivot.xls.

Retrieving Data from the Web

The World Wide Web is a great source of information. From stock quotes to product descriptions, many companies publish useful information on their Web sites. The most common HTML structure used to present financial information is the table, which, like a spreadsheet, organizes the data into rows and columns, as in the following graphic.

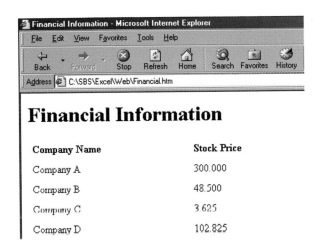

Financial Information

Company Name	Stock Price
Company A	300.000
Company B	48.500
Company C	3.625
Company D	102.825

Copy Paste
Web Query
new for
OfficeXP

Excel 2002 makes creating a Web query easy by letting you copy data directly from a Web page into Excel and then create a query to retrieve data from the HTML table you copied. To create a Copy Paste Web Query, open the target Web page in Internet Explorer, copy the data to the Clipboard, click a cell in the Excel workbook, and then paste the data into the workbook. The data will appear in the workbook, with a **Paste Options** button next to it.

Paste Options

Clicking the **Paste Options** button and then clicking **Create Refreshable Web Query** from the list that appears opens the **New Web Query** dialog box, which contains the data you copied from the Web page.

To select a table to import into Excel, click the table icon next to it. The icon will change to a selected table icon, and the table will be outlined and highlighted to identify it as having been selected. After you select the table, click **Import** to create the query.

Tip

You can select an entire Web page by clicking the top table icon in the display pane.

To refresh query data, right-click any cell in the query and then, from the shortcut menu that appears, click **Refresh Data**. The new data will appear in your workbook.

WebData

In this exercise, you create a Web query to retrieve data using the new Copy Paste Web Query method.

Open

1 On the Standard toolbar, click the **Open** button.

The **Open** dialog box appears.

2 Double-click **WebData.xls**.

WebData.xls opens.

3 Start Internet Explorer, and then, on the **File** menu, click **Open**.

The **Open** dialog box appears.

4 Click **Browse**.

The **Microsoft Internet Explorer** dialog box appears.

5 Navigate to the C:\SBS\Excel\Web directory, and then double-click **Financial.htm**.

The **Microsoft Internet Explorer** dialog box disappears, and *C:\SBS\Excel\Web\Financial.htm* appears in the **Open** box.

6 Click **OK**.

Financial.htm appears in Internet Explorer.

7 Select the table data, and then press [Ctrl]+[C] to copy the data to the Clipboard.

Paste

8 In Microsoft Excel, click cell A1, and then, on the Standard toolbar, click the **Paste** button.

The HTML table data is pasted into the worksheet, and the **Paste Options** button appears next to the data.

9 Click the **Paste Options** button, and then, from the list that appears, click **Create Refreshable Web Query**.

The **New Web Query** dialog box appears, with Financial.htm displayed.

Table icon

10 Click the table icon next to *Company Name*, and then click **Import**.

The HTML table data appears in the worksheet, with its original HTML formatting.

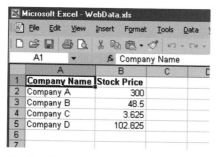

11 On the Standard toolbar, click the **Save** button to save your work.

Close

12 Click the **Close** button to close WebData.xls.

Acquiring Web Data with Smart Tags

Smart Tags
new for
OfficeXP

Another new capability in Excel 2002 is that of bringing information from the Web that is related to the contents of a worksheet cell. This new technology is called Smart Tags.

The clearest example of how Smart Tags work is with stock symbols, the abbreviations of company names on stock market tickers. You can turn on Smart Tags and have Excel look for known stock symbols (such as Microsoft's stock symbol, *MSFT*) and connect to a Web site that has information related to that symbol.

To turn on Smart Tags, on the **Tools** menu, click **AutoCorrect Options** to display the **AutoCorrect** dialog box. In the **AutoCorrect** dialog box, click the **Smart Tags** tab to display the **Smart Tags** tab page.

Select the **Label data with smart tags** check box to activate Smart Tags, and then, in the **Recognizers** box, select the check boxes next to the sets of Smart Tags you want Excel to use. You can also determine how Excel indicates that a cell has a value recognized by Smart Tags by opening the **Show smart tags as** drop-down list and choosing whether the cell will have an indicator in the lower right corner of the cell, a button that appears beside the cell when the mouse pointer is over it, or both. Selecting the **Embed smart tags in this workbook** check box means that Excel will save the reference to any cells with values recognized by Smart Tags and copy the list of Smart Tags into the body of the workbook.

To check the workbook for cell values recognized as Smart Tags, click the **Check Workbook** button. The **AutoCorrect** dialog box will disappear, and cells with recognized values will have an indicator in the lower right corner.

Indicator

Smart Tag
Actions

Moving the mouse pointer over the cell will display an indicator button. Click the indicator button, and then choose the type of information you want from the list that appears. If you click **Stock Quote on MSN MoneyCentral**, for example, Internet Explorer will launch and find the MSN MoneyCentral page for Microsoft.

To delete an individual Smart Tag, click the indicator button next to the cell with the Smart Tag and then click **Remove this Smart Tag**. To turn off Smart Tags entirely, open the **AutoCorrect** dialog box, display the **Smart Tags** tab page, clear the **Label data with smart tags** check box, and then click **OK**.

Smart

Open

In this exercise, you turn on Smart Tags, check a worksheet for Smart Tags, and then use the Smart Tag you find to get stock information about the company represented by a stock symbol.

1 On the Standard toolbar, click the **Open** button.

The **Open** dialog box appears.

2 Double-click **Smart.xls**.

Smart.xls opens.

3 On the **Tools** menu, click **AutoCorrect Options**.

The **AutoCorrect** dialog box appears.

4 Click the **Smart Tags** tab to display the **Smart Tags** tab page.

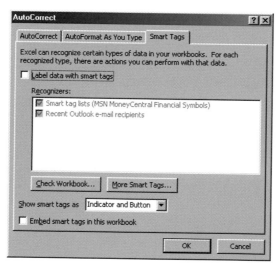

5 Select the **Label data with smart tags** check box.

The **Recognizers** box becomes active.

6 Verify that the **Smart tag lists** check box is selected.

7 Select the **Embed smart tags in this workbook** check box.

Smart Tags will now be saved as part of the workbook file.

8 Click **Check Workbook**.

The **AutoCorrect** dialog box disappears, and a Smart Tag indicator appears in cell B3.

9 Move the mouse pointer over cell B3.

A **Smart Tag Actions** button appears next to the cell.

10 Click the **Smart Tag Actions** button, and then, from the list that appears, click **Insert refreshable stock price**.

The **Insert Stock Price** dialog box appears.

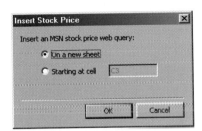

11 Select the **Starting at cell** option button, verify that C3 appears in the **Starting at cell** box, and then click **OK**.

The stock quote appears in the workbook.

12 On the Standard toolbar, click the **Save** button to save your work.

Close

13 Click the **Close** button to close Smart.xls.

Working with Structured Data

Ex2002e-1-2
Ex2002e-7-5
Ex2002e-7-8

Approved Courseware

XML
new for
OfficeXP

Hypertext Markup Language (HTML) lets you determine how a document will be displayed in a Web browser, such as by telling Internet Explorer to display certain text in bold type or to start a new paragraph. However, HTML doesn't tell you anything about the meaning of data in a document. Internet Explorer might "know" it should display a set of data in a table, but it wouldn't "know" that the data represented an Excel spreadsheet.

You can add **metadata**, or data about data, to Web documents using Extensible Markup Language (XML). While a full discussion of XML is beyond the scope of this book, the following bit of XML code shows how to identify an Excel workbook in XML:

```
<?xml version="1.0"?>
<Workbook xmlns="urn:schemas-microsoft-com:office:spreadsheet"
xmlns:o="urn:schemas-microsoft-com:office:office"
xmlns:x="urn:schemas-microsoft-com:office:excel"
xmlns:ss="urn:schemas-microsoft-com:office:spreadsheet"
xmlns:html="http://www.w3.org/TR/REC-html40">
```

Also, XML can identify rows and cells within the spreadsheet, as in the following example:

```
<Row>
    <Cell><Data ss:Type="String">January</Data></Cell>
    <Cell><Data ss:Type="Number">1</Data></Cell>
    <Cell><Data ss:Type="String">Tue</Data></Cell>
    <Cell><Data ss:Type="Number">2</Data></Cell>
    <Cell><Data ss:Type="Number">9</Data></Cell>
    <Cell><Data ss:Type="Number">161</Data></Cell>
</Row>
```

This represents the following worksheet row.

	A	B	C	D	E	F
1	Month	Week	Weekday	Day	Hour	Sales
2	January	1	Mon	1	9	147
3	January	1	Tue	2	9	161
4	January	1	Wed	3	9	182

The goal of XML is to be a universal language, allowing data to move freely from one application to another. In this case, that means that saving an Excel workbook as an XML document would allow any other spreadsheet program to read the XML file, separate out the cell data, and use the metadata to decide how to structure a worksheet to contain that data.

Open

To save an Excel document as an XML file, click **Save As** on the **File** menu to open the **Save As** dialog box. In the **Save As** dialog box, click the **Save as type** down arrow, click **XML Spreadsheet (*.xml)** from the list that appears, and then click **Save**. You can open Excel spreadsheets saved as XML documents by clicking the **Open** button, displaying all Excel files, and then clicking **Open**.

Structured
PivotXML

In this exercise, you save an Excel workbook as an XML document and then import an XML document into Excel.

1 On the Standard toolbar, click the **Open** button.

The **Open** dialog box appears.

2 Double-click **Structured.xls**.

Structured.xls opens.

3 On the **File** menu, click **Save As**.

The **Save As** dialog box appears.

4 Click the **Save as type** down arrow, and then, from the list that appears, click **XML Spreadsheet (*.xml)**.

The file type changes to XML.

5 Click **Save**.

A message box appears, indicating that any Microsoft Visual Basic projects or header or footer image associated with the workbook will not be saved.

6 Click **Yes** to clear the message box and save the workbook as an XML spreadsheet.

Close

7 Click the **Close** button to close Structured.xml.

8 On the Standard toolbar, click the **Open** button.

The **Open** dialog box appears.

9 Navigate to the C:\SBS\Excel\Web folder, and double-click **PivotXML.xml.**

PivotXML.xml, which contains a PivotTable, opens.

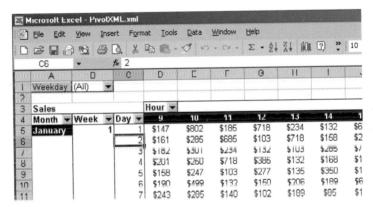

10 Click the **Close** box to close PivotXML.xml.

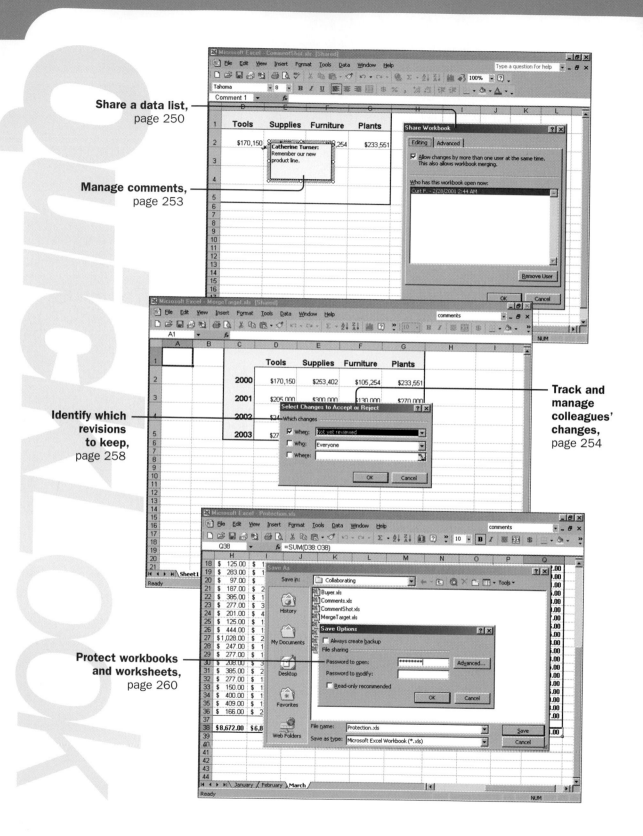

Share a data list, page 250

Manage comments, page 253

Identify which revisions to keep, page 258

Track and manage colleagues' changes, page 254

Protect workbooks and worksheets, page 260

Chapter 16
Collaborating with Colleagues

After completing this chapter, you will be able to:

✔ Share a data list.

✔ Manage comments.

✔ Track and manage colleagues' changes.

✔ Identify which revisions to keep.

✔ Protect workbooks and worksheets.

Even though a single individual might be tasked with managing a company's financial data and related information, there is usually a group of individuals who either enter data into workbooks or can have input into future sales or growth projections. You and your colleagues can also enhance workbook data by adding comments that offer insight into why sales were so good on a particular day or whether a product might be discontinued. If the workbook in which those projections and comments will be stored is available on a local area network or intranet, you can allow more than one user to access the workbook at a time by turning on workbook **sharing**.

Once a workbook has been shared with your colleagues, you can mark and record any changes made to the workbook. Once all changes have been made, the workbook's administrator can decide which changes to keep and which to reject. If several individuals need to make changes to a workbook and they can't access it via a network, you can create several copies of the original file and distribute them via e-mail to your colleagues. After you receive all of the changed files, you can merge the changes into the original file and choose which changes to keep.

Finally, you can limit the ability of other users to make changes to Microsoft Excel documents by adding password protection to a workbook, worksheet, or cell range (including an individual cell). Adding password protection lets you prevent changes to critical elements of your workbooks and, if you like, hide formulas used to calculate values.

In this chapter, you'll learn how to share a data list, manage comments to workbook cells, track and manage changes made by colleagues, identify which changes to a workbook you'll keep, and protect workbooks and worksheets.

This chapter uses the practice files Sharing, Comments, Tracking, MergeTarget, Owner, Buyer, and Protection that you installed from this book's CD-ROM. For details about installing the practice files, see "Using the Book's CD-ROM" at the beginning of this book.

Sharing a Data List

Ex2002e-9-2

Approved Courseware

The first step in making a workbook available to your colleagues is to turn on workbook sharing. When you turn on workbook sharing, you let more than one user edit a workbook simultaneously, which is perfect for a fair-sized business such as The Garden Company, where employees need to look up customer, sales, and product data frequently.

To turn on workbook sharing, on the **Tools** menu, click **Share Workbook**. In the **Share Workbook** dialog box that appears, you turn on workbook sharing by selecting the **Allow changes by more than one user at the same time** check box. You can then set the sharing options for the active workbook by clicking the **Advanced** tab.

There are several settings you can change on the **Advanced** tab page of the **Share Workbook** dialog box, but two settings are of greater interest than the others. The first setting has to do with whether Excel should maintain a history of changes made to the workbook and, if so, for how many days Excel should keep the changes. The default setting is to retain a record of all changes made in the past 30 days, but you can enter any number of days you like. Unless it's critical that you keep all changes made to a workbook, you should probably stay with the default setting of 30 days.

The other important setting on this tab page deals with how Excel will decide which of two conflicting changes in a cell should be applied. For example, a product's price might change, and two of your colleagues could type in what they think is the new price. Selecting the **Ask me which changes win** option button lets you decide which price to keep.

Attach

Attach

Another way to share a workbook is to send a copy of it to your colleagues via e-mail. If, for example, The Garden Company's owner, Catherine Turner, were on a business trip visiting a supplier, she could receive a copy of a workbook as an e-mail attachment. While the specific command to attach a file to an e-mail message will be different in every program, the most common method of attaching a file is to create a new e-mail message and then click the **Attach** button, as in Microsoft Outlook Express.

Sharing

In this exercise, you turn on workbook sharing and then attach the file to an Outlook Express e-mail message.

Important

You will need Outlook Express or Outlook to complete this exercise.

Open

1 On the Standard toolbar, click the **Open** button.

The **Open** dialog box appears.

2 Navigate to the Collaborating folder, and double-click **Sharing.xls**.

Sharing.xls opens.

3 On the **Tools** menu, click **Share Workbook**.

The **Share Workbook** dialog box appears with a list of every user who is accessing the workbook.

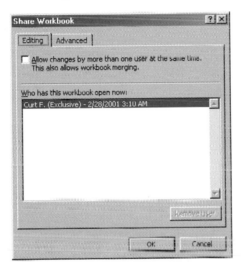

4 Select the **Allow changes by more than one user at the same time** check box, and then click the **Advanced** tab.

The **Advanced** tab page appears.

5 Click **OK** to accept the default settings.

6 Click **OK** to clear the message box that appears and save the workbook.

Close

7 Click the **Close** button to close Sharing.xls.

8 On the Windows taskbar, open the **Start** menu, point to **Programs**, and click **Outlook Express**.

The Outlook Express window opens.

New Mail

9 Click the **New Mail** button.

A new e-mail message appears.

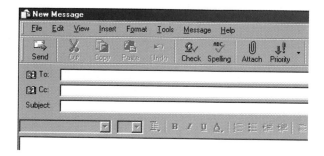

10 Click the **Attach** button.

The **Insert Attachment** dialog box appears.

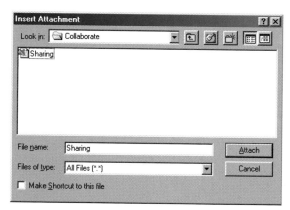

11 Navigate to the C:\SBS\Excel\Collaborating directory, and then double-click **Sharing.xls**.

The **Insert Attachment** dialog box disappears, and Sharing.xls appears in the Attach header field.

12 Click the **Close** button to close the message, and then click **No** in the message box that appears, to close the message without saving it.

Tip

There is no e-mail address in the **To** box, so clicking the **Send** button would have no effect.

13 Click the **Close** button to close Outlook Express.

Managing Comments

Ex2002-7-3

Approved Courseware

Excel makes it easy for you and your colleagues to add comments to workbook cells, adding insights that go beyond the cell data. For example, if sales were exceptionally high for an hour of a particular day, the manager on duty could add a comment to the cell in which she records the sales for that hour, noting that two exceptionally large purchases accounted for the disparity.

When you add a comment to a cell, a flag appears in the upper right corner of the cell. When the mouse pointer hovers over a cell with a comment, the comment appears in a box next to the cell, along with the name of the user logged on to the computer at the time.

Important

Note that the name attributed to a comment may not be the same as the person who actually created it. Enforcing access controls, such as requiring users to enter account names and passwords when they access a computer, can help track who made what comment or change.

You can add a comment to a cell by clicking the cell and clicking **Comment** on the **Insert** menu. When you do, the comment flag appears in the cell and a comment box appears next to the cell. You can type the comment in the box and, when you're done, click another cell to close the box for editing. When you move the mouse pointer over the cell with the comment, the comment will appear next to the cell.

If you want the comment to be shown the entire time the workbook is open, right-click the cell with the comment and then click **Show Comment** from the shortcut menu that appears. You can hide the comment by clicking **Hide Comment** from the same menu, delete the comment by clicking **Delete Comment**, or open the comment for editing by clicking **Edit Comment**.

Tip

When someone other than the original user edits a comment, that person's input is marked with the new user's name and is added to the original comment.

Comments

Open

In this exercise, you add a comment to a cell. You then review and delete the comment.

1 On the Standard toolbar, click the **Open** button.

The **Open** dialog box appears.

2 Double-click **Comments.xls**.

Comments.xls opens.

3   Click cell D3.

4   On the **Insert** menu, click **Comment**.

A comment field appears.

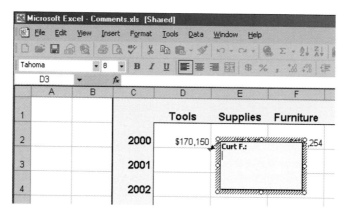

5   In the comment field, type **Remember to figure in our two new lines** and then click cell D5.

A red comment flag appears in the upper right corner of cell D3.

6   Move the mouse pointer over cell D3.

The comment in cell D3 appears.

7   Right-click cell D3, and then, from the shortcut menu that appears, click **Delete Comment**.

The comment is deleted from cell D3.

8   On the Standard toolbar, click the **Save** button to save your work.

Close

9   Click the **Close** button to close Comments.xls.

Tracking and Managing Colleagues' Changes

Ex2002e-9-3

Approved Courseware

Whenever you collaborate with a number of your colleagues in producing or editing a document, you should consider tracking the changes each user makes. When you turn on change tracking, any changes made to the workbook are highlighted in a color assigned to the user who made the changes. One benefit of tracking changes is that if you have a question about a change, you can quickly identify who made the change and verify that it is correct. In Excel, you can turn on change tracking in a workbook by pointing to **Track Changes** on the **Tools** menu and then clicking **Highlight Changes**.

In the **Highlight Changes** dialog box that appears, you select the **Track changes while editing** check box. Selecting this check box saves your workbook, turns on change tracking, and also shares your workbook, allowing more than one user to access the workbook simultaneously. You can use the controls in the **Highlight Changes** dialog box to choose which changes to track, but clearing the **When**, **Who**, and **Where** check boxes will have Excel track all changes. Now whenever anyone makes a change to the workbook, the change will be attributed to the user logged in to the computer from which the change was made. Each user's changes will be displayed in a unique color. As with a comment, when you move the mouse pointer over a change, the date and time the change was made and the name of the user that made it appear as a ScreenTip.

Once you and your colleagues are done modifying a workbook, you can decide which changes to accept and which changes to reject. To start the process, on the **Tools** menu, point to **Track Changes**, and then click **Accept or Reject Changes**. After you clear the message box indicating that Excel will save your workbook, the **Select Changes to Accept or Reject** dialog box appears.

You can use the **When** down arrow to choose which changes to review. The default choice is **Not yet reviewed**, but you can also click **Since date** to open a dialog box into which you can enter the starting date of changes you want to review. To review all changes in your workbook, clear the **When**, **Who**, and **Where** check boxes.

When you are ready to accept or reject changes, click **OK**. The **Accept or Reject Changes** dialog box appears, with the first change described in the body of the dialog box. Clicking the **Accept** button lets the change take effect, while clicking the **Reject** button removes the change and restores the cell to its previous value and erases any record of the change. Clicking **Accept All** or **Reject All** will implement all changes or restore all cells to their original values, but you should choose one of those options only if you are *absolutely certain* you are doing the right thing.

If you want an itemized record of all changes you have made since the last time you saved the workbook, you can add a History worksheet to your workbook. To add a History worksheet, open the **Highlight Changes** dialog box and select the **List changes on a new sheet** check box. When you click **OK**, a new worksheet, named *History*, appears in your workbook. The next time you save your workbook, the History worksheet is deleted.

Tracking

In this exercise, you turn on change tracking in a workbook, accept or reject changes, and create a History worksheet.

Open

1   On the Standard toolbar, click the **Open** button.

The **Open** dialog box appears.

2   Double-click **Tracking.xls**.

Tracking.xls opens.

3   On the **Tools** menu, point to **Track Changes** and then click **Highlight Changes**.

The **Highlight Changes** dialog box appears.

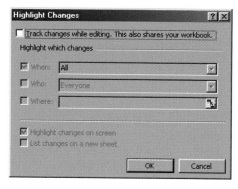

4 Select the **Track changes while editing** check box.

Tip

Selecting the **Track changes while editing** check box also turns on workbook sharing.

5 If necessary, clear the **When** check box.

6 If necessary, clear the **Who** check box.

7 If necessary, select the **Highlight changes on screen** check box.

8 Click **OK**.

The **Highlight Changes** dialog box disappears.

9 Click **OK** to save the workbook and clear the message box that appears.

10 In cell D3, type **235000** and press Enter.

The value $235,000 appears in cell D3, the cell is outlined in the color assigned to the current user, and a flag appears in the upper left corner of the cell.

11 In cell D4, type **300000** and press Enter.

The value $300,000 appears in cell D4, the cell is outlined in the color assigned to the current user, and a flag appears in the upper left corner of the cell.

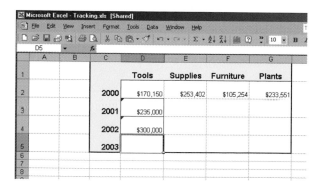

Save

12 On the Standard toolbar, click the **Save** button to save your work.

13 On the **Tools** menu, point to **Track Changes** and then click **Highlight Changes**.

The **Highlight Changes** dialog box appears.

14 Select the **List changes on a new sheet** check box, and then click **OK**.

Tip

If the workbook had sharing turned on when you enabled change tracking, the **List changes on a new sheet** check box would have been available when you opened the **Highlight Changes** dialog box earlier.

A new worksheet named *History* appears in the workbook.

15 If necessary, on the tab bar, click the **History** sheet tab.

The History worksheet appears.

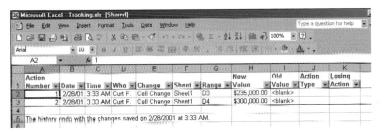

16 On the tab bar, click the **Sheet1** sheet tab.

The Sheet1 worksheet appears.

17 Click cell A1.

18 On the **Tools** menu, point to **Track Changes** and then click **Accept or Reject Changes**.

19 Click **OK** to save the workbook and clear the message box that appears.

The **Select Changes to Accept or Reject** dialog box appears.

20 Verify that the **When** check box is selected and that *Not yet reviewed* appears in the **When** box.

21 Click **OK**.

The **Accept or Reject Changes** dialog box appears with the first change listed.

22 Click **Accept** to accept the change.

The second change appears in the dialog box.

23 Click **Reject**.

The value in cell D4 is removed, and the History worksheet is deleted.

24 On the Standard toolbar, click the **Save** button to save your work.

Close

25 Click the **Close** button to close Tracking.xls.

Identifying Which Revisions to Keep

Ex2002e-9-4

Approved Courseware

Tracking changes lets you and your colleagues modify a document, maintain a record of the changes, and choose which changes to keep in the final version. When every individual with input into a document can't access the same copy of the workbook, such as if a senior manager is away on a business trip, you can still allow your colleagues input into the final version of a document by sending them duplicates of the original document and then merging the changes in their copies into the original document.

To distribute copies of a document and merge the changes into the original, the files involved must meet these criteria:

- All distributed files must be copies of the same workbook, which must have had sharing, change tracking, and change history turned on when it was copied.

- All files must have different file names.

- All files must either have no password or have the same password.

- All distributed files must have maintained a change history continuously since distribution (that is, never had sharing, change tracking, or change history turned off).

When all files meet these criteria, you can merge changes from the distributed copies of a file into the original file and then choose which changes to keep. To begin merging files, open the original file and then, on the **Tools** menu, click **Compare and Merge Workbooks**. When you do, the **Select Files to Merge Into Current Workbook** dialog box appears.

Hold down ⌃ while you click the files to merge into the active workbook, and then click **OK** to make the changes appear in the active workbook.

Troubleshooting

If the changed cells don't have change flags or outlines, on the **Tools** menu, point to **Track Changes**, and then click **Highlight Changes** to open the **Highlight Changes** dialog box. In the **Highlight Changes** dialog box, clear the **When** check box and then click **OK**. The dialog box will disappear, and the changed cells will have change flags and outlines.

To pick which changes to keep, on the **Tools** menu, point to **Track Changes**, and then click **Accept or Reject Changes**. Click **OK** to clear the **Select Changes to Accept or Reject** dialog box and display the **Accept or Reject Changes** dialog box. You can then accept or reject individual changes. If there are conflicting changes for a cell, all changes for that cell will appear in the **Accept or Reject Changes** dialog box. You select which changes to keep by clicking the desired change and then clicking **Accept**.

MergeTarget
Owner
Buyer

In this exercise, you merge changes from two workbooks into a master workbook.

1   On the Standard toolbar, click the **Open** button.

The **Open** dialog box appears.

2   Double-click **MergeTarget.xls**.

MergeTarget.xls opens.

3   On the **Tools** menu, click **Compare and Merge Workbooks**.

The **Select Files to Merge into Current Workbook** dialog box appears.

4   Hold down ⌃ while clicking **Buyer.xls** and **Owner.xls**, and then click **OK**.

The changes from the other files appear in MergeTarget.xls.

Troubleshooting

If the cells with changes don't have comment flags in the corner, on the **Tools** menu, point to **Track Changes**, and then click **Highlight Changes**. In the **Highlight Changes** dialog box, clear the **When** check box and then click **OK**.

Save

5   On the Standard toolbar, click the **Save** button to save your work.

6   On the **Tools** menu, point to **Track Changes** and then click **Accept or Reject Changes**.

The **Select Changes to Accept or Reject** dialog box appears.

7 Verify that the **When** check box is selected and that *Not yet reviewed* appears in the **When** box, that the **Who** check box is cleared, and that the **Where** check box is cleared.

8 Click **OK**.

The **Select Changes to Accept or Reject** dialog box disappears, and the **Accept or Reject Changes** dialog box appears with a list of changes in the **Select a value** box.

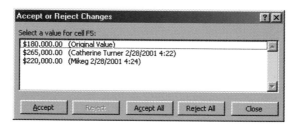

9 Click the change starting with *$265,000.00*, and then click **Accept**.

The change you accepted takes effect, and the next change appears in the **Accept or Reject Changes** box.

10 Click **Accept** to accept the change.

The value in cell F4 changes to *$175,000*, and the **Accept or Reject Changes** box disappears.

11 On the Standard toolbar, click the **Save** button to save your work.

Close

12 Click the **Close** button to close MergeTarget.xls.

Protecting Workbooks and Worksheets

Ex2002e-9-1

Approved Courseware

Excel gives you the ability to share your workbooks over the Web, via a corporate intranet, and by copying files for other users to take with them on business trips. An important part of sharing files, however, is ensuring that only those users you want to have access to the files can open or modify them. For example, The Garden Company might have a series of computers available on the sales floor so that sales associates can look up prices and inventory information. While those computers are a vital tool to making sales, it wouldn't help the company to have customers, even those with good intentions, accessing critical workbooks.

You can limit access to your workbooks, or elements within a workbook, by setting passwords. Setting a password for an Excel workbook means that any users who want to access the protected workbook must enter the workbook's password in a dialog box that appears when they try to open the file. If the person doesn't know the password, he or she will be unable to open the workbook.

To set a password for a workbook, open the workbook to be protected, and on the **File** menu, click **Save As**. The **Save As** dialog box appears, with the name of the open workbook in the **File name** box.

On the toolbar, click the **Tools** menu head and then click **General Options** to open the **Save Options** dialog box. In the **Save Options** dialog box, you can require users to enter one password to open the workbook and another to modify it. After you click **OK**, a **Confirm Password** dialog box will appear so that you can verify the passwords required to access and modify the workbook. After you have confirmed the passwords, click **Save** in the **Save As** dialog box to finish adding password protection to the workbook.

Important

The best passwords are random strings of characters, but random characters are hard to remember. One good method of creating hard-to-guess passwords is to combine elements of two words with a number in between. For example, you might have a password *wbk16pro*, which could be read as "workbook, Chapter 16, protection." In any event, avoid dictionary words in English or any other language, as they can be found easily by password-guessing programs available on the Internet.

If you want to allow anyone to open a workbook but want to prevent unauthorized users from editing a worksheet, you can protect a worksheet by displaying that worksheet, pointing to **Protection** on the **Tools** menu, and then clicking **Protect Sheet** to open the **Protect Sheet** dialog box.

In the **Protect Sheet** dialog box, you select the **Protect worksheet and contents of locked cells** check box to protect the sheet. You can also set a password for the worksheet and choose which elements of the worksheet users who don't have the password will be able to change. To allow a user to change a worksheet element without entering the password, select the check box next to that element's name.

The check box at the top of the worksheet mentions **locked cells**. A locked cell is a cell that can't be changed when worksheet protection is turned on. You can lock or unlock a cell by right-clicking the cell and choosing **Format Cells** from the shortcut menu that appears. In the **Format Cells** dialog box, you click the **Protection** tab to display the **Protection** tab page.

When worksheet protection is turned on, selecting the **Locked** check box prevents unauthorized users from changing the contents or formatting of the locked cell, while selecting the **Hidden** check box hides the formulas in the cell. You might want to hide the formula in a cell if you draw sensitive data, such as customer contact information, from another workbook and don't want casual users to see the name of the workbook in a formula.

Finally, you can password-protect a cell range. For example, you might want to let users enter values in most worksheet cells but also want to protect the cells with formulas that perform calculations based on those values. To password-protect a range of cells, select the cells to protect, and then on the **Tools** menu, point to **Protection** and click **Allow Users to Edit Ranges**. The **Allow Users to Edit Ranges** dialog box appears.

To create a protected range, click the **New** button to display the **New Range** dialog box. Type a name for the range in the **Title** box, and then type a password in the **Range password** box. When you click **OK**, Excel will ask you to confirm the password; after you do, click **OK** in the **Allow Users to Edit Ranges** dialog box to protect the range. Now whenever a user tries to edit a cell in the protected range, he or she will be prompted for a password.

Tip

Remember that a range of cells can mean just one cell!

Protection

In this exercise, you password-protect a workbook, a worksheet, and a range of cells and then hide and unhide the formula in a cell.

Open

1　On the Standard toolbar, click the **Open** button.

The **Open** dialog box appears.

2　Double-click **Protection.xls**.

Protection.xls opens.

3　On the **File** menu, click **Save As**.

The **Save As** dialog box appears.

4　Click the **Tools** menu head, and then click **General Options**.

The **Save Options** dialog box appears.

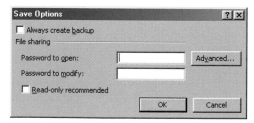

5　In the **Password to open** box, type **wbk16pro** and then click **OK**.

The **Confirm Password** dialog box appears.

6 In the **Reenter password to proceed** box, type **wbk16pro** and then click **OK**.

The **Confirm Password** dialog box disappears.

7 Click **Save**.

8 Click **Yes** to clear the message box that appears.

Excel saves the workbook, and the **Save As** dialog box disappears.

9 On the tab bar, click the **March** sheet tab to move to the March worksheet.

10 On the **Tools** menu, point to **Protection** and then click **Protect Sheet**.

The **Protect Sheet** dialog box appears.

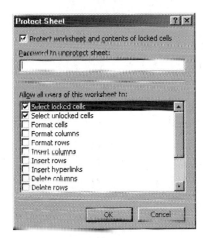

11 In the **Password to unprotect sheet** box, type **wbk16pro** and then click **OK**.

The **Confirm Password** dialog box appears.

12 Type **wbk16pro** in the space provided, and then click **OK**.

The **Confirm Password** dialog box disappears.

13 On the **Tools** menu, point to **Protection** and then click **Unprotect Sheet**.

The **Unprotect Sheet** dialog box appears.

14 In the **Password** box, type **wbk16pro** and then click **OK**.

The **Unprotect Sheet** dialog box disappears, and the password is removed.

15 Select cells L36:O36.

16 On the **Tools** menu, point to **Protection** and then click **Allow Users to Edit Ranges**.

The **Allow Users to Edit Ranges** dialog box appears.

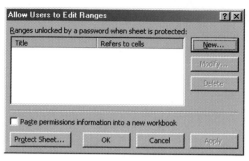

17 Click **New**.

The **New Range** dialog box appears, with =$L$36:$O$36 in the **Refers to cells** box.

18 In the **Title** box, type **LastDay**.

19 In the **Range password** box, type **wbk16pro** and then click **OK**.

The **Confirm Password** dialog box appears.

20 Type **wbk16pro**, and then click **OK**.

The **Confirm Password** dialog box disappears.

21 Click **OK**.

The **Allow Users to Edit Ranges** dialog box disappears.

22 On the **Tools** menu, point to **Protection** and then click **Allow Users to Edit Ranges**.

The **Allow Users to Edit Ranges** dialog box appears.

23 In the **Ranges** box, click **LastDay** and then click **Delete**.

The range disappears from the dialog box.

24 Click **OK** to close the **Allow Users to Edit Ranges** dialog box.

25 Right-click cell Q38, and then, from the shortcut menu that appears, click **Format Cells**.

The **Format Cells** dialog box appears.

26 Click the **Protection** tab to display the **Protection** tab page.

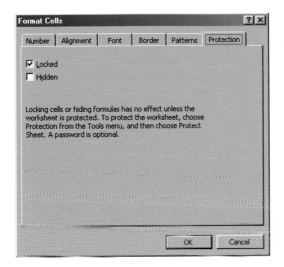

27 Select the **Hidden** check box, and then click **OK**.

The **Format Cells** dialog box disappears.

28 On the **Tools** menu, point to **Protection** and then click **Protect Sheet**.

The **Protect Sheet** dialog box appears.

29 Click **OK** to close the **Protect Sheet** dialog box.

The **Protect Sheet** dialog box disappears. Cell Q38 still has the value calculated by its formula, but the formula doesn't appear on the formula bar.

30 On the **Tools** menu, point to **Protection** and then click **Unprotect Sheet**.

The formula in cell Q38 appears on the formula bar.

31 On the Standard toolbar, click the **Save** button to save your work.

Close

[X]

32 Click the **Close** button to close Protection.xls.

Quick Reference

Page   4   **To open a workbook**

Open

1   On the Standard toolbar, click the **Open** button.

2   Click the **Look In** down arrow, and select the hard disk where you stored the file.

3   Locate and double-click the target folder to display its contents.

4   Double-click the target file to open it.

5   **To save a workbook**

Save

1   On the Standard toolbar, click the **Save** button.

2   Navigate to the folder where you want to save the workbook.

3   In the **File name** box, delete the existing file name and type the name for your file.

4   Click **Save**.

5   **To save a workbook with a different file name and format**

1   On the **File** menu, click **Save As**.

2   Navigate to the folder where you want to save the workbook.

3   In the **File name** box, delete the existing file name and type the name for your file.

4   Click the **Save as type** down arrow to expand the list, and click the desired type.

5   Click **Save**.

7   **To move to a worksheet**

● In the lower left corner of the Microsoft Excel window, click the appropriate sheet tab.

8   **To select one or more cells**

● Click the first cell to be selected, and drag to the last cell to be selected.

8   **To select a noncontiguous group of cells**

● While holding down the Ctrl key, click the cells to be selected.

9   **To select one or more columns or rows**

     1   Click the column or row head for the column or row to be selected.

     2   If necessary, drag to the row or column head at the edge of the group to be selected.

12   **To create a new workbook**

New

     ●   On the Standard toolbar, click the **New** button.

13   **To enter data manually**

     1   Click the cell in which you want to enter the data.

     2   Type the data, and press Enter.

13   **To quickly enter a series of data**

     1   Click the first cell in which you want to enter data.

     2   Type a value, and press Enter.

     3   In the new cell, type the second value in the series.

     4   Grab the fill handle, and drag it to the last cell to be filled with data.

15   **To enter data in multiple cells**

     1   Click a cell, and type the data to appear in multiple cells.

     2   Select the cells in which you want the data in the active cell to appear.

     3   Press Ctrl + Enter.

17   **To find specific data**

     1   On the **Edit** menu, click **Find**.

     2   In the **Find what** box, type the word or text you want to find, and then click **Find Next**.

     3   Click **Find Next** again to find subsequent occurrences of the text.

17   **To replace specific data**

     1   On the **Edit** menu, click **Replace**.

     2   In the **Find what** box, type the word or text you want to replace.

     3   In the **Replace with** box, type the word or text you want to substitute for the text in the **Find what** box.

4   Click **Find Next**.

5   Click **Replace** to replace the value in the highlighted cell.

19   **To replace cell data manually**

1   Click the cell with the data to be replaced.

2   Type the new data, and press Enter.

19   **To modify cell data manually**

1   Click the cell with the data to be modified.

2   Click anywhere on the formula bar.

3   Edit the cell contents on the formula bar, and press Enter.

19   **To change an action**

Undo

1   Click the **Undo** button to remove the last change.

Redo

2   Click the **Redo** button to reinstate the last change you removed.

19   **To check spelling**

Spelling

●   On the Standard toolbar, click the **Spelling** button.

Chapter 2   Setting Up a Workbook

Page   26   **To name a worksheet**

1   In the lower left corner of the workbook window, right-click the desired sheet tab.

2   From the shortcut menu that appears, click **Rename**.

3   Type the new name for the worksheet, and press Enter.

26   **To reposition a worksheet**

●   Click the sheet tab of the worksheet to move, and drag it to the new position on the tab bar.

26   **To adjust column width**

●   Position the mouse pointer over an edge of the column head of the column to be resized, and drag the edge to the side.

27   To adjust row height

- Position the mouse pointer over an edge of the row head of the row to be resized, and drag the edge up or down.

27   To merge cells

Merge and Center

1   Select the cells to be merged.

2   On the Formatting toolbar, click the **Merge and Center** toolbar button.

27   To add a row or column

1   Click any cell in the row below which you want the new row to appear, or click any cell in the column to the right of which you want the new column to appear.

2   On the **Insert** menu, click **Rows** or **Columns**.

28   To hide a row or column

1   Select any cell in the row or column to be hidden.

2   On the **Format** menu, point to **Row** or **Column** and then click **Hide**.

28   To unhide a row or column

- On the **Format** menu, point to **Row** or **Column** and then click **Unhide**.

30   To prevent text spillover

1   Click the desired cell.

2   On the **Format** menu, click **Cells**.

3   If necessary, click the **Alignment** tab.

4   Select the **Wrap Text** check box, and click **OK**.

30   To control how text appears in a cell

1   Click the desired cell.

2   On the **Format** menu, click **Cells**.

3   Use the controls in the **Format Cells** dialog box to change the appearance of the cell text.

31   To freeze column headings

1   Select the rows you want to freeze.

2   On the **Window** menu, click **Freeze Panes**.

31   **To unfreeze column headings**

●   On the **Window** menu, click **Unfreeze Panes**.

32   **To add a picture to a worksheet**

1   Click the cell into which you want to add the picture.

2   On the **Insert** menu, point to **Picture** and then click **From File**.

3   Navigate to the folder with the picture file, and then double-click the file name.

33   **To change a picture's properties**

1   Right click the graphic, and from the shortcut menu that appears, click **Format Picture**.

2   Use the controls in the **Format Picture** dialog box to change the picture's properties.

Chapter   3   **Performing Calculations on Data**

Page   **36**   **To name a range of cells**

1   Select the cells to be included in the range.

2   Click in the Name box.

3   Type the name of the range, and press [Enter].

37   **To name a range of cells using adjacent cell labels**

1   Ensure that the desired name for the cell range is in the topmost or leftmost cell of the range.

2   Select the cells to be part of the range.

3   On the **Insert** menu, point to **Name** and then click **Create**.

4   Select the check box indicating the location of the cell with the name for the range, and then click **OK**.

42   **To write a formula**

1   Click the cell into which the formula will be written.

2   Type an equal sign, and then type the remainder of the formula.

42   **To copy a formula to another cell**

1   Click the cell containing the formula.

Copy

2   On the Standard toolbar, click the **Copy** button.

3   Click the cell into which the formula will be pasted.

Paste

4   On the Standard toolbar, click the **Paste** button.

43   **To create a formula with a function**

1   Click the cell where you want to create the formula.

2   On the **Insert** menu, click **Function**.

3   Click the function you want to use, and then click **OK**.

4   Type the arguments for the function in the argument boxes, and then click **OK**.

43   **To create a formula with a conditional function**

1   Click the cell where you want to create the formula.

2   On the **Insert** menu, click **Function**.

3   In the Select A Function pane, click **IF**, and then click **OK**.

4   In the **Logical_test** box, type the test to use.

5   In the **Value_if_true** box, type the string to be printed if the logical test evaluates to true. (Enclose the string in quotes.)

6   In the **Value_if_false** box, type the string to be printed if the logical test evaluates to false. (Enclose the string in quotes.)

46   **To trace precedents or dependents**

1   Click the cell from which to trace precedents or dependents.

2   On the **Tools** menu, point to **Formula Auditing** and then click **Trace Precedents** or **Trace Dependents**.

47   **To remove tracer arrows**

●   On the **Tools** menu, point to **Formula Auditing** and then click **Remove All Arrows**.

Chapter 4   Changing Document Appearance

Page   52   **To change cell formatting**

1   Click the cell you want to change.

2   On the Formatting toolbar, click the button corresponding to the formatting you want to apply.

53 **To add cell borders**

Borders

1 On the Formatting toolbar, click the **Borders** button's down arrow and then, from the list that appears, click **Draw Borders**.

2 Click the cell edge on which you want to draw a border.

3 Drag the mouse pointer to draw a border around a group of cells.

53 **To add cell shading**

1 Click the cell to be shaded.

Fill Color

2 On the Formatting toolbar, click the **Fill Color** button.

3 In the **Fill Color** color palette, click the desired square, and then click **OK**.

55 **To create a style**

1 On the **Format** menu, click **Style**.

2 In the **Style name** box, delete the existing value and then type a name for the new style.

3 Click **Modify**, and define the style with the controls of the **Format Cells** dialog box.

4 Click **OK** in the **Format Cells** dialog box and the **Styles** dialog box.

55 **To copy a format**

1 Click the cell with the format to be copied.

Format Painter

2 On the Standard toolbar, click the **Format Painter** button.

3 Click the cell or cells to which the styles will be copied.

58 **To format a number**

1 Click the cell with the number to be formatted.

2 On the **Format** menu, click **Cells**.

3 If necessary, click the **Number** tab.

4 In the **Category** list, click the general category for the formatting.

5 In the **Type** list, click the specific format, and then click **OK**.

50 **To format a number as a dollar amount**

1 Click the cell with the number to be formatted.

Currency Style

2 On the Formatting toolbar, click the **Currency Style** button.

59 **To create a custom format**

1   On the **Format** menu, click **Cells**.

2   In the **Category** list, click **Custom**.

3   In the **Type** list, click the item to serve as the base for the custom style.

4   In the **Type** box, modify the item, and then click **OK**.

63 **To create a conditional format**

1   Click the cell to be formatted.

2   On the **Format** menu, click **Conditional Formatting**.

3   In the second list box, click the down arrow and then click the operator to use in the test.

4   Type the arguments to use in the condition.

5   Click the **Format** button, and use the controls in the **Format Cells** dialog box to create a format for this condition.

6   Click **OK**.

63 **To set multiple conditions for a cell**

1   Click the cell to be formatted.

2   Create a conditional format, and then click **Add**.

3   Create a new condition and format in the spaces provided.

65 **To add a header or a footer**

1   On the **View** menu, click **Header and Footer**.

2   Click the **Custom Header** or **Custom Footer** button.

3   Add text or images, and click **OK**.

66 **To add a graphic to a header or footer**

1   Create a header or footer.

Insert Picture

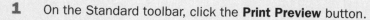

2   Click anywhere in one of the section boxes, and then click the **Insert Picture** button.

3   Navigate to the folder with the image file, double-click the file name, and then click **OK**.

69 **To change margins**

Print Preview

1   On the Standard toolbar, click the **Print Preview** button.

2   Click **Margins**.

3   Drag the margin lines in the window to the desired positions.

70 **To change page alignment**

1 On the **File** menu, click **Page Setup**.

2 If necessary, click the **Page** tab.

3 Select the appropriate alignment option.

Chapter 5 Focusing on Specific Data Using Filters

Page 75 **To find the top ten values in a list**

1 Click the top cell in the column to filter.

2 On the **Data** menu, point to **Filter** and then click **AutoFilter**.

3 Click the down arrow that appears, and then click **(Top 10...)** in the list.

4 In the **Top 10 AutoFilter** dialog box, click **OK**.

75 **To find a subset of data in a list**

1 Click the top cell in the column to filter.

2 On the **Data** menu, point to **Filter** and then click **AutoFilter**.

3 Click the down arrow that appears, and from the list of unique column values that appears, click the value to use as the filter.

76 **To create a custom filter**

1 Click the top cell in the column to filter.

2 On the **Data** menu, point to **Filter** and then click **AutoFilter**.

3 Click the down arrow, and then click **(Custom...)** in the list.

4 In the upper left box of the **Custom AutoFilter** dialog box, click the down arrow, and from the list that appears, click a comparison operator.

5 Type the arguments for the comparison in the boxes at the upper right, and click **OK**.

76 **To remove a filter**

● On the **Data** menu, point to **Filter** and then click **AutoFilter**.

76 **To filter for a specific value**

1 Click the top cell in the column to filter.

2 On the **Data** menu, point to **Filter** and then click **AutoFilter**.

3 Click the down arrow, and then, from the list of unique column values that appears, click the value for which you want to filter.

77　**To select a random row from a list**

1　In the cell next to the first cell with data in it, type **=RAND()<#%**, replacing #
with the number that represents the percentage.

2　Press ⌨Tab.

3　Click the cell into which you entered the RAND() formula, grab the fill handle,
and drag to the cell next to the last cell in the data column.

77　**To extract a list of unique values**

1　Click the top cell in the column to filter.

2　On the **Data** menu, point to **Filter** and then click **Advanced Filter**.

3　Select the **Unique records only** check box, and then click **OK**.

79　**To find a total**

●　Select the cells with the values to be summed. The total appears on the status bar, in the lower right corner of the Excel window.

79　**To edit a function**

1　Click the cell with the function to be edited.

2　On the **Insert** menu, click **Function**.

3　Edit the function in the **Function** dialog box.

81　**To set acceptable values for a cell**

1　Click the cell to be modified.

2　On the **Data** menu, click **Validation**.

3　In the **Allow** box, click the down arrow, and from the list that appears, click
the type of data to be allowed.

4　In the **Data** box, click the down arrow, and from the list that appears, click
the comparison operator to be used.

5　Type values in the boxes to complete the validation statement.

6　Click the **Input Message** tab.

7　In the **Title** box, type the title for the message box that appears when the
cell becomes active.

8　In the **Input Message** box, type the message the user will see in the message box.

9　Click the **Error Alert** tab.

10 In the **Style** box, click the down arrow, and from the list that appears, choose the type of box you want to appear.

11 In the **Title** box, type the title for the message box that appears when a user enters invalid data. Then click **OK**.

83 **To allow only numeric values in a cell**

1 Click the cell to be modified.

2 On the **Data** menu, click **Validation**.

3 In the **Allow** box, click the down arrow, and from the list that appears, click **Whole number**.

4 Click **OK**.

Chapter 6 Combining Data from Multiple Sources

Page 87 **To delete a worksheet**

● On the tab bar, in the lower left corner of the workbook window, right-click the tab of the sheet to be deleted, and from the shortcut menu that appears, click **Delete**.

87 **To save a document as a template**

1 On the **File** menu, click **Save As**.

2 Click the **Save as type** down arrow, and click **Template**.

88 **To create a workbook from a template**

1 On the **View** menu, click **Task Pane**.

2 In the **New from template** section of the task pane, click **General Templates**.

3 In the **Templates** dialog box, double-click the template to use as the basis for the new workbook.

90 **To open multiple workbooks**

Open

1 On the Standard toolbar, click the **Open** button.

2 Hold down Ctrl while you click the files to open, and then click **Open**.

90 **To change how a workbook is displayed in Excel**

1 Open the files to be displayed.

2 On the **Window** menu, click **Arrange**.

3 In the **Arrange Windows** dialog box, click the option button corresponding to the desired display pattern and click **OK**.

91 **To insert a worksheet in an existing workbook**

1 On the tab bar, right-click the tab of the sheet to move, and then, from the shortcut menu that appears, click **Move or Copy**.

2 Click the **To book** down arrow, and then, from the list that appears, click the book to which you want to move the worksheet.

3 In the **Before sheet** list, click the sheet to appear behind the moved sheet.

4 At the bottom of the **Move or Copy** dialog box, select the **Create a copy** check box.

5 Click **OK**.

92 **To change worksheet tab colors**

1 On the tab bar, right-click the tab to be changed, and then, from the shortcut menu that appears, click **Tab Color**.

2 Click the square of the desired color, and click **OK**.

95 **To link to a cell in another worksheet**

1 Click the cell from which to link, and then type **=**.

2 Click the title bar of the workbook containing the cell to link to.

3 Click the cell to link to.

4 Click the title bar of the workbook from which to link, and then press [Enter].

95 **To fix a broken link**

1 In the alert box that appears when you open a workbook with a broken link, click **Update**.

2 Click **Edit Links**.

3 Click **Change Source**.

4 Open the target workbook, navigate to the proper worksheet, and click the target cell.

5 In the **Edit Links** dialog box, click **Close**.

98 **To consolidate data**

1 Open all of the files to be consolidated.

2 On the **Data** menu, click **Consolidate**.

3 On the **Window** menu, click the name of a file with data to be consolidated.

4 Select the cells to consolidate, and click **Add**.

5 Repeat steps 3 and 4 to choose corresponding cells in other worksheets.

6 On the **Window** menu, click the name of the file that will hold the data summary.

7 In the **Consolidate** dialog box, click **OK**.

100 **To save workbooks in a workspace**

1 Open the files to be saved in the workspace.

2 On the **File** menu, click **Save Workspace**.

3 In the **File name** box, type the name of the workspace, and click **Save**.

101 **To open a workspace**

Open

1 On the Standard toolbar, click the **Open** button.

2 Double-click the workspace.

Chapter 7   **Reordering and Summarizing Data**

Page   105   **To sort a data list**

Sort Ascending

A↓
Z

1 Select the column of cells to be sorted.

Sort Descending

Z↓
A

2 On the Standard toolbar, click the **Sort Ascending** or **Sort Descending** button.

106 **To sort a data list by multiple columns**

1 Select the columns of cells to be sorted.

2 On the **Data** menu, click **Sort**.

3 If necessary, click the **Sort by** down arrow, and then, from the list that appears, click the first column to sort by.

4 Click the **Then by** down arrow, and then, from the list that appears, click the next column to sort by.

5 Repeat step 4 with the next **Then by** down arrow.

6 Click **OK**.

107 **To set a custom sort order**

1 On the **Tools** menu, click **Options**.

2 Click the **Custom Lists** tab.

3 Click **Import**, and click **OK**.

111 **To find a subtotal**

1 Select the rows for which you want to calculate a subtotal.

2 On the **Data** menu, click **Subtotals**.

3 Click **OK**.

112 **To create an outline**

1 Select the row heads of the rows to be included in the outline.

2 On the **Data** menu, point to **Group and Outline** and then click **Group**.

112 **To create an outline with multiple levels**

1 Select the row heads of the rows to be included in the first, smaller level of the outline.

2 Select the row heads of the rows to be included in the second, larger level of the outline.

112 **To hide levels of detail**

Hide Detail

● Click the **Hide Detail** button for the level you want to hide.

113 **To show levels of detail**

Show Detail

● Click the **Show Detail** button for the level you want to show.

Chapter 8 **Analyzing Alternative Data Sets**

Page 118 **To create a scenario**

1 On the **Tools** menu, click **Scenarios**.

2 In the **Scenario Manager** dialog box, click **Add**.

3 In the **Scenario name** box, type the name of the new scenario.

4 At the right edge of the **Changing cells** box, click the **Collapse Dialog** button.

5 Delete the contents of the **Add Scenario** dialog box, and then hold down [Ctrl] while you click the cells to include in the scenario.

6 At the right edge of the **Changing cells** box, click the **Expand Dialog** button.

7 Click **OK**.

8 In the **Scenario Values** dialog box, enter the alternative values for each cell in the scenario.

9 Click **OK**, click **Show**, and then click **Close**.

118   **To edit a scenario**

     1   On the **Tools** menu, click **Scenarios**.

     2   In the **Scenario Manager** dialog box, click the name of the scenario to be edited.

     3   Click **Edit**.

     4   To change the scenario name, edit the value in the **Scenario Name** box.

     5   To add or delete cells from the scenario, at the right edge of the **Changing cells** box, click the **Collapse Dialog** button.

     6   Click **OK**.

     7   In the **Scenario Values** dialog box, enter the alternative values for each cell in the scenario.

     8   Click **OK**, and click **Close**.

120   **To create multiple scenarios**

     1   On the **Tools** menu, click **Scenarios**.

     2   In the **Scenario Manager** dialog box, click **Add**.

     3   In the **Scenario name** box, type the name of the new scenario.

     4   At the right edge of the **Changing cells** box, click the **Collapse Dialog** button.

     5   Delete the contents of the **Add Scenario** dialog box, and then hold down `Ctrl` while you click the cells to include in the scenario.

     6   At the right edge of the **Changing cells** box, click the **Expand Dialog** button.

     7   Click **OK**.

     8   In the **Scenario Values** dialog box, enter the alternative values for each cell in the scenario.

     9   Click **OK**.

   10   Repeat steps 2 through 9 for each additional scenario.

121   **To view scenarios**

     1   On the **Tools** menu, click **Scenarios**.

     2   In the Scenarios pane, click the name of the scenario to show.

     3   Click **Show**.

122   **To summarize scenarios**

     1   On the **Tools** menu, click **Scenarios**.

     2   In the **Result cells** box, click the **Collapse Dialog** button.

     3   Select the cells to appear in the summary.

4   In the **Result cells** box, click the **Expand Dialog** button.

5   Click **OK**.

6   On the tab bar, click the **Scenario Summary** sheet tab to view the summary.

124   **To find required values for reaching a target value**

1   Click the cell to hold the target value.

2   On the **Tools** menu, click **Goal Seek**.

3   In the **To value** box, type the target value for the active cell.

4   In the **By changing cell** box, type the address of the cell to vary.

5   Click **OK**.

6   In the **Goal Seek Status** dialog box, click **OK**.

Chapter   9   Creating Dynamic Lists with PivotTables

Page   132   **To create a PivotTable**

1   Click any cell in the data list.

2   On the **Data** menu, click **PivotTable and PivotChart Report**.

3   Ensure that the **Microsoft Excel list or database** option button is selected in the top pane, identifying your worksheet as the data source, and that the **PivotTable** option button is selected in the bottom pane.

4   Click **Next** to move to the next page of the wizard.

5   Ensure that the proper cell range appears in the **Range** box.

6   Click **Next** to move to the next page of the wizard.

7   Click **Finish**.

8   From the **PivotTable Field List** dialog box, drag the fields for the horizontal axis to the **Drop Column Fields Here** box.

9   From the **PivotTable Field List** dialog box, drag the fields for the vertical axis to the **Drop Row Fields Here** box.

10   From the **PivotTable Field List** dialog box, drag the data field to the **Drop Data Field Here** box.

11   From the **PivotTable Field List** dialog box, drag the fields for the page area to the **Drop Page Fields Here** box.

139   **To filter a PivotTable**

1   Click the down arrow at the right edge of any column heading.

2   From the list of values that appears, click the value to use as the filter.

3 If the list appears as a list of values with check boxes next to the values, select the check boxes beside the values to appear in the PivotTable.

4 Click **All** from the list to remove a filter.

134 **To format PivotTable data**

1 Select the cells in the PivotTable data area.

2 On the **Format** menu, click **Cells**.

3 Use the controls in the **Format Cells** dialog box to format the cells in the PivotTable, and click **OK**.

134 **To apply a predefined format to a PivotTable**

1 If the **PivotTable** toolbar is hidden, right-click any toolbar and then, from the shortcut menu that appears, click **PivotTable**.

2 Click any cell in the PivotTable.

3 On the **PivotTable** toolbar, click the **Format Report** button.

4 Click the desired **AutoFormat**.

133 **To add a field to a PivotTable**

1 Click any cell in the PivotTable.

2 If the **PivotTable** toolbar is hidden, right-click any toolbar and then, from the shortcut menu that appears, click **PivotTable**.

3 On the **PivotTable** toolbar, click the **Show Field List** button.

4 From the **PivotTable Field List** dialog box, drag the new field to the desired area of the PivotTable.

140 **To change a PivotTable's layout**

1 On the **PivotTable** toolbar, click **PivotTable** and then click **Wizard**.

2 Click **Layout**.

3 Drag fields to new areas.

4 Click **OK**, and click **Finish**.

140 **To refresh PivotTable data**

1 Click any cell in the PivotTable.

2 If the **PivotTable** toolbar is hidden, right-click any toolbar and then, from the shortcut menu that appears, click **PivotTable**.

3 On the **PivotTable** toolbar, click the **Refresh Data** button.

140 **To show underlying PivotTable data**

● Double-click a column head in a PivotTable to collapse or expand the rows defined by the column head.

141 **To create a link to a PivotTable field**

1 Click the cell from which you want to link to the PivotTable field, and type =.

2 On the tab bar, click the sheet tab of the worksheet with the PivotTable.

3 Click the PivotTable cell to supply the data for the other cell.

4 Press ⌷Enter⌷ to accept the *GETPIVOTDATA* formula Excel creates.

144 **To import a text file**

1 On the **Data** menu, point to **Import External Data** and then click **Import Data**.

2 Navigate to the folder with the file to be imported, and double-click the file name.

3 If necessary, select the **Delimited** or **Fixed Width** option button to identify how columns are marked in the text file. Click **Next** to accept the **Text Import Wizard's** summary of the text file's data and move to the second page of the wizard.

4 If necessary, select the check box next to the proper delimiter for the text file. Click **Next** to accept the **Text Import Wizard's** analysis of the text file's data and move to the third page of the wizard.

5 Click **Finish** to accept the values and data types as assigned by the wizard.

6 Click **OK** to paste the imported data into the active worksheet, beginning at the active cell.

7 Create the PivotTable using the steps outlined in the *To create a PivotTable* section.

Chapter 10 **Creating Charts**

Page 153 **To create an embedded chart**

1 Select the cells to provide data for the chart.

Chart Wizard

2 On the Standard toolbar, click the **Chart Wizard** button.

3 In the Chart Type pane, click the desired chart type; and then, in the Chart Sub-Type pane, click the desired subtype.

4 Click **Next** to move to the next wizard page.

5 Verify that the axis and data series names are correct.

6 Click **Next** to move to the next wizard page.

7   In the **Chart title** box, type the name of the chart and then press `Tab`.

8   Type names for the axes and data series in the boxes provided, and then click **Next**.

9   Click **Finish** to accept the default choice to create the chart as part of the active worksheet.

154   To resize a chart

●   Grab the sizing handle at the edge of the chart, and drag it to resize the chart.

154   To change a chart's background

1   Right-click anywhere in the Chart Area of the chart, and then, from the shortcut menu that appears, click **Format Chart Area**.

2   In the Area pane of the **Format Chart Area** dialog box, click the **Fill Effects** button.

3   Click the **Texture** tab to display the **Texture** tab page.

4   Click the desired texture.

5   Click **OK** twice to close the **Fill Effects** dialog box and the **Format Chart Area** dialog box.

157   To customize chart labels

1   Double-click the chart label to be customized.

2   Use the controls in the **Format Chart** dialog box that appears, to customize the chart label.

3   To change the text of a chart label, click the label and edit it in the text box that appears.

158   To customize chart number formats

1   Double-click the axis of the chart with the numbers to be customized.

2   In the **Format** dialog box that appears, click the **Number** tab.

3   Use the controls on the **Number** tab page to format the chart numbers.

4   Click **OK**.

161   To perform trend line analysis

1   In a chart, right-click a data point in the body of the chart and then, from the shortcut menu that appears, click **Add Trendline**.

2   If necessary, in the **Trend/Regression type** section, click **Linear**.

3 Click the **Options** tab.

4 In the Forecast pane, type the number of horizontal axis units to look ahead in the **Forward** box. Then click **OK**.

164 **To create a PivotChart**

1 Click any cell in the data list.

2 On the **Data** menu, click **PivotTable and PivotChart Report**.

3 Ensure that the **Microsoft Excel list or database** option button is selected in the top pane, identifying your worksheet as the data source, and that the **PivotChart report (with PivotTable report)** option button is selected in the bottom pane.

4 Click **Next** to move to the next page of the wizard.

5 Ensure that the proper cell range appears in the **Range** box.

6 Click **Next** to move to the next page of the wizard.

7 Click **Finish**.

8 From the **PivotTable Field List** dialog box, drag the fields for the horizontal axis to the **Drop Column Fields Here** box.

9 From the **PivotTable Field List** dialog box, drag the fields for the vertical axis to the **Drop Row Fields Here** box.

10 From the **PivotTable Field List** dialog box, drag the data field to the **Drop Data Field Here** box.

11 From the **PivotTable Field List** dialog box, drag the fields for the page area to the **Drop Page Fields Here** box.

165 **To save a PivotChart as a custom chart type**

1 On the **Chart** menu, click **Chart Type**.

2 If necessary, click the **Custom Types** tab to display the **Custom Types** tab page.

3 In the **Select from** section, select the **User-defined** option button and then click **Add**.

4 In the **Name** box, type a name for the chart type.

5 In the **Description** box, type a description for the chart type. Then click **OK**.

166 **To change a PivotChart's chart type**

1 Open the **Chart** menu, and click **Chart Type**.

2 Click the **Standard Types** tab.

3 In the **Chart type** section, click the desired chart type. Then click **OK**.

Chapter 11 Printing

Page   174   **To preview a worksheet**

● On the Standard toolbar, click the **Print Preview** button.

174   **To change printer setup**

1 On the Standard toolbar, click the **Print Preview** button.

2 Click **Setup**.

3 In the Orientation pane, select the **Landscape** option button.

4 Click **OK**.

175   **To zoom in on part of a page**

1 On the Standard toolbar, click the **Print Preview** button.

2 Click **Setup**.

3 Click the **Zoom** button.

175   **To preview page breaks**

1 On the Standard toolbar, click the **Print Preview** button.

2 Click **Setup**.

3 Click **Page Break Preview**.

4 Click **OK** to clear the message box that appears.

5 Drag the page break line to the desired location on the page.

6 On the **View** menu, click **Normal**.

175   **To change page printing order**

1 On the **File** menu, click **Page Setup**.

2 Click the **Sheet** tab to display the **Sheet** tab page.

3 In the **Page order** section, select the option button for the desired page order.

173   **To print a multipage worksheet**

1 On the **File** menu, click **Print**.

2 In the **Print range** section, select the **All** option button.

3 Click **Print**.

176   **To print nonadjacent worksheets in a workbook**

1 On the tab bar, hold down Ctrl while you click the sheet tabs of the worksheets to print.

Print

2 On the Standard toolbar, click the **Print** button.

176   **To suppress error messages when printing**

1   On the **File** menu, click **Page Setup**.

2   Click the **Sheet** tab to display the **Sheet** tab page.

3   In the **Print** section, click the **Cell errors as** down arrow and then, from the list that appears, click the desired representation.

179   **To print selected pages of a multipage worksheet**

1   On the **File** menu, click **Print**.

2   In the **Print range** section, select the **Page(s)** option button.

3   In the **From** box, type the first page to print.

4   In the **To** box, type the last page to print.

5   Click **OK**.

179   **To print a worksheet on a specific number of pages**

1   On the **File** menu, click **Page Setup**.

2   If necessary, click the **Page** tab.

3   In the **Scaling** section, select the **Fit to** option button and then type the desired number of pages in the **page(s) wide by** and **tall** boxes.

4   Click **OK**.

180   **To define a print area and center it on a page**

1   Select the cells to be printed.

2   On the **File** menu, point to **Print Area** and then click **Set Print Area**.

3   On the Standard toolbar, click the **Print Preview** button.

4   Click the **Setup** button.

5   Click the **Margins** tab to display the **Margins** tab page.

6   In the **Center on page** section, select the **Horizontally** check box and the **Vertically** check box.

7   Click **OK**.

180   **To hide columns or rows during printing**

1   Select the column or row heads of the columns or rows to be hidden.

2   On the **Format** menu, point to **Columns** or **Rows** and then click **Hide**.

181 **To unhide columns or rows during printing**

● On the **Format** menu, point to **Columns** or **Rows** and then click **Unhide**.

178 **To repeat rows or columns at the top or left of printed pages**

1 On the **File** menu, click **Page Setup**.
2 Click the **Sheet** tab to display the **Sheet** tab page.
3 Click the **Collapse Dialog** button next to the **Rows to repeat at top** or **Columns to repeat at left** box.
4 Select the rows or columns to repeat.
5 Click the **Expand Dialog** button.
6 Click **OK**.

182 **To print a chart without printing the worksheet**

1 Click the chart.
2 On the **File** menu, click **Print**.
3 In the **Print what** section, ensure that the **Selected Chart** option button is selected.
4 Click **OK** to print the chart.

183 **To print a worksheet without printing a chart**

1 Right-click the **Chart Area** of the chart, and then, from the shortcut menu that appears, click **Format Chart Area**.
2 Click the **Properties** tab.
3 Clear the **Print object** check box, and then click **OK**.

183 **To resize and print a chart**

1 Right-click the **Chart Area** of the chart, and then, from the shortcut menu that appears, click **Format Chart Area**.
2 Click the **Properties** tab.
3 Select the **Print object** check box, and then click **OK**.
4 On the Standard toolbar, click the **Print Preview** button.
5 Click the **Setup** button.
6 Click the **Chart** tab.
7 Select the **Custom** option button, and then click **OK**.

Chapter 12   Automating Repetitive Tasks with Macros

Page   190   **To open and view a macro**

    1   Open a workbook with a macro attached.

    2   Click **Enable Macros** to allow macros to run.

    3   On the **Tools** menu, point to **Macro** and then click **Macros**.

    4   In the Macro Name pane, click the name of the macro to view.

    5   Click **Edit**.

    6   Click **Close** to close the macro.

191   **To step through a macro**

    1   On the **Tools** menu, point to **Macro** and then click **Macros**.

    2   In the Macro Name pane, click the name of the macro to step through.

    3   Click **Step Into**.

    4   Right-click the taskbar, and then, from the shortcut menu that appears, click **Tile Windows Vertically**.

    5   Click the Microsoft Visual Basic editor title bar, and then press [F8] twice to start the macro.

    6   Press [F8] to execute each macro step.

    7   After the last macro step, in the Microsoft Visual Basic editor, click the **Close** button.

    8   Click **OK** to close the dialog box that appears.

192   **To run a macro**

    1   On the **Tools** menu, point to **Macro** and then click **Macros**.

    2   In the Macro Name pane, click the name of the macro to run.

    3   Click **Run**.

193   **To create a macro**

    1   On the **Tools** menu, point to **Macro** and then click **Record New Macro**.

    2   In the **Macro name** box, delete the existing name and then type a name for the new macro.

    3   Click **OK**.

    4   Execute the steps that make up the macro.

    5   On the Stop Recording toolbar, click the **Stop Recording** button.

193   To modify an existing macro

1   On the **Tools** menu, point to **Macro** and then click **Macros**.

2   In the **Macro name** section, click the macro name and then click **Edit**.

3   Change the VBA code that makes up the macro.

4   On the Standard toolbar, click the **Save** button to save your change.

5   Click the **Close** button.

196   To create a toolbar

1   On the **Tools** menu, click **Customize**.

2   If necessary, click the **Toolbars** tab to display the **Toolbars** tab page.

3   Click **New**.

4   In the **Toolbar name** box, type the name of the new toolbar.

5   Click **OK**.

197   To add a macro button to a toolbar

1   On the **Tools** menu, click **Customize**.

2   In the **Customize** dialog box, click the **Commands** tab.

3   In the Categories pane, click **Macros**.

4   Drag the **Custom Button** command to the target toolbar.

5   On the **Custom Macros** toolbar, right-click the **Custom** button and then, from the shortcut menu that appears, click **Name**.

6   Type a name for the button, and then press [Enter].

7   On the target toolbar, right-click the new button and then, from the shortcut menu that appears, click **Assign Macro**.

8   Click the name of the macro to be assigned to the button.

9   Click **OK**.

10   In the **Customize** dialog box, click **Close**.

198   To delete a custom toolbar

1   On the **Tools** menu, click **Customize**.

2   If necessary, click the **Toolbars** tab.

3   In the **Toolbars** list, click the name of the toolbar to be deleted.

4   Click **Delete**.

5   Click **OK** in the warning dialog box that appears.

6   Click **Close** to close the **Customize** dialog box.

200 To create a new menu

1   On the **Tools** menu, click **Customize**.

2   If necessary, click the **Commands** tab to display the **Commands** tab page.

3   In the **Categories** list, click **New Menu**.

4   Drag **New Menu** from the **Commands** list to the end of the main menu bar.

5   Right-click the **New Menu** heading, and then, from the shortcut menu that appears, click **Name**.

6   Type a new name for the menu, and then press `Enter`.

7   In the **Customize** dialog box, click **Close**.

200 To add a macro to a menu

1   On the **Tools** menu, click **Customize**.

2   If necessary, click the **Commands** tab to display the **Commands** tab page.

3   In the **Categories** list of the **Customize** dialog box, click **Macros**.

4   In the **Commands** list, drag the **Custom Menu Item** command to the new menu head. When a box appears under the menu head, drag **Custom Menu Item** onto it.

5   On the new menu, right-click **Custom Menu Item** and then, from the shortcut menu that appears, click **Name**.

6   Type a name for the item, and then press `Enter`.

7   On the new menu, right-click the new menu item and then, from the shortcut menu that appears, click **Assign Macro**.

8   In the **Macro name** box, click the name of the macro to assign to the menu item.

9   Click **OK**.

10 Click **Close** to close the **Customize** dialog box.

201 To delete a custom menu

1   On the **Tools** menu, click **Customize**.

2   Right-click the menu head of the menu to be deleted, and then, from the shortcut menu that appears, click **Delete**.

3   In the **Customize** dialog box, click **Close**.

202 To run a macro when a workbook is opened

1   On the **Tools** menu, point to **Macro** and then click **Record New Macro**.

2   In the **Macro name** box, type **Auto_Open**.

3 Click **OK**.

4 Carry out the steps to be saved in the macro.

5 On the Stop Recording toolbar, click the **Stop Recording** button.

Chapter 13 **Working with Other Microsoft Office Programs**
Page 207 **To link to an external document**

1 On the **Insert** menu, click **Object**.

2 Click the **Create from File** tab to display the **Create from File** tab page.

3 Click **Browse**.

4 Navigate to the target folder, and double-click the file to include in the workbook.

5 Select the **Link to file** check box.

6 Click **OK**.

208 **To edit a linked file**

● Right-click the linked file, and then, from the shortcut menu that appears, point to **Presentation Object** (in the case of a Microsoft PowerPoint presentation) and then click **Edit**.

210 **To store a workbook as part of another file**

1 Open the Office XP file.

2 On the **Insert** menu, click **Object**.

3 Select the **Create from File** option button.

4 Click the **Browse** button.

5 Navigate to the target folder, and double-click the workbook to include in the file.

6 Click **OK**.

211 **To edit an embedded workbook**

● Right-click the linked file, and then, from the shortcut menu that appears, point to **Worksheet Object** (in the case of a PowerPoint presentation) and then click **Edit**.

215 **To create a hyperlink within a document**

1 Right-click the cell into which you want to insert the hyperlink, and then, from the shortcut menu that appears, click **Hyperlink**.

2 Click the **Place in This Document** button.

3 In the **Or select a place in this document** box, click the target for the hyperlink.

4 In the **Text to display** box, type the text to be shown as the link.

5 Click **OK**.

214 **To create a hyperlink between documents**

1 Right-click the cell into which you want to insert the hyperlink, and then, from the shortcut menu that appears, click **Hyperlink**.

2 If necessary, click the **Existing File or Web Page** button.

3 Navigate to the folder with the target file.

4 Click the name of the target file.

5 In the **Text to display** box, type the text to be shown as the link.

6 Click **OK**.

216 **To paste a chart into another document**

1 Right-click a blank spot on the chart, and then, from the shortcut menu that appears, click **Copy** to copy the chart image to the clipboard.

2 Open the file into which the chart will be pasted.

3 Right-click a blank spot in the active document, and from the shortcut menu that appears, click **Paste**.

Chapter 14 **Working with Database Data**
Page 222 **To find a value**

1 Create a data range in which the leftmost column contains a unique value for each row.

2 In a cell, type **=VLOOKUP(Cell2, Range, Column, FALSE)** (where *Cell2* is the cell for someone to enter a value for Excel to find in the leftmost column, *Range* is the name of the named range, and *Column* is the number of the column—counting from the left—for the value to be returned), and press Enter .

3 In *Cell2*, type the value to be found in the named range, and press Enter .

225 **To define a new data source**

1 On the **Data** menu, point to **Import External Data** and then click **New Database Query**.

2 If necessary, click the **Databases** tab in the **Choose Data Source** dialog box.

3   Click **<New Data Source>**, and then click **OK**.

4   In the first box, type the name of the source.

5   In the second box, click the down arrow and then, from the list that appears, click **Microsoft Access Driver (*.mdb)**.

6   Click **Connect**.

7   Click **Select**.

8   Navigate to the target folder, click the target database, and then click **OK**.

9   Click **OK** again.

10   In the fourth box, click the down arrow and then, from the list that appears, click the default table for the data source.

11   Click **OK**.

225   **To create a database query**

1   On the **Data** menu, point to **Import External Data** and then click **New Database Query**.

2   If necessary, click the **Databases** tab in the **Choose Data Source** dialog box.

3   Click the name of the data source, and then click **OK**.

4   Add the table columns you want to use in your query by clicking the column name and then clicking **Add**.

5   Click **Next**.

6   In the Column To Filter pane, click the name of the column by which you want to filter the results.

7   In the first comparison operator box, click the down arrow and then, from the list that appears, click the comparison operator to be used.

8   In the first value box, type the first value to use in the comparison.

9   If necessary, type a second value in the second value box.

10   Click **Next**.

11   In the **Sort by** box, click the down arrow and then, from the list that appears, click the name of the column by which to sort the query results.

12   Click **Next**.

13   Click **Save Query**.

14   In the **File name** box, type a name for the query and then click **Save**.

15   Click **Finish**.

16   In the **Import Data** dialog box, click **OK**.

Chapter 15   Publishing Information on the Web
Page   233   **To save a workbook as an HTML document**

1   On the **File** menu, click **Save as Web Page**.

2   If necessary, in the Save pane, select the **Entire Workbook** option button.

3   Verify that Saving.htm appears in the **File name** box, and then click **Save**.

233   **To view a workbook via the Web**

1   Start Internet Explorer.

2   In Internet Explorer, open the **File** menu and then click **Open**.

3   Click **Browse**.

4   Navigate to the target folder, and then double-click the file to be viewed.

5   Click **OK**.

235   **To publish a worksheet on the Web**

1   On the **File** menu, click **Save as Web Page**.

2   In the **Save** section of the dialog box, select the **Selection: Sheet** option button to publish the active worksheet on the Web.

3   In the **Save** section of the dialog box, select the **Add interactivity** check box and then click **Publish**.

4   In the **Publish as** section of the dialog box, click the **Change** button.

5   In the **Title** box, type a new title for the page and then click **OK**.

6   Select the **AutoRepublish every time this workbook is saved** check box.

7   Select the **Open published web page in browser** check box, and then click **Publish**.

236   **To update Excel Web pages automatically**

1   On the **File** menu, click **Save as Web Page**.

2   In the **Save** section of the dialog box, select the **Selection: Sheet** option button to publish the active worksheet on the Web.

3   In the **Save** section of the dialog box, select the **Add interactivity** check box and then click **Publish**.

4   In the **Publish as** section of the dialog box, click the **Change** button.

5   In the **Title** box, type a new title for the page and then click **OK**.

6   Select the **AutoRepublish every time this workbook is saved** check box.

7   Select the **Open published web page in browser** check box, and then click **Publish**.

237 **To edit a workbook over the Web**

1 On the **File** menu, click **Save as Web Page**.

2 In the **Save** section of the dialog box, select the **Selection: Sheet** option button to publish the active worksheet on the Web.

3 In the **Save** section of the dialog box, select the **Add interactivity** check box and then click **OK**.

4 Open the file in Internet Explorer.

5 Use the tools on the Interactivity toolbar to edit the worksheet.

238 **To save a PivotTable as a PivotList**

1 Click any cell in the PivotTable.

2 On the **File** menu, click **Save as Web Page**.

3 In the **Save** section of the dialog box, select the **Selection: Sheet** option button.

4 In the **Save** section of the dialog box, select the **Add interactivity** check box and then click **Publish**.

5 If necessary, click the **Choose** down arrow, and then, from the list that appears, click **Items on Pivot**.

6 In the list below the **Choose** box, click the item beginning with *PivotTable*.

7 If necessary, in the bottom section of the dialog box, select the **Open published web page in browser** check box.

8 Click **Publish**.

239 **To work with a PivotList via the Web**

1 Open the Web page with the PivotList in Internet Explorer.

2 Use the down arrows and column heads to modify the PivotList's organization.

242 **To link to Web data**

1 In Internet Explorer, open the Web page with the table data to which you want to link.

2 Select the table data, and then press ⒸⓉⓇⓁ+Ⓒ to copy the data to the Clipboard.

3 In Microsoft Excel, click the desired cell, and then, on the Standard toolbar, click the **Paste** button.

4 Click the **Paste Options** button, and then, from the list that appears, click **Create Refreshable Web Query**.

5 Click the table icon next to *Company Name*, and then click **Import**.

244 **To acquire real-time data**

1   On the **Tools** menu, click **AutoCorrect Options**.

2   Click the **Smart Tags** tab to display the **Smart Tags** tab page.

3   Select the **Label data with smart tags** check box.

4   Verify that the **Smart tag lists** check box is selected.

5   Select the **Embed smart tags in this workbook** check box.

6   Click **Check Workbook**.

7   Move the mouse pointer over a cell with the Smart Tag indicator.

8   Click the **Smart Tag Actions** button, and then, from the list that appears, click the desired action.

9   Select the **Starting at cell** option button, verify that the proper cell appears in the **Starting at cell** box, and then click **OK**.

246 **To export Excel documents as XML**

1   On the **File** menu, click **Save As**.

2   Click the **Save as type** down arrow, and then, from the list that appears, click **XML Spreadsheet (*.xml)**.

3   Click **Save**.

4   Click **Yes** to clear the message box and save the workbook as an XML spreadsheet.

247 **To import an XML file into Excel**

Open

1   On the Standard toolbar, click the **Open** button.

2   Navigate to the target folder, and double-click the target file with the .xml extension.

Chapter 16   **Collaborating with Colleagues**

Page   251   **To turn workbook sharing on**

1   On the **Tools** menu, click **Share Workbook**.

2   Select the **Allow changes by more than one user at the same time** check box, and then click the **Advanced** tab.

3   Click **OK** to accept the default settings.

4   Click **OK** to clear the message box that appears and save the workbook.

251 **To send a workbook to colleagues by e-mail**

1   On the Windows taskbar, open the **Start** menu, point to **Programs**, and click **Outlook Express**.

2   Click the **New Mail** button.

3   Click the **Attach** button.

4   Navigate to the target folder, and double-click the file to attach.

5   Click **Send**.

254   **To add a comment**

1   Click the cell to which to add the comment.

2   On the **Insert** menu, click **Comment**.

3   In the comment field, type the comment.

4   Click a different cell.

254   **To view a comment**

●   Move the mouse pointer over a cell with a comment.

254   **To delete a comment**

●   Right click the cell with the comment, and then, from the shortcut menu that appears, click **Delete Comment**.

255   **To turn on change tracking**

1   On the **Tools** menu, point to **Track Changes** and then click **Highlight Changes**.

2   Select the **Track changes while editing** check box.

3   If necessary, clear the **When** check box.

4   If necessary, clear the **Who** check box.

5   If necessary, select the **Highlight changes on screen** check box.

6   Click **OK**.

257   **To accept or reject changes in a single workbook**

1   On the **Tools** menu, point to **Track Changes** and then click **Accept or Reject Changes**.

2   Click **OK** to save the workbook and clear the message box that appears.

3   Verify that the **When** check box is selected and that *Not yet reviewed* appears in the **When** box.

4   Click **OK**.

5   Click **Accept** to accept the change, or click **Reject** to reject the change

257 **To add a history worksheet to a workbook**

1 On the **Tools** menu, point to **Track Changes** and then click **Highlight Changes**.

2 Select the **List changes on a new sheet** check box.

3 Click **OK**.

259 **To merge changes from multiple workbooks**

1 On the **Tools** menu, click **Compare and Merge Workbooks**.

2 Hold down `Ctrl` as you click the files with the changes to be merged, and then click **OK**.

3 On the Standard toolbar, click the **Save** button to save your work.

4 On the **Tools** menu, point to **Track Changes** and then click **Accept or Reject Changes**.

5 Verify that the **When** check box is selected and that *Not yet reviewed* appears in the **When** box, that the **Who** check box is cleared, and that the **Where** check box is cleared.

6 Click **OK**.

262 **To password-protect a workbook**

1 On the **File** menu, click **Save As**.

2 Click the **Tools** menu head, and then click **General Options**.

3 In the **Password to open** box, type a password and then click **OK**.

4 In the **Reenter password to proceed** box, type the same password and then click **OK**.

5 Click **Save**.

6 Click **Yes** to clear the message box that appears.

263 **To remove a password from a workbook**

1 On the **File** menu, click **Save As**.

2 Click the **Tools** menu head, and then click **General Options**.

3 In the **Password to open** box, erase the existing password and then click **OK**.

263 **To password-protect a worksheet**

1 Activate the worksheet to be protected.

2 On the **Tools** menu, point to **Protection** and then click **Protect Sheet**.

3 In the **Password to unprotect sheet** box, type the password and then click **OK**.

4 In the **Confirm Password** dialog box, type the same password in the space provided, and then click **OK**.

263 **To remove a password from a worksheet**

1 On the **Tools** menu, point to **Protection** and then click **Unprotect Sheet**.

2 In the **Password** box, type the password and then click **OK**.

263 **To password-protect a range**

1 Select the cells to be protected.

2 On the **Tools** menu, point to **Protection** and then click **Allow Users to Edit Ranges**.

3 Click **New**.

4 In the **Title** box, type the name for the new range.

5 In the **Range password** box, type a password and then click **OK**.

6 In the **Confirm password** box, type the same password and then click **OK**.

264 **To remove a password from a cell range**

1 On the **Tools** menu, point to **Protection** and then click **Allow Users to Edit Ranges**.

2 In the **Ranges** box, click the range to be unprotected and then click **Delete**.

3 Click **OK**.

Glossary

3-D reference   A pattern for referring to the workbook, worksheet, and cell from which a value should be read

active cell   The cell that is currently selected and open for editing

alignment   The manner in which a cell's contents are arranged within that cell (for example, centered)

arguments   Specific data a function requires to calculate a value

aspect ratio   The relationship between a graphic's height and width

auditing   The process of examining a worksheet for errors

AutoComplete   The ability to complete data entry for a cell based on similar values in other cells in the same column

AutoFill   The ability to extend a series of values based on the contents of a single cell

AutoFilter   An Excel tool you can use to create filters

AutoFormats   Predefined formats that can be applied to a worksheet

AutoRepublish   A new Excel 2002 technology that maintains a link between a Web document and the worksheet on which the Web document is based and updates the Web document whenever the original worksheet is saved

browser   A program that lets users view Web documents

cell   The box at the intersection of a row and a column

cell range   A group of cells

cell reference   The letter and number combination, such as C16, that identifies the row and column intersection of a cell

charts   Visual summaries of worksheet data, also called graphs

columns   Cells that are on the same vertical line in a worksheet

conditional formats   Formats that are applied only when cell contents meet certain criteria

conditional formula   A formula that calculates a value using one of two different expressions, depending on whether a third expression is true or false

data consolidation   Summarizing data from a set of similar cell ranges

dependents   The cells with formulas that use the value from a particular cell

driver   A program that controls access to a file or device

dynamic-link library   A file with programming code that can be called by a worksheet function

embed   To save a file as part of another file, as opposed to linking one file to another

error code   A brief message that appears in a worksheet cell, describing a problem with a formula or a function

Extensible Markup Language (XML)   A content marking system that lets you store data about the contents of a document in that document

field   A column in a data list

fill handle   The square at the lower right corner of a cell you drag to indicate other cells that should hold values in the series defined by the active cell

FillSeries   The ability to extend a series of values based on the contents of two cells, where the first cell has the starting value for the series and the second cell shows the increment

filter   A rule that Excel uses to determine which worksheet rows to display

formats   Predefined sets of characteristics that can be applied to cell contents

formula   An expression used to calculate a value

freeze   To assign cells that will remain at the top of a worksheet regardless of how far down the worksheet a user scrolls

function   A predefined formula

Goal Seek   An analysis tool that finds the value for a selected cell that would produce a given result from a calculation

graphs   Visual summaries of worksheet data, also called charts

hyperlink   A reference to a file on the World Wide Web

Hypertext Markup Language (HTML)   A document formatting system that tells a Web *browser* such as Internet Explorer how to display the contents of a file

landscape mode   A display and printing mode whereby columns run parallel to the short edge of a sheet of paper

link   A formula that has a cell show the value from another cell

locked cells   Cells that cannot be modified if their worksheet is protected

macro   A series of recorded automated actions that can be replayed

mailto   A special type of hyperlink that lets a user create an e-mail message to a particular e-mail address

metadata   Data that describes the contents of a file

named range   A group of related cells defined by a single name

Open DataBase Connectivity (ODBC)   A protocol that facilitates data transfer between databases and related programs

Pick from List   The ability to enter a value into a cell by choosing the value from the set of values already entered into cells in the same column

pivot   To reorganize the contents of a PivotTable

PivotChart   A chart that is linked to a PivotTable and that can be reorganized dynamically to emphasize different aspects of the underlying data

PivotTable   A dynamic worksheet that can be reorganized by a user

portrait mode   A display and printing mode whereby columns run parallel to the long edge of a sheet of paper

precedents   The cells that are used in a formula

primary key   A field or group of fields with values that distinguish a row in a data list from all other rows in the list

query   A statement that locates records in a database

range   A group of related cells

refresh   To update the contents of one document when the contents of another document are changed

report   A special document with links to one or more worksheets from the same workbook

rows   Cells that are on the same horizontal line in a worksheet

scenarios   Alternative data sets that let you view the impact of specific changes on your worksheet

sharing   Making a workbook available for more than one user to open and modify simultaneously

sheet tab   The indicator for a worksheet, located in the lower left corner of the workbook window

Smart Tags   A new Excel 2002 technology that recognizes values in a spreadsheet and finds related information on the Web

sort   To reorder the contents of a worksheet based on a criterion

split bar   A line that defines which cells have been frozen at the top of a worksheet

subtotals   Partial totals for related data in a worksheet

tables Data lists in a database

tags Marks used to indicate display properties or to communicate data about the contents of a document

template A workbook used as a pattern for creating other workbooks

trend line A projection of future data (such as sales) based on past performance

validation rule A test that data must pass to be entered into a cell without generating a warning message

what-if analysis Analysis of the contents of a worksheet to determine the impact that specific changes have on your calculations

workbook The basic Excel document, consisting of one or more worksheets

worksheet A page in an Excel workbook

workspace An Excel file type (.xlw) that allows you to open several files at once

Index

Numbers and Symbols

, (commas), 50, 141
= (equal signs), 38, 95
= (equal to) comparisons, 76, 82, 221, 224, 227
> (greater than) comparisons, 76, 227
< (less than) comparisons, 61, 82, 221, 224
+ (plus sign) pointer, 13, 195, 199
# (pound signs) in error codes, 45
errors, 45
#DIV/0! errors, 45
#N/A errors, 221, 222
#NAME? errors, 44, 45
#REF! errors, 45, 94
#VALUE! errors, 45
" (quotation marks), 58, 59
0 in number formats, 57
3-D references, 94, 97, 98, 213

A

absolute references to cells, 42
accepting workbook changes, 255, 258
Access, 219, 223, 225
Accounting number format, 156
account names, 253
active cells, 6, 8
active directories, 86, 87
active workbooks, 88, 90
active worksheets, 169, 170
Add button, 61, 63
adding
    buttons to toolbars, 1
    conditions, 61, 63
    custom chart types, 165
    scenarios, 116–17, 118, 120, 121
    trendlines, 159–61
    words to dictionaries, 20
addresses for HTML pages, 232

Add Scenario dialog box, 116–17, 118, 120, 121
Add Trendline dialog box, 159–61
administrators of shared workbooks, 249
Advanced Filter dialog box, 77
Advanced tab (Share Workbook dialog box), 250, 251
alerts. *See also* error messages
    cell references, 94, 95
    invalid data entries, 81, 82
    printing when conditions are met, 40–41
aligning text in cells, 29, 30, 50, 52, 55
Align Left button, 50
Align Right button, 50
allowing
    specific data types, 81, 82
    users to edit cell ranges, 262, 263
alphabetical order, sorting rows into, 104
alternative data sets
    analyzing data, 115
    creating scenarios, 116–19
    Goal Seek feature, 123–25
    multiple scenarios, 119–22
applications, sharing data with, 205
applying styles, 51, 53–56
approximate matches in querying, 220–21
area codes in phone numbers, 57
arguments in functions
    defined, 39
    entering, 40–41, 43
    errors involving, 45
    VLOOKUP function, 220–21
Arrange Windows dialog box, 89, 90, 94
arranging
    workbooks in windows, 89, 90
    worksheets in workbooks, 90, 92
arrows
    blue tracer arrows, 45, 46
    down arrows on buttons, 51

ascending sorts, 104, 105, 221, 224, 227
Ask A Question box, 2, 3
Ask me which changes win option, 250
aspect ratio of images, 32, 33, 66
assigning macros
    to menu items, 198–201
    to toolbar buttons, 195–96, 197
Assign Macro dialog box, 196, 197, 199, 201
attachments to e-mail, 250, 251–52
auditing worksheets for errors, 44
AutoCalculate feature, 78
AutoComplete feature, 11, 14
AutoCorrect dialog box, 243, 244
AutoFill feature, 11–12, 13, 64
Auto Fill Options button, 11–12, 64
AutoFilter feature, 74, 75
AutoFormat dialog box, 132, 134
AutoFormats for PivotTables, 132, 134
Auto_ macro names, 202
AutoRepublish feature, 235, 236
AutoSum button, 79
AVERAGE function, 39, 40, 43
averages, calculating, 39, 40, 43, 79–80
axes in charts and graphs, 152, 153

B

background colors for charts, 153
basing files on templates, 86–87, 88
between comparisons, 61, 63
black plus sign pointer (+), 13
blank cells, printing, 173
blank pages, preventing printing, 178

Index

M

Macro dialog box, 188–92
macros
 arranging windows for coding, 191
 automatically running, 187, 201–3
 creating and editing, 192–94
 defined, 187
 deleting, 192
 naming, 202
 overview, 188–90
 running, 190, 192, 194
 security settings problems, 189
 toolbar buttons, 187, 194–98
magnifying Print Preview view, 171, 175
mailto hyperlinks, 213
main menu bar, 2
margins, 68, 69–70, 170–71, 174–75
markers
 comment and change flags, 253–54, 256, 259
 error markers, 93
 grouped data outline indicators, 103, 112
 Smart Tag (XML) indicator buttons, 243, 244
marking changes in files, 249, 250, 254–58
Match Destination Formatting paste option, 6
matching cells
 generating lists of, 17
 VLOOKUP function, 220–21, 222
MAX function, 39
memory limitations, 88
menus and menu items
 adding, 199, 200
 assigning items to, 198–201
 deleting, 199, 201
 macro items, 187
Merge and Center button, 25, 27, 50
merging
 cells, 25, 27, 50
 changes from multiple workbooks, 249, 258–60
 unmerging cells, 67
messages. *See* **alerts; error messages**

metadata, 245–47
Microsoft Access, 219, 223, 225
Microsoft Internet Explorer, 232, 233, 242
Microsoft Office XP
 including data in other files, 209–11
 including other files in Excel, 206–9
 linking and pasting files, 205
Microsoft Outlook or Outlook Express, 213, 251–52
Microsoft Visual Basic editor, 189, 190–92, 193
MIN function, 39
misspellings, 16
models for workbooks (templates), 85, 86–88
monthly payments, 39–40
Move or Copy dialog box, 90, 91, 92
moving
 charts and graphs, 154
 columns, 6
 logos or pictures, 32
 margins, 70, 170–71, 175
 page break lines, 171, 175
 PivotTable fields, 131, 133
 to specific cells, 5
 through HTML pages, 232, 234
 through Print Preview pages, 170
 to top of worksheet, 10
 worksheets to other files, 90, 91
 worksheet tabs, 24, 26, 90, 92
multiple cells. *See* **cell ranges**
multiple copies of documents, 258–60
multiple workbooks. *See* **linking data; merging; workspaces**
multiple worksheets, printing, 173–74, 176

N

#N/A errors, 221, 222
#NAME? error, 44, 45
Name box, 8, 9, 36, 38
named ranges
 in formulas, 40
 Name box, 36, 38
 password protection, 262

named ranges, *continued*
 VLOOKUP function, 220–21, 222
names
 associated with comments, 253
 chart types, 163, 165
 data sources, 223, 225
 macros, 192, 193, 202
 menus and menu items, 199, 200
 ranges of cells, 35–38
 styles, 55
 worksheets, 23–24, 26
navigating. *See* **moving**
negative numbers, 57
networks, sharing workbooks on, 249
New Database Query command, 223, 225
New from template section, 87, 88
New Menu command, 198–99, 200
New Range dialog box, 262, 264
New Toolbar dialog box, 194, 196
New Web Query dialog box, 241, 242
new workbooks, 10, 12
noncontiguous cells, 40, 177
nonscrolling rows, 29–30, 31
normal scenarios, 120
notations in workbooks, 253–54
Not in Dictionary box, 19
Not yet reviewed changes, 255, 257
NOW() function, 39
numbering pages, 50, 65
numbers and numeric values
 formatting in charts, 155–58
 pasting with formatting, 7
 readability of, 56–60
 validation rules for, 81, 82
Number tab (Format Cells dialog box), 56–57

O

Object dialog box, 206, 207
objects, charts as, 152
ODBC (Open DataBase Connectivity), 223

Curtis Frye

Curtis Frye is a freelance writer from Portland, Oregon. He is the author of *Master Access 2000 Visually* from IDG/Maran, Microsoft Press's *Microsoft Access 2000 Step by Step Courseware Expert Skills Student Guide* for ActiveEducation, and *Active-Education's Introduction to ASP*, as well as three online courses for DigitalThink (*Excel 2000: Data Formatting and Customization*, *Excel 2000: Data Analysis and Dissemination*, and *Advanced Database Design*). He was also a major contributor to Eric and Deborah Ray's *Microsoft Access 2000 for Windows: Visual QuickStart*, from Peachpit Press, and writes "The Interoperability Corner," a monthly column for Jerry Olsen's *All About Microsoft Word* newsletter.

His academic and policy writing ventures include sole authorship of *Privacy-Enhanced Business* (Quorum Books), lead authorship of *The State of Web Commerce* (a 1997 market research report from O'Reilly & Associates), a chapter on Internet commerce in Osborne's *Internet: The Complete Reference, Millennium Edition*, and an article on cryptography policy entitled "Regulated Privacy" in the premier issue of *Infobahn* magazine. He is also the editor and lead reviewer for *Technology & Society Book Reviews* (*http://www.techsoc.com/*).

Before beginning his writing career in June 1995, Curt spent four years with The MITRE Corporation as a defense trade analyst and one year as Director of Sales and Marketing for Digital Gateway Systems, an Internet service provider. Curt graduated from Syracuse University in 1990 with an honors degree in political science. When he's not writing, Curt is a professional improvisational comedian with ComedySportz.

Self-paced
training
that works
as hard as you do!

Information-packed STEP BY STEP courses are the most effective way to teach yourself how to complete tasks with Microsoft® Office XP. Numbered steps and scenario-based lessons with practice files on CD-ROM make it easy to find your way while learning tasks and procedures. Work through every lesson or choose your own starting point—with STEP BY STEP modular design and straightforward writing style, *you* drive the instruction. And the books are constructed with lay-flat binding so you can follow the text with both hands at the keyboard. Select STEP BY STEP titles also provide complete, cost-effective preparation for the Microsoft Office User Specialist (MOUS) credential. It's an excellent way for you or your organization to take a giant step toward workplace productivity.

- **Microsoft Office XP Step by Step**
  ISBN 0-7356-1294-3

- **Microsoft Word Version 2002 Step by Step**
  ISBN 0-7356-1295-1

- **Microsoft Excel Version 2002 Step by Step**
  ISBN 0-7356-1296-X

- **Microsoft PowerPoint® Version 2002 Step by Step**
  ISBN 0-7356-1297-8

- **Microsoft Outlook® Version 2002 Step by Step**
  ISBN 0-7356-1298-6

- **Microsoft FrontPage® Version 2002 Step by Step**
  ISBN 0-7356-1300-1

- **Microsoft Access Version 2002 Step by Step**
  ISBN 0-7356-1299-4

- **Microsoft Project Version 2002 Step by Step**
  ISBN 0-7356-1301-X

- **Microsoft Visio® Version 2002 Step by Step**
  ISBN 0-7356-1302-8

Microsoft Press® products are available worldwide wherever quality computer books are sold. For more information, contact your book or computer retailer, software reseller, or local Microsoft Sales Office, or visit our Web site at mspress.microsoft.com. To locate your nearest source for Microsoft Press products, or to order directly, call 1-800-MSPRESS in the United States. (in Canada, call 1-800-268-2222).

Prices and availability dates are subject to change.

mspress.microsoft.com

Target your
solution and fix it
yourself—fast!

When you're stuck with a computer problem, you need answers right now. *Troubleshooting* books can help. They'll guide you to the source of the problem and show you how to solve it right away. Use easy diagnostic flowcharts to identify problems. Get ready solutions with clear, step-by-step instructions. Go to quick-access charts with *Top 20 Problems* and *Prevention Tips*. Find even more solutions with handy *Tips* and *Quick Fixes*. Walk through the remedy with plenty of screen shots to keep you on track. Find what you need fast with the extensive, easy-reference index. And keep trouble at bay with the Troubleshooting Web site—updated every month with new FREE problem-solving information. Get the answers you need to get back to business fast with *Troubleshooting* books.

Get a **Free**
e-mail newsletter, updates,
special offers, links to related books,
and more when you

register on line!

Register your Microsoft Press® title on our Web site and you'll get
a FREE subscription to our e-mail newsletter, *Microsoft Press
Book Connections.* You'll find out about newly released and upcoming
books and learning tools, online events, software downloads, special
offers and coupons for Microsoft Press customers, and information
about major Microsoft® product releases. You can also read useful
additional information about all the titles we publish, such as de-
tailed book descriptions, tables of contents and indexes, sample
chapters, links to related books and book series, author biographies,
and reviews by other customers.

Registration is easy. Just visit this Web page and fill in your information:

http://mspress.microsoft.com/register

Microsoft®

- -

MICROSOFT LICENSE AGREEMENT

Book Companion CD

IMPORTANT—READ CAREFULLY: This Microsoft End-User License Agreement ("EULA") is a legal agreement between you (either an individual or an entity) and Microsoft Corporation for the Microsoft product identified above, which includes computer software and may include associated media, printed materials, and "online" or electronic documentation ("SOFTWARE PRODUCT"). Any component included within the SOFTWARE PRODUCT that is accompanied by a separate End-User License Agreement shall be governed by such agreement and not the terms set forth below. By installing, copying, or otherwise using the SOFTWARE PRODUCT, you agree to be bound by the terms of this EULA. If you do not agree to the terms of this EULA, you are not authorized to install, copy, or otherwise use the SOFTWARE PRODUCT; you may, however, return the SOFTWARE PRODUCT, along with all printed materials and other items that form a part of the Microsoft product that includes the SOFTWARE PRODUCT, to the place you obtained them for a full refund.

SOFTWARE PRODUCT LICENSE

The SOFTWARE PRODUCT is protected by United States copyright laws and international copyright treatics, as well as other intellectual property laws and treaties. The SOFTWARE PRODUCT is licensed, not sold.

1. **GRANT OF LICENSE.** This EULA grants you the following rights:

   a. **Software Product.** You may install and use one copy of the SOFTWARE PRODUCT on a single computer. The primary user of the computer on which the SOFTWARE PRODUCT is installed may make a second copy for his or her exclusive use on a portable computer.

   b. **Storage/Network Use.** You may also store or install a copy of the SOFTWARE PRODUCT on a storage device, such as a network server, used only to install or run the SOFTWARE PRODUCT on your other computers over an internal network; however, you must acquire and dedicate a license for each separate computer on which the SOFTWARE PRODUCT is installed or run from the storage device. A license for the SOFTWARE PRODUCT may not be shared or used concurrently on different computers.

   c. **License Pak.** If you have acquired this EULA in a Microsoft License Pak, you may make the number of additional copies of the computer software portion of the SOFTWARE PRODUCT authorized on the printed copy of this EULA, and you may use each copy in the manner specified above. You are also entitled to make a corresponding number of secondary copies for portable computer use as specified above.

   d. **Sample Code** Solely with respect to portions, if any, of the SOFTWARE PRODUCT that are identified within the SOFTWARE PRODUCT as sample code (the "SAMPLE CODE"):

      i. **Use and Modification.** Microsoft grants you the right to use and modify the source code version of the SAMPLE CODE, provided you comply with subsection (d)(iii) below. You may not distribute the SAMPLE CODE, or any modified version of the SAMPLE CODE, in source code form.

      ii. **Redistributable Files.** Provided you comply with subsection (d)(iii) below, Microsoft grants you a nonexclusive, royalty free right to reproduce and distribute the object code version of the SAMPLE CODE and of any modified SAMPLE CODE, other than SAMPLE CODE, or any modified version thereof, designated as not redistributable in the Readme file that forms a part of the SOFTWARE PRODUCT (the "Non-Redistributable Sample Code"). All SAMPLE CODE other than the Non-Redistributable Sample Code is collectively referred to as the "REDISTRIBUTABLES."

      iii. **Redistribution Requirements.** If you redistribute the REDISTRIBUTABLES, you agree to: (i) distribute the REDISTRIBUTABLES in object code form only in conjunction with and as a part of your software application product; (ii) not use Microsoft's name, logo, or trademarks to market your software application product; (iii) include a valid copyright notice on your software application product; (iv) indemnify, hold harmless, and defend Microsoft from and against any claims or lawsuits, including attorney's fees, that arise or result from the use or distribution of your software application product; and (v) not permit further distribution of the REDISTRIBUTABLES by your end user. Contact Microsoft for the applicable royalties due and other licensing terms for all other uses and/or distribution of the REDISTRIBUTABLES.

2. **DESCRIPTION OF OTHER RIGHTS AND LIMITATIONS.**

   - **Limitations on Reverse Engineering, Decompilation, and Disassembly.** You may not reverse engineer, decompile, or disassemble the SOFTWARE PRODUCT, except and only to the extent that such activity is expressly permitted by applicable law notwithstanding this limitation.

   - **Separation of Components.** The SOFTWARE PRODUCT is licensed as a single product. Its component parts may not be separated for use on more than one computer.

   - **Rental.** You may not rent, lease, or lend the SOFTWARE PRODUCT.

   - **Support Services.** Microsoft may, but is not obligated to, provide you with support services related to the SOFTWARE PRODUCT ("Support Services"). Use of Support Services is governed by the Microsoft policies and programs described in the user manual, in "online" documentation, and/or in other Microsoft-provided materials. Any supplemental software code provided to you as part of the Support Services shall be considered part of the SOFTWARE PRODUCT and subject to the terms and conditions of this EULA. With respect to technical information you provide to Microsoft as part of the Support Services, Microsoft may use such information for its business purposes, including for product support and development. Microsoft will not utilize such technical information in a form that personally identifies you.

- **Software Transfer.** You may permanently transfer all of your rights under this EULA, provided you retain no copies, you transfer all of the SOFTWARE PRODUCT (including all component parts, the media and printed materials, any upgrades, this EULA, and, if applicable, the Certificate of Authenticity), **and** the recipient agrees to the terms of this EULA.

- **Termination.** Without prejudice to any other rights, Microsoft may terminate this EULA if you fail to comply with the terms and conditions of this EULA. In such event, you must destroy all copies of the SOFTWARE PRODUCT and all of its component parts.

3. **COPYRIGHT.** All title and copyrights in and to the SOFTWARE PRODUCT (including but not limited to any images, photographs, animations, video, audio, music, text, SAMPLE CODE, REDISTRIBUTABLES, and "applets" incorporated into the SOFTWARE PRODUCT) and any copies of the SOFTWARE PRODUCT are owned by Microsoft or its suppliers. The SOFTWARE PRODUCT is protected by copyright laws and international treaty provisions. Therefore, you must treat the SOFTWARE PRODUCT like any other copyrighted material **except** that you may install the SOFTWARE PRODUCT on a single computer provided you keep the original solely for backup or archival purposes. You may not copy the printed materials accompanying the SOFTWARE PRODUCT.

4. **U.S. GOVERNMENT RESTRICTED RIGHTS.** The SOFTWARE PRODUCT and documentation are provided with RESTRICTED RIGHTS. Use, duplication, or disclosure by the Government is subject to restrictions as set forth in subparagraph (c)(1)(ii) of the Rights in Technical Data and Computer Software clause at DFARS 252.227-7013 or subparagraphs (c)(1) and (2) of the Commercial Computer Software—Restricted Rights at 48 CFR 52.227-19, as applicable. Manufacturer is Microsoft Corporation/One Microsoft Way/Redmond, WA 98052-6399.

5. **EXPORT RESTRICTIONS.** You agree that you will not export or re-export the SOFTWARE PRODUCT, any part thereof, or any process or service that is the direct product of the SOFTWARE PRODUCT (the foregoing collectively referred to as the "Restricted Components"), to any country, person, entity, or end user subject to U.S. export restrictions. You specifically agree not to export or re-export any of the Restricted Components (i) to any country to which the U.S. has embargoed or restricted the export of goods or services, which currently include, but are not necessarily limited to, Cuba, Iran, Iraq, Libya, North Korea, Sudan, and Syria, or to any national of any such country, wherever located, who intends to transmit or transport the Restricted Components back to such country; (ii) to any end user who you know or have reason to know will utilize the Restricted Components in the design, development, or production of nuclear, chemical, or biological weapons; or (iii) to any end user who has been prohibited from participating in U.S. export transactions by any federal agency of the U.S. government. You warrant and represent that neither the BXA nor any other U.S. federal agency has suspended, revoked, or denied your export privileges.

DISCLAIMER OF WARRANTY

NO WARRANTIES OR CONDITIONS. MICROSOFT EXPRESSLY DISCLAIMS ANY WARRANTY OR CONDITION FOR THE SOFTWARE PRODUCT. THE SOFTWARE PRODUCT AND ANY RELATED DOCUMENTATION ARE PROVIDED "AS IS" WITHOUT WARRANTY OR CONDITION OF ANY KIND, EITHER EXPRESS OR IMPLIED, INCLUDING, WITHOUT LIMITATION, THE IMPLIED WARRANTIES OF MERCHANTABILITY, FITNESS FOR A PARTICULAR PURPOSE, OR NONINFRINGEMENT. THE ENTIRE RISK ARISING OUT OF USE OR PERFORMANCE OF THE SOFTWARE PRODUCT REMAINS WITH YOU.

LIMITATION OF LIABILITY. TO THE MAXIMUM EXTENT PERMITTED BY APPLICABLE LAW, IN NO EVENT SHALL MICROSOFT OR ITS SUPPLIERS BE LIABLE FOR ANY SPECIAL, INCIDENTAL, INDIRECT, OR CONSEQUENTIAL DAMAGES WHATSOEVER (INCLUDING, WITHOUT LIMITATION, DAMAGES FOR LOSS OF BUSINESS PROFITS, BUSINESS INTERRUPTION, LOSS OF BUSINESS INFORMATION, OR ANY OTHER PECUNIARY LOSS) ARISING OUT OF THE USE OF OR INABILITY TO USE THE SOFTWARE PRODUCT OR THE PROVISION OF OR FAILURE TO PROVIDE SUPPORT SERVICES, EVEN IF MICROSOFT HAS BEEN ADVISED OF THE POSSIBILITY OF SUCH DAMAGES. IN ANY CASE, MICROSOFT'S ENTIRE LIABILITY UNDER ANY PROVISION OF THIS EULA SHALL BE LIMITED TO THE GREATER OF THE AMOUNT ACTUALLY PAID BY YOU FOR THE SOFTWARE PRODUCT OR US$5.00; PROVIDED, HOWEVER, IF YOU HAVE ENTERED INTO A MICROSOFT SUPPORT SERVICES AGREEMENT, MICROSOFT'S ENTIRE LIABILITY REGARDING SUPPORT SERVICES SHALL BE GOVERNED BY THE TERMS OF THAT AGREEMENT. BECAUSE SOME STATES AND JURISDICTIONS DO NOT ALLOW THE EXCLUSION OR LIMITATION OF LIABILITY, THE ABOVE LIMITATION MAY NOT APPLY TO YOU.

MISCELLANEOUS

This EULA is governed by the laws of the State of Washington USA, except and only to the extent that applicable law mandates governing law of a different jurisdiction.

Should you have any questions concerning this EULA, or if you desire to contact Microsoft for any reason, please contact the Microsoft subsidiary serving your country, or write: Microsoft Sales Information Center/One Microsoft Way/Redmond, WA 98052-6399.

New Features in Excel 2002

Task pane   Ask A Question box

Borders toolbar

PivotTable toolbar

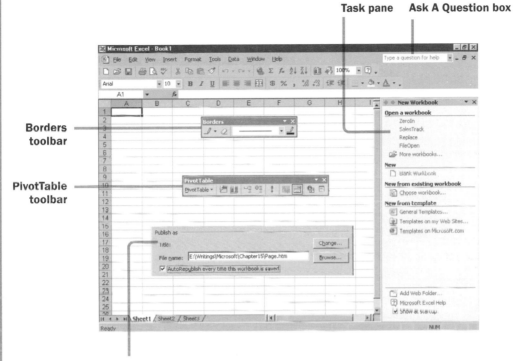

AutoReplenish to the Web

Common Keyboard Shortcuts

Shortcut	Action
Ctrl + C	Copy the selected cell or cells
Ctrl + X	Cut the contents of the selected cell or cells
Ctrl + V	Paste the contents of the Clipboard
Ctrl + Z	Undo the last action
Ctrl + Y	Redo the last action
Ctrl + S	Save the active file
Ctrl + !	Format the active cell or cells
Ctrl + F	Find specified text
Ctrl + H	Replace specified text
Ctrl + K	Insert or edit a hyperlink
F7	Check spelling
Alt + F8	Display available macros
Ctrl + B	Make text bold
Ctrl + I	Make text italic

To select a noncontiguous group of cells

1. While holding down the Ctrl key, click the cells to be selected.

To locate specific data

1. On the **Edit** menu, click **Find**.
2. In the **Find what** box, type the word or text you want to find, and then click **Find Next**.
3. Click **Find Next** again to find subsequent occurrences of the text.

To change your actions

- Click the **Undo** button to remove the last change.
- Click the **Redo** button to reinstate the last change you removed.

To prevent text spill-over

1. Click the desired cell.
2. On the **Format** menu, click **Cells**.
3. If necessary, click the **Alignment** tab.
4. Select the **Wrap text** check box, and click **OK**.

To add cell borders

1. On the Formatting toolbar, click the down arrow at the right of the **Borders** button and then, from the list that appears, click **Draw Borders**.
2. Click the cell edge on which you want to draw a border.
3. Drag the mouse pointer to draw a border around a group of cells.

To add a graphic to a header or footer

1. Create a header or footer.
2. Click anywhere in the one of the section boxes, and then click the **Insert Picture** button.
3. Navigate to the folder with the image file and then double-click the file name. Then click **OK**.

To create a custom filter

1. Click the top cell in the column to filter.
2. On **Data** menu, point to **Filter**, and then click **AutoFilter**.
3. Click the down arrow and then, from the list that appears, click (**Custom...**).
4. In the upper left box of the **Custom AutoFilter** dialog box, click the down arrow and, from the list that appears, click a comparison operator.

5. Type the arguments for the comparison in the boxes at the upper right and click **OK**.

To insert a worksheet in an existing workbook

1. On the tab bar, right-click the tab of the sheet to move and then, from the shortcut menu that appears, click **Move or Copy**.
2. Click the **To book** down arrow, and then, from the list that appears, click the book to which you want to move the worksheet.
3. In the **Before sheet** list, click the sheet to appear behind the moved sheet.
4. At the bottom of the **Move or Copy** dialog box, select the **Create a copy** check box. Then click **OK**.

To sort a data list by multiple columns

1. Select the columns of cells to be sorted.
2. On the **Data** menu, click **Sort**.
3. If necessary, click the **Sort by** down arrow and then, from the list that appears, click the first column to sort by.
4. Click the **Then by** down arrow and then, from the list that appears, click the second column to sort by.
5. Repeat step 4 in the next **Then by** down arrow, and then click **OK**.

To print non-adjacent worksheets in a workbook

1. On the tab bar, hold down Ctrl while you click the sheet tabs of the worksheets to print.
2. On the Standard toolbar, click the **Print** button.

To save a workbook as an HTML document

1. On the **File** menu, click **Save as Web Page**.
2. If necessary, in the **Save** section, select the **Entire Workbook** option button.
3. Type a name for the document in the **File name** box, and then click **Save**.